In this volume of essays – which emerges from an SNTS seminar on the Shepherd Discourse in 1985–1986 – an international team of specialists analyses one of the most intriguing of Jesus' discourses within the Fourth Gospel. While previous studies of the Shepherd Discourse have tended to concentrate either on its historical setting in the life of Jesus (Simonis) or on the prehistory of the text (Bultmann and his school) this collection adopts a more contextual approach. By situating the discourse in the text of the gospel as a whole, with particular emphasis on the preceding chapter 9 and on the subsequent Passion Narrative, the contributors are able to point to its internal coherence, and indicate that – in spite of links with Gnostic ideas – the roots of the Shepherd Discourse are based in Old Testament and Jewish texts about the shepherds of Israel.

While demonstrating the important conclusions that can be drawn from a contextual examination of this fascinating text, the book at the same time provides an introduction to previous research on the Shepherd Discourse, including work on its structure, its literary history, and the syncretistic milieu out of which it came.

SOCIETY FOR NEW TESTAMENT STUDIES

MONOGRAPH SERIES

General Editor: G. N. Stanton

67

THE SHEPHERD DISCOURSE OF JOHN 10 AND ITS CONTEXT

The Shepherd Discourse of John 10 and its Context

Studies by members of the Johannine Writings Seminar

Edited with introduction by
**JOHANNES BEUTLER, SJ, AND
ROBERT T. FORTNA**

*The right of the
University of Cambridge
to print and sell
all manner of books
was granted by
Henry VIII in 1534.
The University has printed
and published continuously
since 1584.*

CAMBRIDGE UNIVERSITY PRESS

CAMBRIDGE

NEW YORK   PORT CHESTER
MELBOURNE   SYDNEY

CAMBRIDGE UNIVERSITY PRESS
Cambridge, New York, Melbourne, Madrid, Cape Town, Singapore, São Paulo

Cambridge University Press
The Edinburgh Building, Cambridge CB2 2RU, UK

Published in the United States of America by Cambridge University Press, New York

www.cambridge.org
Information on this title: www.cambridge.org/9780521392112

First published 1991
This digitally printed first paperback version 2005

A catalogue record for this publication is available from the British Library

Library of Congress Cataloguing in Publication data
The Shepherd Discourse of John 10 and its context: Studies by
members of the Johannine Writings Senimar: edited with introduction
by Johannes Beutler and Robert T. Fortna.
    p.   cm. – (Monograph series: 67)
English and German.
Papers from a seminar sponsored by the Society for New Testament
Studies.
ISBN 0-521-39211-X
1. Bible. N.T. John X – Criticism, interpretation, etc. –
Congresses.   I. Beutler, Johannes.   II. Fortna, Robert Tomson.
III. Society for New Testament Studies.   IV. Series: Monograph
series (Society for New Testament Studies): 67.
BS2615.2.S47   1990
226.5 – dc20   89–78219 CIP

ISBN-13 978-0-521-39211-2 hardback
ISBN-10 0-521-39211-X hardback

ISBN-13 978-0-521-02060-2 paperback
ISBN-10 0-521-02060-3 paperback

CONTENTS

ABBREVIATIONS

ABR	*Australian Biblical Review*
AJBI	*Annual of the Japanese Biblical Institute*
AnBib	Analecta biblica
ANET	*Ancient Near Eastern Texts* (J.B. Pritchard, ed.)
ATD	Das Alte Testament deutsch
AThR	*Anglican Theological Review*
BBET	Beiträge zur biblischen Theologie und Exegese
BETL	Bibliotheca Ephemeridum Theologicarum Lovaniensium
BFChTh.M	Beiträge zur Forderung christlicher Theologie. 2 Reihe. Sammlung wissenschaftlicher Monographien
BHTh	Beiträge zur historischen Theologie
BJRL	*Bulletin of the John Rylands Library*
BR	*Biblical Research*
BSt(F)	Biblische Studien (Freiburg)
BThB	*Biblical Theological Bulletin*
BU	Biblische Untersuchungen
BZ	*Biblische Zeitschrift*
CB.NT	Coniectanea biblica. New Testament Series
CBQ	*Catholic Biblical Quarterly*
CNT	*Coniectanea neotestamentica*
DTh	*Deutsche Theologie*
EKK.V	Evangelisch-Katholischer Kommentar zum Neuen Testament. Vorarbeiten
EThL	*Ephemerides Theologicae Lovanienses*
EvTh	*Evangelische Theologie*
EvQ	*Evangelical Quarterly*
Exp.	*The Expositor*
FRLANT	Forschungen zur Religion und Literatur des Alten und Neuen Testaments
FzB	Forschung zur Bibel

HC	Hand-Commentar zum Neuen Testament
HeyJ	*Heythrop Journal*
HibJ	*Hibbert Journal*
HJ	*Historisches Jahrbuch*
HNT	Handbuch zum Neuen Testament
HThK	Herders theologischer Kommentar zum Neuen Testament
HThR	*Harvard Theological Review*
HTS	*Harvard Theological Studies*
ICC	International Critical Commentary
IntB	*Interpreter's Bible*
Interp.	*Interpretation*
JBL	*Journal of Biblical Literature*
JDTh	*Jahrbücher für deutsche Theologie*
JPTh	*Jahrbücher für protestantische Theologie*
JSHRZ	Jüdische Schriften aus hellenistisch-römischer Zeit
JSNT	*Journal for the Study of the New Testament*
JTS	*Journal of Theological Studies*
KEK	Kritisch-exegetischer Kommentar über das Neue Testament
KNT	Kommentar zum Neuen Testament
KuD	*Kerygma und Dogma*
NGTT	*Nederduitse Gereformdeerde Teologiese Tydskrif*
NGWG.PH	Nachrichten der Gesellschaft der Wissenschaften Göttingen. Philologisch-historische Klasse
NHC	Nag Hammadi Codices
NT	*Novum Testamentum*
NT.S	Novum Testamentum. Supplement
NTD	Das Neue Testament deutsch
NTS	*New Testament Studies*
ÖTK	Ökumenischer Taschenbuchkommentar zum Neuen Testament
PVTG	Pseudepigrapha veteris testamenti Graece
RGG	*Die Religion in Geschichte und Gegenwart*
SANT	Studien zum Alten und Neuen Testament
SBL.DS	Society of Biblical Literature. Dissertation Series
SBL.SP	Society of Biblical Literature. Seminar Papers
SBS	Stuttgarter Bibelstudien
Scrip.	*Scripture* (Edinburgh)
SEA	*Svensk exegetisk Årsbok*

SHAW.PH	Sitzungsberichte der Heidelberger Akademie der Wissenschaften. Philosophisch-historische Klasse
SNT	Die Schriften des Neuen Testaments (ed. J. Weiss et al.)
SNTA	Studiorum Novi Testamenti Aupilia
SNTSMS	Society for New Testament Studies Monograph Series
SThZ	*Schweizerische theologische Zeitschrift*
StTh	*Studia theologica*
SVTP	Studia in veteris testamenti pseudepigrapha
TDNT	*Theological Dictionary of the New Testament*
TEH	*Theologische Existenz heute*
ThBl	*Theologische Blätter*
ThJb (T)	*Theologische Jahrbücher* (Tübingen)
ThR	*Theologische Rundschau*
ThStKr	*Theologische Studien und Kritiken*
ThT	*Theology Today*
ThZ	*Theologische Zeitschrift*
TRE	*Theologische Realenzyklopädie*
TThT	*Teyler's theologisch tijdschrift*
ThWNT	*Theologisches Wörterbuch zum Neuen Testament*
TZTh	*Tübinger Zeitschrift für Theologie*
UNT	Untersuchungen zum Neuen Testament
VigChr	*Vigiliae Christianae*
VoxTh	*Vox theologica*
WMANT	Wissenschaftliche Monographien zum Alten und Neuen Testament
WUNT	*Wissenschaftliche Untersuchungen zum Neuen Testament*
ZNW	*Zeitschrift für die neutestamentlichen Wissenschaft*
ZSTh	*Zeitschrift für systematische Theologie*
ZThK	*Zeitschrift für Theologie und Kirche*
ZWTh	*Zeitschrift für wissenschaftliche Theologie*

INTRODUCTION

The present volume reproduces, in modified form, papers presented
to the continuing Seminar on Johannine Writings of the international
association of New Testament scholars, Studiorum Novi Testamenti Societas. They were given at the General Meetings of the Society
at Trondheim (Norway) in 1985, and at Atlanta, Georgia (USA),
in 1986. The editors, who have shared the leadership of the seminar,
had proposed the tenth chapter of John's gospel as the theme for
both sessions, and it proved unusually successful. Indeed, that
chapter of the Fourth Gospel serves as a focal point for most of the
issues of current Johannine scholarship. Does the chapter belong in
its present context within the gospel? Does the received text of the
chapter preserve the correct order? Was it written down in a single
stage or did it come into existence by stages? Could the author or
authors depend on written sources, or at least oral traditions, and if
so, what history of religions currents gave the impetus? To what
extent can historical questions properly be asked of the text? Or must
it be explained above all in itself and as part of its context within the
entire work?

The papers begin with a survey of the literary and theological
problems of the Shepherd Discourse as a whole (Busse), then deal with
the question of background — the Biblical/Jewish (Beutler) and the
Hellenistic/Gnostic (Turner). These three papers were presented in
Trondheim in 1985. The discussion continued with four papers in
Atlanta the following year. Painter deals with the question of the
chapter's origin. Also using a historical perspective, Sabbe treats the
relation of the text to the Synoptic Gospels. Then Du Rand looks at
the structure of John 10 in connection with chapter 9, and Thyen the
chapter in the context of the gospel as a whole.

At first glance the *variety of approaches* is surprising. They can be
divided into two groups: those that consider the text in the light of

its pre-history (*diachronically*) and those that treat it as a given unity (*synchronically*). Busse initiates the diachronic approach with a survey of the literary problems of the passage. In addition to textual criticism, he discusses hypotheses of rearrangement and source, and the literary genre of the Shepherd Discourse. Beutler and Turner scan the history of religions horizon of the discourse; the former primarily examines the 'Old Testament' and Jewish ideas behind the discourse, the latter compares it to Hellenistic and Gnostic texts. Both use the tradition-critical method to concentrate on the roots of Johannine terminology and thought in their cultural and religious environment.

Both Painter's and Sabbe's contributions also belong to the area of historical issues. Painter traces the possibility of stages in the development of this passage, and of the gospel as a whole, seeking to depict its development, whether literary or still traditional, but always so as to recognise the theological changes that occur in the evolution of the chapter (and gospel) into its present form.

Of the literature comparable to the Fourth Gospel, Sabbe focusses on the Synoptic Gospels and examines them alongside the Johannine text, using Jesus' trial as portrayed in the Synoptics for the comparison. But while he explicitly holds the Synoptics to be sufficient sources of the present text of John, he does not consider stages of development in the gospel traditions. Thus, in a way, he is the first to interpret the text synchronically, along with the remaining contributors, who altogether disregard its prior development, as well as its later influence.

Du Rand widens the unit of text to be studied to include the healing of the man born blind, and its ensuing dialogue, in chapter 9. He uses the intricate 'syntactical' and 'narratological' techniques of the new literary criticism to expose dimensions of meaning otherwise unnoticed in the text of chapters 9–10. Thyen is primarily interested in a still larger context, the entire gospel as a macro-text of the Shepherd Discourse, and he definitively rejects as a 'dangerous illusion' a diachronic approach to the text, especially the attempt to make our interpretation conform to the original author's intention.

The fact that the more synchronically oriented contributions were presented in the later session did not at first seem to be more than accidental. But in retrospect its significance becomes evident: except for Painter, who had been prevented from attending the previous year, the seminar's interest had shifted from theories about the text's origin to a thorough analysis of its present form. In this way the previously elaborated historical insights reappear in a new light.

In view of the variety of approaches, the *unity of results* is also surprising. In the editors' opinion, one of the most important results of the two-year study appears to be the agreement of the authors and participants in the discussion concerning the close coherence of John 9 and 10. The Shepherd Discourse is therefore to be regarded as a continuation of Jesus' argument with the Pharisees and 'the Jews' in chapter 9. Only thus can the pervasively polemical overtones of the discourse be accounted for.

Some agreement is found also in regard to the validity of the preserved order of John 10. The only exception is Turner, who suggests as a working hypothesis that the chapter be read in the following order: verses 19–30, 1–18, 31–42.

Basic agreement is found in the view that the author of the gospel draws on the world of ideas of the Hebrew Bible, particularly on the post-exilic prophets and their texts about the coming eschatological shepherd (whether God himself or his anointed one). There is less agreement as to how far Hellenistic and early Gnostic or even proto-Gnostic thought exercised influence on the evangelist, and whether the Biblical motifs came to that author directly or were mediated by a tradition.

This raises the question of sources. That the fourth evangelist knew one or more of the three Synoptic Gospels and used them in some way was not a matter of explicit discussion; nor was the question of the nature and proportion of such dependence resolved. Sabbe's paper shows the ways such a view sheds light on the present text; alternative views of how synoptic-like material may have been conveyed to the evangelist, as by either tradition or sources, are not represented. Until just a few years ago most scholars accepted the Gospel's independence of the Synoptics. It is significant that this consensus can no longer be taken for granted.

A major consensus was reached concerning the overall structure of the Shepherd Discourse; in particular, the character of verses 7–10 and 11–19 as interpretations of the *paroimia* of verses 1–5 had wide acceptance. The same is true on a more detailed level as to the definition of both interpretative sections by means of their introductory I–AM sayings (verses 7, 11).

Viewing the Shepherd Discourse, and its elaboration in verses 22–39 and 40–2, as an expression of the dispute between the Johannine congregation and the synagogue was not a matter of controversy, nor does there appear to be difference of opinion as to the originating germ of the dispute going back somehow to the life of Jesus himself.

Finally, although the history of religions background of the ideas of John 10 is evaluated differently, the various contributors agree in characterising the main lines of the chapter's theology.

Despite these largely converging results for the interpretation of John 10 there do remain some *unanswered questions*. They have to do both with details of interpretation and the proper method of interpretation itself.

Divergence on details starts with the text of verse 7: which text is to be read – 'I am the shepherd' (Busse) or 'I am the door' (the others)? The choice has ramifications for the structure of the entire discourse of 10:1–18. And the textual order of the chapter was not entirely resolved, as we saw.

Whether and to what extent we have to assume our text to contain layers, and whether these deserve attention, is left open. Painter is clearly the strongest advocate of the view that assumes a developing tradition behind the discourse; others, like Sabbe, exclude this possibility. A further group leaves the question unresolved, or holds it to be insignificant for interpretation. Nevertheless, an answer to the question is important for the problem of assessing the discourse historically. Does it mirror primarily the dispute between church and synagogue, or does it reflect, at least in its later layers, a rank dispute within the Johannine community, so that in its present form it is to be placed on a level with the First Epistle of John (Painter)?

The question also remains unanswered how far, in addition to the Hebrew scripture and Jewish thought in general, the Shepherd Discourse was influenced by Hellenism and early Gnosticism. This cannot be resolved on the basis of a single text, of course, since it leads to the heart of present discussion about the definition, nature, and age of 'gnosis' and Gnosticism. This debate has been occasioned by extensive studies of the Nag Hammadi texts now available; surely, however, they will need more study.

Possibly the most interesting issue, in reviewing both sessions of the seminar is this: how do individual interpretative approaches relate to each other? Especially, the more and more urgent problem of the reciprocal relation between diachronic and synchronic readings of a text comes to the fore. The tendency of most of the seminar partici-pants is to hold that both more time and greater priority need to be assigned to the synchronic reading of texts. This stands in accord with the results of recent methodological discussions on either side of the Atlantic. Not least of the benefits for all the seminar participants is that of contributing to such dialogue on the basis of a rewarding sample of text, and of doing so in a collaborative way that both preserves the integrity of each scholar and provides the benefit of work undertaken jointly and honed by collective evaluation.

The Editors

Frankfurt a.M./Poughkeepsie, NY

1

OPEN QUESTIONS ON JOHN 10*
Ulrich Busse

John 10, on the shepherd, is a passage which, while undoubtedly attractive, is laden with all the exegetical problems characteristic of John's gospel.[1] Not only is the beginning disputed, but also its form, inner structure, in part its wording, and most of all its place in the larger context and also the thrust of the chapter.

Here the task will be limited to examining in light of the text the validity of answers given by scholars to some of the problems. Accordingly, questions of the origin and later use of the imagery, as well as the significance of Biblical allusions for the interpretation, will only be dealt with in passing.[2] Our plan results from the task before us. Literary questions will be discussed before we turn to theological issues.

1. Literary problems

1.1 One literary problem of chapter 10 consists in what is often felt to be a loose insertion of the shepherd speech into its present context.[3] This 'impression' is usually substantiated by pointing to the supposedly abrupt change of topic, and to the surprising transition to a different narrative genre[4] between 9:39 and 10:1. Yet these observations apply only to the beginning of the speech. As the chapter develops, verses 26b–28 are presupposed in the preceding material. The classic solution for this supposed enigma is provided by literary criticism. From a literary point of view two possible solutions have been offered over the past hundred years. One explores the tradition-historical 'growth' model, according to which various sources have been arranged redactionally by a third party, or one piece of text has been inserted later. The other suggestion employs the 'rearrangement'

* A contribution, which formed part of the project 'Johannes und die Synoptiker', sponsored by the Ministerium für Wissenschaft und Forschung of Nordrhein-Westfalen (FRG). – The original version of this paper appeared as 'Offene Fragen zu Joh 10', in *NTS*, 33 (1987), 516–31.

hypothesis. It has the advantage of easing the abrupt new beginning of 10:1 by means of skillfully rearranging the text. Most adherents of this latter proposal are content to move the entire shepherd speech (10:1–18) to follow verse 28.[5] The leading exponents of the former suggestion, on the other hand, are mainly dependent on a hypothesis which arose last century[6] and which, despite the individual differences, sought to distinguish sharply between Jesus' speeches and the narrative texts in John's gospel (= JG). H. H. Wendt,[7] for instance, reconstructed an older source made up of speeches (9:4f., 49–41; 10:1–18, 24–38) which was expanded by the evangelist (9:1–3, 6–38; 10:19–22, 39–42) through narrative material. A new variant of the 'growth' model is presented by Langbrandtner and J. Becker.[8] They attempt to show that the shepherd speech was inserted subsequently into chapter 10 by the so-called 'ecclesiastical redactor'. Among other reasons, it was the observation that verse 16 is sometimes regarded as a secondary insertion[9] which led them to pursue this hint.

Each of these suggested solutions is as attractive as its presuppositions are plausible. Therefore doubts may certainly be raised. It should be noted that the chapter is firmly integrated both as to narrative and speech. The asides of verses 19–21, 31 and 39a presuppose earlier events,[10] as is clear from the introductory πάλιν.[11] In Jesus' response to the challenge (verse 24de) to say frankly and openly whether he is the Christ (this in itself is a reflection of 8:25 and 7:26), Jesus points to his deeds which can lead to faith. He thus draws on 9:4b. That verse, however, together with verses 3 and 5, forms an interpretive addition by the author. On the one hand he sheds light on the *sign* character (cf. 9:16e) of the healing of the blind man just as he points backwards to 8:12 and forwards to 11:9f. by employing the light motif. In regard to the former verse (8:12) it was already F. C. Baur's[12] judgement that it forms the chief idea of chapters 8–11. This has been recognised also by the literary critics who used it as support for their conclusion that only 10:1–18 is to be viewed as an independent text unit. But even this unit is rooted in the context. Only rarely has its dialectical structure received due attention. Throughout, contrasting persons are compared with one other. For instance, rather surprisingly, the comparison of verse 1 does not start with the 'good' shepherd but instead with the antitype, the thief and robber.[13] The reason for this is to be found in the scene's framework. Already since 9:40 the Pharisees[14] have been in view. As early as the preceding verse (39) Jesus, in taking up the interpretation of the healing of the blind man, had drawn the conclusion from his miracle that it would separate some from others. The blind will come to have faith (verse 38b); the ones who can see physically, however, will remain in the continuing darkness of sin (verse 41). Thus the Pharisees have lost the right to lead the people, the salvation community of Israel; this right has now gone to Jesus, the stumbling stone (verse 39b).

The development of thought (which is present latently as a metaphor already in verses 39ff.) suggests at this point the transition to the portrayal of the everyday life of a shepherd, a picture which was prepared for in the OT.[16] Already there the major characteristic of the shepherd caringly guarding and securing life as part of his task as ruler took shape, and ideals of how to rule as well. This idea is now used as a weapon to judge the legitimacy of any claim of authority, as well as to point to the contrast between the Pharisees and Jesus in terms of competence.[17] The basic clarification at which the author aims is fruitfully displayed by the mental image of the shepherd. Verses 1–5a rather sweepingly contrast a number of individuals. In an almost synonymous characterisation of those who illegitimately climb over the wall to the sheep, various patterns of activity (secret–violent) are hinted at. It is not until verse 5c that the contrast can be further unfolded by way of the summarising plural, 'the strangers' (parallel to thief/robber/day labourer?).

Therefore 10:1ff. cannot be separated from chapter 9, and notably 9:39–41, without difficulty.[18] Verse 39 creates a new scene, and verse 41 (the Pharisees' blindness) together with verse 6 (the listeners' inability to comprehend) ties the speech together even closer.[19] Apart from this one should notice what is mentioned mostly by earlier interpreters,[20] namely that the confrontation with Jesus' deeds (compare the Sabbath healing, chapter 5, with the healing of the blind man on the Sabbath, chapter 9), which issues in either salvation or judgement, extends over a number of chapters (at least chapters 7–11). Verbally (ῥῆμα) the peak of the argument is reached in the chapter about the shepherd and after the Lazarus miracle (ἔργον) his death is decided in principle by the people's leaders.[21] Thus in chapter 10 the confrontation between Jesus and the leaders of the people, which started in chapter 5, moves towards its first climax. This takes place after Jesus' refutation as illegitimate and wrong of the seemingly legitimate claim of the Pharisees to lead Israel. The basis for this is found in 9:40, where Jesus' deeds result in a separation of the ways leading to salvation on the one hand and to disaster on the other.

Analogous with the interlacing of the chapter about the shepherd with preceding statements of chapter 9 there are also strong links with the chapters which follow. Chapter 11 verses 8—10 builds not only on the attempts to stone Jesus (10:31 and verse 39) but draws also on the symbolism of light in 8:12 and 9:5 (cf. 11:37). The interpretive insertion 11:4 is also patterned in analogy to 9:3—5. It sheds light on the significance of the resurrection: the sign of the glorification of the Son of God. Since JG refers the glorification motif to Jesus' passion, the author here not only alludes to the final decision of the High Priests and Pharisees to kill Jesus (11:47—53); the application of the title of honour, Son of God, to Jesus points back also to his confession of 10:36f. If, however, 11:47—53 replaces the synoptic account of the trial by the Sanhedrin,[22] — which in its synoptic form is missing from the Johannine passion account — then the proleptic accusation of blasphemy in 10:33 is the occasion for 18:20[23] (cf. 5:18) and 19:7, where Jesus points to his public teaching in the synagogue and temple, and where the 'Jews' stubbornly object to his self-revelation as Son of God. Besides these rather obvious peculiarities, 10:18 and 39b also include a hidden allusion to the Johannine passion account. Not only does Jesus voluntarily and as an act of sovereignty offer his own life (cf. 18:4—7);[24] it is also the case that the hour which the Father had determined had not yet arrived at 10:39b, which is why Jesus could escape once more.[25] Jesus' request in 18:8f. to let his disciples go may also have been prepared for as early as 10:28f. Equally the statement in 18:37 that all those on the side of truth hear Jesus' voice draws on what has been said in 10:1—5.

Thus the close interlacing of all parts of the text of chapter 10 with the wider context renders any version of rearrangement unlikely. It is not just Haenchen[26] who thinks that the time for 'rearrangement hypotheses' is over. Already Jülicher suggested that

> Critics all too often use as criteria their own sense of logic, their attention to detail and their desire for a correct flow of thought. In short, they call for a gospel written the way they would have written it.

This is true also of Bultmann's large commentary.[27] In spite of the recent literary-critical attempt to assign John 10:1—18 to secondary redaction, this does not promise to emerge as a convincing solution either. Rather, the attempt must be made to comprehend the author's complex line of argument before assuming a subsequent interweaving of alleged traditions.

1.2 A clarification, of great import for the interpretation of 10:1–18, is called for in the case of the wording of verse 7. If the noun ἡ θύρα, which is regarded as a difficult variant,[28] is still the preferred reading, even though P[75] (cop[sa]) renders the variant ὁ ποιμήν possible, then an ecclesiological interpretation which takes Jesus to be the door to the sheep, through which the leaders of Christian churches enter into the church,[29] becomes compelling. Yet, it destroys the coherence of the text. 'The picture of the door breaks into the speech ... The contrast between the shepherds should remain at the centre, both in terms of topic and of execution and expansion.'[30] Attempts have been made to remove in various ways the disruption in the flow of thought without having recourse to a text-critical decision.[31] Yet, a text-critically reasonable solution has to be sought. Schnackenburg[32] put the decisive question thus: How could a text which is so much more suitable disappear? The answer is found in the later use of the metaphor 'door'. In ecclesiastical apologetics it gradually came to denote a fixed idea, i.e. opposition to false church leaders.[33] Only the shepherd who appeals to Christ and who was appointed by Christ could be certain of his legitimacy. Here we find the reason for the poor attestation of the original reading ὁ ποιμήν. It now fits nicely into the context[34] since, the hearers' inability to comprehend having been declared in verse 6, there is a need to decipher the shepherd's *paroimia*. The text is formulated accordingly. The contrast between ὁ μή εἰσερόμενος διά in verse 1 and ὁ δέ εἰσερχόμενος διά in verse 2 is not drawn upon until verse 9. There the metaphor is commented on in soteriological terms by reference to Num. 27:17 (Micah 5:4). The use of διά in 3:17 and 14:6 corresponds to this. Therefore the soteriologically significant distinction between the legitimate shepherd and the illegitimate ones is made explicit a number of times. This is done by first pointing to this separation on the level of metaphor before it is transferred to the quasi-historical level of action in the second part of the chapter, i.e. verses 22–39.

1.3 A problem much debated among scholars is that of determining the genre of 10:1–18 or of 10:1–5. The definitions found in the literature are sometimes more and sometimes less well founded. These verses have been called allegory,[35] similitude,[36] parable,[37] concept[38] or simply image.[39] This uncertainty of definition testifies to the distinctive feature of this figurative language in comparison with the other gospels. Already Strauss[40] claimed a lack of development in terms of plot, and B. Bauer, with his intuitive feel for literary forms, realised the high extent of abstraction involved:

> Here the point is not like that in the story of the sower, for example, where a specific event is reported which is resolved in general terms only at the end. The author does not report what this particular good or bad shepherd did to a particular flock − rather, both shepherd and flock are portrayed in general terms right from the start. To be sure, the relationship between shepherd and flock does not lack alternation[41] (bad/good; following/not following; knowing/not knowing).

Only by means of such abstraction was the narrator able to unfold the significance of the *paroimia* a number of times consecutively and to strike a balance in terms of the depth of its significance. The literary procedure can therefore, with K. Berger,[42] be labelled an 'image field' 'which is approached from all angles; the author "plays" with the entire metaphorical range available.' This enables him to connect Jesus a number of times with the various metaphors of keeping sheep and so to use them for the purpose of identification, a procedure so common in his gospel.[43] In contrast to his counterparts (thief/robber; stranger/labourer), Jesus really is who he claims to be.

1.4 The final literary peculiarity which needs discussion is the author's use of what appears to be historically accurate data. Even though verses 22f. give a new time for the following argument between Jesus and the 'Jews' (verses 24−38), the author presupposes that his audience knows Jesus' 'shepherd' speech (verses 26bff.) as well as his earlier deeds. H. J. Holtzmann[44] highlights this as a consistent method of the writer.

> The period of at least three months is fictitious; in reality the space in between consists of 30 lines. The quarter of a year which separates the two events is real only on paper. The truth is that the author reminds himself as well as the readers of what he wrote just shortly before. The same applies to the reminder at Lazarus' grave (11:37) of the one who was born blind and equally to the even more peculiar reference to 3:14, 8:28 (not 12:23) in 12:34.

The author's peculiarity in having the audience regard the narrative as historical should no longer be taken as true historical reminiscence. Rather, it signals theological considerations. The christological−

soteriological reflection is meant to be exempted in all circumstances from a sense of unreality. The Johannine Logos has become flesh in space and time. This is where the roots of any subsequent reflection on the soteriological event revealed in him are to be found, an event in which the readers participate.

2. Theological problems

The insights gained so far have displayed the central significance of the chapter about the shepherd within the overall framework of the gospel. As it is embedded in the surrounding chapters it also forms an important part of a christological reflection. Literarily this reflection is presented as part of a dramatic quarrel between Jesus and his audience in Jerusalem revolving around the fact and meaning of his divine commission. From a dramatic point of view the argument works by means of the rather cryptic christological allusions by Jesus as well as by means of the doubt, lack of comprehension and open rejection on the part of his audience. Jesus, in turn, responds to this in an insulting fashion.

In the second part of chapter 10 the audience finally wants clarification (verse 24c−e). The Johannine Jesus meets this expectation only reluctantly by pointing to his works. His disclosures (verses 30; 36f. and 38fg) lead to weighty consequences for him. The dispute, covering a number of chapters and the Lazarus miracle, results in his final condemnation by the High Priests and the Pharisees (11:46−53). This last consequence has been deliberately fitted by the author into the entire section, even though the synoptics place the scene within the passion narrative. For the writer this scene justifies those parts of Jesus' speeches where he comments on his own death. Weizsäcker[45] would have reproduced the meaning and style of the depiction more appropriately had he taken the Sanhedrin trial, which is anticipated in chapter 11, into account. He describes the composition of chapters 7−10 correctly:

> One can apply to the passage whatever one would say about the entire gospel: it seems constantly to intensify the argument and dispute, but in fact it only sheds light on the latter from many different angles. One objection after the other is contrasted with the various explanations, which in substance are all identical. All this creates a picture of tension which forces a decision without actually issuing in it.

Not until chapter 11 is the decision made. However, the point itself, i.e. the christological conception of the author as far as can be elaborated from John 10, will be dealt with in what follows.

2.1 The image of the legitimate and the illegitimate shepherd can be understood properly only against the background of the events reported in chapter 9. The healing of the blind man[46] occasions mention of an eschatological division and its effect in and for the present (as well as the future: cf. verse 16).[47] Even though in verse 39cd it is the followers of Jesus (cf. verse 38) who became the μὴ βλέποντες in contrast to Mk. 4:12 par. while the Pharisees (cf. verse 40c) became the βλέποντες,[48] the synoptic motif of hardening is taken up, yet different conclusions are drawn (cf. 12:37ff.). It is not so much their present lack of faith that deprives the Pharisees of their credentials, but rather the state of sin which is grounded in the hardening. This is the only way to make sense of the argument put forward in verse 41. The first clause − 'if you were blind' − finds its logical complement in the thought expressed in the last clause: then your previous deeds would not be considered sinful because of your lack of knowledge. However, because you consider yourselves wise, you remain in sin[49] (cf. 8:21, 24; 15:22, 24). These verses explain the image as it is used thereafter. Sometimes it makes use of contrasting terms (robber/ thief/day labourer) for the description of Jesus' commission. The Johannine Jesus identifies himself exclusively[50] (cf. verse 8) with the role of the caring shepherd. It would be a waste of time to try to determine those persons who might be lurking behind the contrasting figures. Their only function is to emphasise the centrality of the person of Jesus and his deeds. For instance, the debate about whom[51] the robbers and thieves who preceded Jesus represent is superfluous, since on the one hand the rhetorical character of verse 8b is obvious from the use of ὅσοι, and on the other hand it is christological with respect to the shepherd. Therefore the robbers and thieves are those who preceded him and who pretended to be what he is exclusively:[52] the life-giving Saviour (verse 9c; 10fg). The image of the day labourer also serves to define more clearly the shepherd's role which Jesus claims exclusively. His commission does not terminate because of a life-threatening danger, rather his death is understood − in contrast to the medieval theology of atonement[53] − as a saving death (cf. 18:8; 17:11f.). The 'good' shepherd saves the sheep from the wolf. At the same time (secondarily?) a further aspect of his commission is named. Death is not the total end for Jesus; rather it makes possible the enlarging of the present flock to the size envisaged in God's commission (verse 18).[54] Thus Jesus' giving himself up and his self-resurrection are rooted functionally in God's salvation plan. The understanding of Jesus' resurrection as a deed performed by himself is expressed by the note in John 20:5−7 concerning the unfolded bandages and the cloth lying by itself.

Accordingly Jesus released himself from the grip of death. He could only do so as a result of the authority bestowed upon him by the Father. At the same time this concluding statement marks the post-Easter standpoint of the author in the fourth Christian generation. For him the death of Jesus has primarily attained significance in terms of its salvific function. Jesus thus performs his commission from God (cf. 19,30[55]). JG speaks only of ἡ ἐντολή τοῦ θεοῦ when Jesus is in view. It is he who obediently fulfills God's commission.[56] Therefore the death of Jesus is not just a matter of voluntarily giving himself up (cf. 10:18bc and 13:1) as a result of caring love. It comes to have salvation-historical significance. After his self-resurrection Jesus is exalted, yet, it is by other means that he fulfills his commission. He is deliberately glorified by God in order to be empowered to create what God desired (cf. the salvation-historical δεῖ in verse 16c), i.e. community among his children. For this reason the idea of the humiliation Jesus experienced on the cross recedes to the background. But this must not be overstressed theologically,[57] as if the author wanted to present Jesus as a god striding over the earth. What can finally be said is that he aims to present the salvation-historical significance of Jesus' commission.

2.2 If, however, the salvation-historical function of Jesus' death is an integral part of JG's reflexion, then this has far-reaching consequences for the interpretation of the gospel as a whole. Within the author's horizon it would still be conceivable to consider the post-Easter continuation of the Jesus story not just as the history of its effect, but also as Jesus' own continuing function. The differentiation between Easter eye-witnesses and later Christian generations, such as appears to be presupposed by the makarism in 20:29[58] (cf. 4:38; 11:52; 17:20), and the repeated use of the shepherd metaphor in chapter 21, could be accounted for within that horizon. The promise of the paraclete in the farewell discourse, which surprisingly is not referred to in 20:22, would also gain plausibility for later generations of Christians. Since most, however, have decided against a thorough-going historical consciousness and in favour of realised eschatology as the presupposition of the author, a literary-critical manoeuvre becomes inescapable. Verse 16 therefore is removed by most as the later insertion of an ecclesiastical redactor. The price to be paid for this is that the functional resurrection statement of verse 18 as the basis for the preceding thesis is left without point of reference.

2.3 One final burning problem is mentioned already (though indirectly) in 10:14–18. Yet, it only becomes active in the two-part debate between Jesus and the 'Jews' (verses 24–38).[59] The 'Jews' take Jesus' claim to be one with the Father as a blasphemous attempt to put himself on a level with God. The statement is not sufficiently clarified by the later definitions of the councils. It is a striking feature of the debate in the last century that the so-called progressive interpreters[60] are mostly found on the side of the councils' definitions, while the more moderate and conservative theologians[61] are seen to go their own ways. Before one attempts – like Cludius[62] – to argue, on the grounds of 14:28 and chapter 17, against the unity in substance of the Son with Father, the statement should be interpreted within its context. In my view it contains clues only for a functional unity. In the context (verses 24–9) only the deeds (e.g. chapter 9) and the profession of the shepherd (10:1–18) which God conferred upon Jesus are in view. Thus God acts through him, as is confirmed by the Johannine Jesus himself in verses 37f. (cf. 14:10). This is alluded to already in verses 14–18. Yet, it is not until verses 24–38 that the christological conviction comes to full expression. By means of the image of the shepherd, then, the author metaphorically describes the office held by Jesus.[63]

Even verse 36, which can be put forward against this interpretation,[64] actually supports it. This verse is part of an extended chain of argument by Jesus against the charge of having intended to put himself on a par with God. His pointing to the Scriptures and arguing *a minori ad majus* would be unfitting if they were meant to serve as proof for a unity of substance. None of the audience could possibly have concluded from Ps. 82:6 that judges, in their function as God's representatives, partook in divine substance. The most that could be concluded is that they stood in a special relationship with the one who commissioned them. The proximity to God of the one who may exclusively call himself 'Son of God' must be much greater. All this is only recognisable to Jesus' audience via his deeds (verse 38c–e). He and the Father are one because he performs only God's deeds. Only the one who is commissioned by God, the one who does and says everything in accordance with the Father is capable of being God's representative.[65] At the incarnation he has set aside the pre-existent Logos' being since God can only be recognised truly by means of a functional unity with the one commissioned. In this sense theology and christology finally coincide. This has been expressed superbly by Weizsäcker:[66]

> We must not say: He is the salvation of the world because he is himself conscious of being God's Logos. Instead: Because of his intention to give salvation to the world, to reveal the Father ... he knows himself to be the one in whom God's Logos dwells. Because of this intention he knows himself to have been sent by the Father, cf. 10:36. His self-consciousness is not grounded in the personality of the divine Logos, but rather in his *certainty about his commission*, it is this which gives him this awareness of God's presence in himself.

3. Conclusion

The discussion has demonstrated a coherent literary composition and flow of argument in so far as the main interest of the author is christological–soteriological.[67] He aims at offering a basic definition and presentation of Jesus' commission by using the image of the shepherd, the fulfilling of this commission (chapters 9 and 11), and the negative reaction to it by certain circles. In the debate at the Chanukka festival in the temple Jesus' activity is used as an argument for proving the functional unity between Father and Son *in history* (cf. 1:4). Here the christological confession that Jesus is Son of God from eternity finds its subsequent legitimation because the shepherd's caring attitude, which leads to his giving up himself, is seen to have revealed God's love for the world. If one follows Wrede[68] when he describes the author's interest as that of 'securing Jesus' divine son-ship', an interest which dominates 'the entire gospel', then the nearest parallel to this chapter is found in John 20:31. There also the main question is not so much that of the Son's pre-existence; rather it is the identity of the 'historical Jesus' with the pre-existent Son which is held on to for soteriological reasons. For the same reason the caring attitude of Jesus which, to adhere to the image, assures the sheep of 'food' (verse 9f) and consequently life (verse 10fg), is pushed to the forefront of the argument of John 10. Simultaneously the confession of faith, that Jesus is the pre-existent Son of God, is retracted. In addition, the legitimacy of his claim to pasture the sheep of Israel is meant to be deduced from his exemplary behaviour.

The evangelist sees the danger that the concreteness of the salvation which is revealed in Jesus, fulfilled by him and tied to him, be watered down by an overemphasis on a christology of pre-existence which features all the negative aspects of speculation. Haenchen's[69] opinion that the Johannine church was pneumatically oriented, has once again, though in a modified form, been shown to be sound.

2

DER ALTTESTAMENTLICH-JÜDISCHE HINTERGRUND DER HIRTENREDE IN JOHANNES 10

Johannes Beutler, SJ

Neben dem Prolog ist die Hirtenrede Jesu wohl immer noch der umstrittenste Text des Joh(annesevangeliums). Eine Einführung in den neuesten Stand der hier verhandelten Fragen hat jüngst R. Schnackenburg[1] gegeben. Sie braucht hier darum nicht wiederholt zu werden. Wir beschränken uns im vorliegenden Beitrag im wesentlichen auf die Frage nach dem Hintergrund der eigentümlichen Bildwelt der Jesusrede in Joh 10. Noch immer stehen sich hier zwei Lager mehr oder minder unversöhnt gegenüber. Für die einen ist die Bildwelt von Hirt, Herde, Mietling, Räuber und Wolf nur vom AT und frühjüdischen Texten her verständlich,[2] für die anderen greift der Evangelist auf die Bildwelt der Gnosis zurück.[3] Dabei ist freilich im Auge zu behalten, daß solche Ableitungsversuche sich nicht notwendigerweise gegenseitig ausschließen. Zum einen ist es durchaus möglich, daß das Joh einerseits auf alttestamentlich-jüdisches Sprach- und Gedankengut zurückgreift, andererseits aber Beziehungen zur sich bildenden gnostischen Gedankenwelt aufweist;[4] zum andern ist daran zu erinnern, daß die Gnosis ihrerseits ihre Wurzeln nicht zuletzt im AT hat, so daß sich auch ihre Bildwelt aus alttestamentlich-jüdischen Quellen speist.[5] Bei der religionsgeschichtlichen Erklärung der Hirtenrede in Joh 10 kann es also nicht um ein Entweder – Oder bezüglich des alttestamentlich-jüdischen und des gnostischen Hintergrundes gehen, sondern nur um eine Standortbestimmung innerhalb einer von dem einen zum anderen Bereich verlaufenden 'Entwicklungslinie'.[6]

Wir schicken unserer Untersuchung einige Einleitungsfragen voraus, bei denen wir uns auf das vorangehende Referat von U. Busse beziehen können. In manchen Fragen, wie der des Kontextes, werden wir uns mit ihm einig wissen, in anderen, wie der Textbestimmung in Vers 7, werden wir von ihm abweichen. Ergänzend soll genauer zwischen Form und Gattung der Jesusrede in Joh 10: 1 – 18 unterschieden werden. Auch zu dem hinter dieser Rede stehenden vermutlichen kompositions- oder redaktionsgeschichtlichen Prozeß sei ein Wort gesagt. Innerhalb der traditionsgeschichtlichen Untersuchungen im engeren Sinne muß zwischen der Motivwelt von schlechtem und gutem Hirten einerseits und derjenigen von der Tür unterschieden werden. Letztere wird sich gegen eine religionsgeschichtliche Einordnung in den von uns untersuchten Herkunftsbereich sträuben. Für beide Motivkomplexe ist dabei zwischen sprachlichen Entsprechungen einzelner Worte und Ausdrücke in der alttestamentlich-jüdischen Tradition einerseits und bei Joh anderseits und religionsgeschichtlichen Zusammenhängen zu unterscheiden. Letztere werden sich vor allem dann erhärten lassen, wenn sich ganze Motivkomplexe durchhalten, wobei die sprachliche Formulierung leicht variieren kann. Gegenüber den sprachlichen Berührungen läßt sich so die Zahl der relevanten Stellen aus der alttestamentlich-jüdischen Überlieferung einerseits erweitern, andererseits aber auch eingrenzen.

1. Einleitungsfragen

1.1 Kontext

Wie auch von anderer Seite bemerkt,[7] fallen wichtige Vorentscheidungen für die Auslegung der johanneischen Hirtenrede auf der Ebene von Tradition und Redaktion bei der Entscheidung über ihre Zuordnung zu ihrem Kontext.

Auf der einen Seite stehen Autoren, die sie als Fremdkörper an ihrer Stelle empfinden[8] und auch innerhalb des Verlaufs der Rede Umstellungen vornehmen, um Aufbau und Gedankenfolge klarer hervortreten zu lassen.[9] Auf der anderen Seite hält sich aber die Meinung durch, ja sie gewinnt derzeit an Boden, daß die Hirtenrede in Joh 10 an ihrer Stelle steht, ja nur so sinnvoll ausgelegt werden kann.[10] Wir halten diese Auffassung für überzeugender, und zwar aus folgenden hier noch einmal kurz rekapitulierten Gründen: die Rede Jesu ist vor allem in den Versen 1–13, aber auch darüber hinaus von Antithesen bestimmt. Diese prägen das Bild so sehr, daß sie auch strukturell hervortreten. So steht in Vers 1–3a das negative Bild des über die Mauer steigenden Fremden voran, dem der durch die Tür kommende Hirt entgegengestellt wird. In Vers 3b–5 kontrastiert in umgekehrter Reihenfolge der Hirt, dessen Stimme die Schafe kennen, mit dem Fremden, dessen Stimme ihnen unbekannt ist. In Vers 7–10 stehen die Aussagen über die Diebe und die Räuber erneut vor denen über Jesus als denjenigen, dem die Schafe gehören. In wiederum umgekehrter Reihenfolge sprechen Verse 11–13 von Jesus als gutem Hirten im Gegensatz zum Mietling, dem nichts an den Schafen liegt. Dieser polemische Charakter der Hirtenrede findet seine plausibelste Erklärung in deren näherem Kontext.[11] Der das Bildwort von Vers 1–5 abschließende Vers 6 hält ausdrücklich fest: 'Diese Bildrede sagte ihnen Jesus, sie aber verstanden nicht, was er ihnen sagen wollte.' Alles spricht dafür, dies Wort auf die zuvor in Kapitel 9 genannten Gegner Jesu zu beziehen. Sie werden in 9:13, 15–16, 40 als 'Pharisäer', in Vers 18, 22 als 'Juden' bezeichnet. Während der Blindgeborene, geheilt, zum Glauben an Jesus kommt (Vers 38), verharren die Gegenspieler Jesu im Unglauben und müssen den Vorwurf bleibender Blindheit hören (Verse 39–41). Eben gegen sie richtet sich zumindest auf der Ebene des vorliegenden Evangeliums die nachfolgende Rede. Sie fügt sich mit ihrer Auseinandersetzung mit den Führern Israels lückenlos in ihren größeren Kontext der Kapitel 7–10 oder sogar 5–12 des Joh,[12] so daß eine Notwendigkeit, sie aus diesem herauszulösen, nicht besteht.

1.2 Text

Da es für die Strukturbestimmung wie Auslegung der Hirtenrede nicht unerheblich ist, sei kurz auf die textkritische Frage in Joh 10.7 zurückgekommen. Die in letzter Zeit gelegentlich favorisierte Lesart 'ich bin der Hirt der Schafe'[13] hat auch dadurch neue Nahrung erhalten, daß P. Weigandt die Unabhängigkeit der sie stützenden koptischen Handschriftengruppen und die größere Ursprünglichkeit des sie gleichfalls stützenden P^{75} vor Codex B (Vaticanus) betont hat.[14]

Das Gewicht der gesamten übrigen Textüberlieferung ist jedoch so eindrucksvoll, daß das Greek New Testament die Lesart vom 'Hirten' nicht einmal in Erwägung gezogen hat. Daß sich die inneren Gründe für beide Lesarten die Wage halten, hat dabei auch P. Weigandt zugegeben.[15] Wir lesen also mit allen neueren Textausgaben und fast allen Kommentatoren in Vers 7 'ich bin die Tür der Schafe' und setzen diese Lesart auch für die nachfolgende Strukturbestimmung voraus.

1.3 Form/Gattung

Vor der Gattungsbestimmung der Hirtenrede und vor allem ihrer einleitenden Verse Joh 10:1–5 steht sinnvollerweise die Formanalyse. Sie muß und kann hier in aller Kürze behandelt werden.

Seit E. Fascher[16] wird in der Forschung[17] darauf hingewiesen, daß die Verse 7–18 offenbar eine deutende Aufgabe gegenüber der Bildrede in Vers 1–5 haben. Ähnlich wie beim Gleichnis vom Unkraut unter dem Weizen (Mt 13:24–30) die Deutung seiner wichtigsten Stichworte in der Reihenfolge ihres Vorkommens erfolgt (Mt 13:36–43), so werden auch in Joh 10:7–18 zwei Stichworte der Bildreihe in der Reihenfolge ihres Vorkommens herausgegriffen und je doppelt gedeutet. Voran steht das Stichwort 'Tür' in Vers 7 und 9. Es folgt das Stichwort 'Hirt' in Verse 11 und 14. Die Verse 7–8 gehen nach dem einleitenden 'Ich-bin-Wort' vom Negativbild derer aus, die 'vor Jesus' kamen.[18] In Vers 9–10 steht die positive Aussage voran. Dabei wird dann in Vers 10 noch einmal das unterschiedliche Motiv des 'Kommens' vom Räuber und von Jesus herausgestellt.

Weitgehend analog sind die Verse 11–18 aufgebaut. An die Selbstprädikation und Gliederungsformel 'Ich bin der gute Hirte' schließt sich in Vers 11 die positive Aussage über die Lebenshingabe des guten Hirten. Die Verse 12–13 sind dann vom negativen Gegenbild des Mietlings bestimmt. In Vers 14–18 beherrschen dann die positiven Aussagen über den 'guten Hirten' den Gedankengang. Wechselseitige Kenntnis von Hirt und Schafen und Lebenshingabe des Hirten für die Schafe sind thematisch miteinander verwoben. Der gelegentlich als störend empfundene Vers 16[19] bleibt im weiteren Sinne innerhalb der Bildwelt von Hirt, Hürde, Herde und Schafen, wobei er stärker auf Vers 1–5 zurückbezogen erscheint. Insofern er vom Hirten das 'Führen' weiterer Schafe aussagt, fügt er sich zu den weiteren Aussagen von Verse 11–18.

Versteht man, wie unter 1.1 zu begründen versucht, die Hirtenrede insgesamt polemisch, so fügen sich die Verse 19–21 bruchlos an Vers 1–18 an. Auch der Rückbezug auf die Heilung des Blindgeborenen in Kapitel 9 erscheint dann nicht mehr befremdlich.[20]

Verse 22–30 schließen insofern lückenlos an, als Jesu Berufung auf seine Werke zur Legitimation seines messianischen Anspruchs auch aus dem gesamten vorhergehenden Kontext vorbereitet erscheint (vgl. schon 5:36 im Kontext von Kapitel 5). Die Aussagen der Verse 26–30 greifen, wie P.-R. Tragan gezeigt hat,[21] auf die Hirtenrede von Vers 1–18 zurück und bringen ihr gegenüber, was den Hirten und die Schafe betrifft, nichts Neues. Nur wird der Gedanke der Handlungseinheit von Vater und Sohn vertieft.[22] Er bestimmt auch die abschließenden Verse 31–8 mit der Reaktion der Juden in Vers 39, worauf die Rückzugsnotiz von Vers 40–2 erfolgt. Es besteht also kein zwingender Grund, die vorgefundene Textanordnung in Kapitel 10 durch Umstellungen zu verändern.

1.4 Redaktion

Wenn im vorhergehenden Abschnitt die Verse 11–18 als Deutung der παροιμία aufgefaßt wurden und auch auf den sekundären Charakter von Vers 26–30 gegenüber der Bildrede von Vers 1–18 hingewiesen wurde, so folgt daraus noch nicht, daß wir es in Vers 7–18 und 26–30 mit Ergänzungen, 'relectures' des Hirtengleichnisses zu tun hätten, die aufeinander folgenden Redaktoren zuzuschreiben wären. Diese These von P.-R. Tragan[23] steht und fällt mit der ekklesiologischen Deutung der Verse 7–18 (26–30), die in den 'Dieben' und 'Räubern' sowie dem 'Mietling' christliche Falschlehrer sieht, denen sich Jesus als der einzig wahre 'gute Hirt' gegenüberstellt. Wenn auch zugegeben werden kann, daß sich die Motivwelt von 'Hirt', 'Herde' und 'reißenden Wölfen' in Joh 10 mit 'pastoralen' Abschnitten der Evangelien (vgl. Joh 21:15–17), der Apostelgeschichte (vgl. Apg 20:28f.) und der neutestamentlichen Briefe (vgl. 1 Petr 2:25; 5:2f.) deckt, so ist damit doch noch nicht über die Zugehörigkeit der johanneischen Hirtenrede zu solchen Texten entschieden. Es könnte sein, und dies soll im folgenden aufgezeigt werden, daß frühkirchliche Mahnungen zu rechter Hirtensorge gegenüber Irrlehrern aus dem kirchlichen Bereich selbst, wie wir sie in den genannten Texten finden, und die johanneische Auseinandersetzung mit falschen Hirten, Dieben und Räubern eine gemeinsame Wurzel haben, nämlich alttestamentliche und frühjüdische Texte gegen unrechte Hirten Israels. Der vierte Evangelist hätte sie dann in ihrer ursprünglichen Zielsetzung übernommen, die übrige, eher spätere neutestamentliche Literatur übersetzt in eine neue Situation, die durch die gegen Ende des 1. Jahrhunderts beginnende Kirchenspaltung gekennzeichnet war. Innerhalb der johanneischen Schriften wird dieses Stadium vor allem durch die Johannesbriefe und die auch im Evangelium anzunehmende 'johanneische Redaktion' repräsentiert.[24] Sie auch in Joh 10:1–18, 26–30 anzunehmen, erscheint so lange nicht zwingend, als eine direkte Abhängigkeit der johanneischen Hirten-Motivwelt von spät- und nachbiblischen jüdischen Texten plausibel gemacht werden kann, für die auch der johanneische Kontext spricht.

2. Der alttestamentlich-jüdische Hintergrund von Joh. 10:1–18, 26–30

2.1 Abgrenzung der Untersuchung

Wir beschränken unsere Untersuchung im folgenden auf die johanneische Hirtenrede im engeren Sinne, das heißt die Jesusrede in Joh 10:1–18 unter Berücksichtigung ihres Echos in Vers 26–30. Außer Betracht bleibt die Argumentation in Vers 32–8 mit dem Schriftwort in Vers 34 und dessen christologischer Auswertung durch Jesus.[26] Allein die Tatsache, daß Jesus hier seine Einheit mit dem Vater aus der Schrift begründet, spricht für eine Schriftnähe auch des Kontextes – will man nicht dem Problem durch Zuweisung der Verse 34–6 an einen nachjohanneischen Redaktor entgehen.[26]

Was den religionsgeschichtlichen Hintergrund der Verse 1–18 (26–30) anlangt, so klammern wir (absprachegemäß) den hellenistischen und gnostischen Bereich aus. Innerhalb der jüdischen Vergleichstexte verfolgen wir die spärlichen Spuren nicht weiter, die zum Rabbinismus hinführen. Eine doppelte Ursache scheint dazu geführt zu haben, daß sich für den 'guten Hirten' im messianischen Sinne rabbinisch so gut wie keine Belege beibringen lassen. Zum einen legte die geringe Einschätzung des Hirten in Israel zur Zeit des NT nahe, auf dieses Bild als Hoheitsaussage zu verzichten. Zum andern dürfte die frühe Verwendung des Hirtenbildes für Jesus dazu geführt haben, entsprechende alttestamentlich-frühjüdische Traditionen nicht weiter zu verfolgen.[27] Auch die Verwendung der Hirtenmetaphorik in der jüdisch-hellenistischen Theologie eines Philo sei hier nur erwähnt, aber nicht dargestellt, da dies an anderer Stelle von kompetenter Seite geschehen ist[28] und der dortige Gebrauch mit dem johanneischen wenig Berührungspunkte aufweist.

So verbleibt als engerer Untersuchungsraum für unsere Studie die 'Entwicklungslinie' vom AT über das pseudepigraphische jüdische Schrifttum und die Qumrantexte bis zum NT. Sie gilt es im folgenden aufzuzeigen.

2.2 Zeichen von Überlieferung

Daß hinter Joh 10: 1 – 18 (26 – 30) überhaupt Überlieferung steht, läßt sich schon aufgrund von sprachlichen Beobachtungen wahrscheinlich machen. Während die Verse 26 – 30 offenbar auf die vorangehende Hirtenrede zurückgreifen und keine neuen, sonst nicht oder kaum bei Johannes bezeugten Stichwörter bieten, sind die Verse 1 – 18 in hohem Maße von solchen Stichwörtern bestimmt. Insgesamt gibt es nicht weniger als 11 Substantive, Adjektive, Verben oder Adverbien, die bei Johannes nur in der Hirtenrede von Joh 10: 1 – 18 (26 – 30) vorkommen. Es sind dies in der Reihenfolge des Vorkommens: 'von anderswoher' (ἀλλαχόθεν, Vers 1, nur hier im NT, 'Hirt' (ποιμήν, Verse 11 2x, 14, 16), 'hinausführen' (ἐξάγω, Vers 3), 'fremd' (ἀλλότριος, Vers 5 2x), 'fliehen' (φεύγω, Verse 5, 12), 'Weide' (νομή, Vers 9, nur noch 2 Tim 2: 17), 'stehlen' (κλέπτω, Vers 10), 'schlachten' (θύω, Vers 10), 'Mietling' (μισθωτός, Verse 12, 13, nur noch Mk 1: 20), 'Wolf' (λύκος, Vers 12 2x) und 'Herde' (ποίμνη, Vers 16).

Eine Reihe anderer Ausdrücke stehen außer Joh 10: 1 – 18 (26 – 30) bei Johannes selten und außerhalb der Hirtenrede vornehmlich in überlieferten Zusammenhängen.[29] Auf die Beauftragung des Petrus in Joh 21: 15 – 17 verweist dabei nur das Stichwort 'Schaf' (πρόβατον) zusammen mit dem bei Johannes häufigen 'nachfolgen' (ἀκολουθεῖν).[30]

2.3 Sprachliche Entsprechungen und vereinzelte Anspielungen

Wenn die Hirtenrede von Joh 10: 1 – 18 (26 – 30) weitgehend von nicht-johanneischem Vokabular geprägt ist, so folgt daraus noch nicht, daß sich für die vermutlich der Überlieferung entnommenen Ausdrücke ohne weiteres literarische Vorlagen namhaft machen ließen. Dies gilt auch nicht für den biblischen und unmittelbar nachbiblisch-jüdischen Bereich.

E. D. Freed verzeichnet in seiner Monographie *Old Testament Quotations in the Gospel of John*[31] kein alttestamentliches Zitat innerhalb unseres Redetextes. Erst in Vers 34 ist bekanntlich ein solches gegeben. Auch G. Reim kommt in seiner erweiterten Oxforder Dissertation *Studien zum alttestamentlichen Hintergrund des Johannesevangeliums*[32] zu dem Ergebnis, daß in der johanneischen Hirtenrede keine direkten Zitate aus dem Alten Testament vorliegen. Nur Anspielungen sind gegeben, die teils mehr formaler, teils mehr inhaltlicher Art sind. Deren wahrscheinlichste hat P.-R. Tragan in seiner mehrfach erwähnten Straßburger Dissertation[33] überprüft und auf den Stand gebracht. Nach erneuter Prüfung und Korrektur (Joh 10:7 'Ich bin der Hirt der Schafe' als Anspielung auf Jes 63:11 mußte aufgrund der in 1.2 gefällten textkritischen Entscheidung entfallen) ergeben sich folgende wahrscheinliche Anspielungen in Joh 10:1–18 auf alttestamentliche Stellen:

- der Hirt, der seine Herde führt (Jes 40:11);
- der Knecht, der sich 'dem Tode ausliefert' (Jes 53:12);
- die 'Sammlung' der Schafe (Jes 56:8; Ez 34:13; 37:21–2);
- der 'eine' Hirte (Ez 34:23; 37:21–4);
- der Hirt, der den Gerechten 'auf frische Weide führt' (Ps 23:1–3);
- Gott als Hirte Israels, des 'Volkes seiner Weide, der Herde, von seiner Hand geführt' (Ps 95:7).

Weitere Entsprechungen bleiben mehr oder weniger unsicher. Hierhin gehören das 'Rufen beim Namen' (Jes 43:1; Joh 10:3), das 'Ein- und Ausziehen' (Dtn 31:2) bzw. 'Herein- und Herauskommen' oder '-führen' und 'vor ihnen Hergehen' (Num 27:17; Joh 10:4; vgl. 9), die Liebe Gottes zur Weisheit bzw. zum Sohn (Weish 8:3; Joh 10:17) oder die Verheißung des Lebens für den, der sich auf Gottes Wort einläßt (Lev 18:5; Joh 10:10).

2.4 Sachliche Entsprechungen

Auch wenn solche Berührungen von Einzelversen und -begriffen in Joh 10:1–18 (26–30) mit alttestamentlichen Parallelen selten bleiben, so ist doch damit nicht ausgeschlossen, daß Grundmotive der johanneischen Hirtenrede in alttestamentlichen und nachbiblischen jüdischen Texten vorbereitet sind. Solchen möglichen Entsprechungen soll im folgenden nachgegangen werden.

2.4.1 Schlechte Hirten und Wölfe

Spätestens seit dem Artikel von J. Jeremias[34] wird darauf hinge-wiesen, daß Israel sich scheut, seine Könige als 'Hirten' zu bezeichnen. Das AT bietet keinen einzigen Beleg, der den regierenden König als 'Hirten' bezeichnet, ganz im Unterschied zum Gebrauch der angren-zenden orientalischen Völker. Erst rückblickend wird im AT von den Königen und politischen Führern Israels als 'Hirten' gesprochen. Wohl unter deuteronomischem Einfluß klagen die Propheten zur Zeit des Untergangs der Monarchie auch im Südreich die Monarchen und

Regierenden als 'Hirten' an, die ihre Aufgabe vernachlässigten und nur ihren Vorteil suchten. Erste Belege finden sich hier bei Jeremia. In Jer 23:1 –8 findet sich ein Gerichtswort an die Hirten Israels bzw. Judas (Vers1 –2). Wie in Jer 10:21 wird als Folge ihrer Vernachlässigung der Herde deren Zerstreuung festgestellt. Es folgt in Jer 23:3 –4 die Ankündigung, daß Gott sein Volk selber sammeln wird aus allen Ländern und daß er ihm neue Hirten geben wird (vgl. schon 3:14 –15). Diese Ankündigung wird in Vers 5 –6 präzisiert durch die Voraussage eines neuen Davidssprosses. Gottes Werk einer neuen Heraufführung seines Volkes bildet den Inhalt der abschließenden Verse 7 –8.[35]

Eine ähnliche Abfolge findet sich in Ez 34. Das Kapitel hat offenbar eine längere Entstehungsgeschichte durchlaufen, wenn auch über deren einzelne Etappen bis heute keine Klarheit herrscht.[36] So, wie der Text heute vorliegt und mit Sicherheit schon zur Abfassungszeit des NT vorlag, beginnt auch er mit einem Gerichtswort über die Hirten Israels, 'die nur sich selber weiden' (Verse 1 –10). Der Kern der Aussage steht bereits in Vers 1 –2. Es folgt eine – vielleicht schon sekundäre – Entfaltung des unrechten Verhaltens in Vers 3 –4, der, wie in Jer 23, die Schilderung der Auswirkung des Fehlverhaltens der Hirten folgt: die Zerstreuung der Herde und ihre Gefährdung durch wilde Tiere (Verse 5 –6). Nach abermaligem Rückgriff auf das Fehlverhalten der Hirten (Verse 7 –8) folgt dann der Urteilsspruch: die Absetzung der untauglichen Hirten (Verse 9 –10). Es folgt die Ankündigung, daß Gott sich als Hirt seiner Herde annehmen werde (Verse 11 –16) und daß er – Wechsel des Bildes – zwischen Schafen und Schafen, Widdern und Böcken richten werde (Verse 17 –22). Auch hier folgt dann die Ankündigung eines kommenden Hirten, der die Schafe auf die Weide führen werde (Verse 23 –4, siehe unten, 4.4.2), und die Schilderung des kommenden Friedensbundes Jahwes mit seinem Volk (Verse 25 –31). Nach der ausführlichen Studie von B. Willmes[37] zu diesem Kapitel ist es nicht sicher, daß Jer 23 direkt auf unseren Text eingewirkt hat. Dann lag das Thema der Hirten, die sich selbst weiden, mit dem Ausgang der Monarchie Israels in der Luft, wobei in Ez 34:17 –22 die Rivalität zwischen fetten und schwachen Schafen über den König hinaus an eine ganze, schuldig gewordene Führungsschicht denken läßt.

Daß diese erweiterte Perspektive richtig ist, zeigt auch der Vergleich der Beamten Judas mit Wölfen in Ez 22:27: mit ihrem Gewinnstreben sind sie schuld am Blut ihrer Mitbürger. Die Metapher hat eine Parallele in Zef 3:3, wo es im Gericht über Jerusalem heißt: 'Ihre

Priester sind brüllende Löwen. Ihre Richter sind wie Wölfe der Steppe, die bis zum Morgen keinen Knochen mehr übriglassen.' Hier wie dort schließt sich ein Gerichtswort über die Propheten an, das zeigt, daß sich das Gotteswort nicht nur gegen einen einzelnen richtet.

In die Spätzeit alttestamentlicher Prophetie verweisen Texte aus Deuterosacharja (Sach 9−14), die vom Gericht Gottes über die Hirten Israels sprechen. Die Wendung von 'Schafen ohne Hirten' (10:2) verweist dabei auf Texte wie Num 27:17; 1 Kön 22:17; Jdt 11:19 (vgl. Mk 6:34 und Mt 9:36). Das Gericht über die Hirten klingt bereits an in 10:3 und wird breiter entfaltet in 11:4−17. Dabei ist freilich nicht sicher, ob es sich hier um die Führer Israels oder die Herrscher der Fremdvölker handelt.[38]

Die Metaphorik von schlechten Hirten als Herrschern Israels oder über Israel läßt sich nun durch die Pseudepigraphen des AT bis in die Zeit des Vierten Evangeliums verfolgen. Innerhalb der Traumgesichte Henochs (1 Hen 83−90)[39] sieht der Seher die Heilsgeschichte seit Noach und darin die Geschichte Israels seit der Patriarchenzeit. Die 12 Söhne Jakobs und ihre Nachfahren werden dabei entsprechend der Bildwelt dieser Kapitel als Schafe dargestellt (89:12ff.). Ägypten taucht unter dem Bild von Wölfen auf (89:13−27). Saul erscheint unter dem Bild eines Widders, der seine Herde stößt und verletzt (89:42−4). Die auf die Zerstörung Jerusalems folgenden Fremdherrscher werden mit 70 Hirten verglichen, die ihre Herde vernachlässigen und den wilden Tieren preisgeben (89:59−70), über die Zahl der ihnen von Gott zur Vernichtung übergebenen Tiere hinaus. Das gleiche Bild wird gebraucht von 35 Herrschern zwischen der Rückkehr aus der babylonischen Gefangenschaft und der Makkabäerzeit (89:74−6). Für die Zukunft kündigt der Verfasser Gottes Gericht über diese Hirten an (90:22−5). Aufgrund des Abbrechens der heilsgeschichtlichen Darstellung in der frühen Makkabäerzeit und aufgrund aramäischer Fragmente datiert M. Black diesen Teil von 1 Hen auf ca. 175 bis 165 vor Chr.[40]

In die Zeit zwischen 63 v. Chr., das heißt die römische Eroberung Palästinas, und 50 n. Chr., ungefähre Abfassungszeit der Antiquitates Judaicae des Flavius Josephus, datiert A.-M. Denis[41] ein von ihm herausgegebenes fragmentarisches Ezechiel-Apokryphon.[42] Es paraphrasiert in dem neu edierten Text in freier Form Ez 34, beginnend mit der Anklagerede gegen die Hirten Israels in Ez 34:1−10 und fortfahrend mit der Ankündigung des Gerichts zwischen Widder und Widder, Kalb und Kalb (vgl. Ez 34:17−22).

Daß auch zur Zeit des Vierten Evangelisten treulose Hirten ein
sprichwörtlicher Vergleich für politische oder religiöse Führer waren,
die ihr Volk im Stich ließen, zeigt ein Text aus dem in diese Zeit
datierten[43] 4. Buch Esra. Hier sagt Phaltiel, der Fürst des Volkes, zu
Esra: 'laß uns nicht im Stich, dem Hirten gleich, der seine Herde den
bösen Wölfen preisgibt' (Text nach Kautzsch).

Nicht metaphorisch, sondern direkt spricht von der Verteidigung
der Herde vor Löwen, Wölfen und anderen wilden Tieren TestGad I
2–4. Der Text zeigt noch einmal die Geläufigkeit der Vorstellung in
neutestamentlicher Zeit.[44]

2.4.2 Der endzeitliche gute Hirte

Eine Fülle von alttestamentlichen Texten sprechen von Gott als dem
Hirten seines Volkes – sei es, daß sie ihn direkt als Hirten bezeichnen,
sei es, daß sie ihm Tätigkeiten des Hirten gegenüber seiner Herde
zuschreiben. In diesem Sinne hat B. Willmes[45] die Belege jüngst
gesammelt, chronologisch versuchsweise geordnet und kurz kommen-
tiert. Hier können nur kurz die Ergebnisse berichtet werden. In die
vorexilische Zeit reichen Gen 49:24; 48:15; Hos 4:16; Ps 28:9; 80:2
sowie vermutlich 23:1–3. Die folgenden Psalmen sind schon als
exilisch oder nachexilisch einzustufen: 78:52; 74:1; 79:13; 77:21;
95:7; 100:3.

Von besonderer Bedeutung sind für unsere Untersuchung die
Stellen in den Propheten des herannahenden, hereingebrochenen oder
überstandenen Exils, die von Gott als dem kommenden Hirten seines
Volkes sprechen. Als früheste Texte nennt Willmes hier Jer 31:10;
13:17 und 23:3 – letzteren Text hatten wir bereits in seinem Kontext
kennengelernt (siehe oben, 4.4.1). Aus Deuterojesaja und damit
bereits exilischer Zeit sind hier Jes 40:11; 49:9b, 10 zu nennen (vgl.
auch Jer. 50:17–19). Schwer zu datieren bleiben wegen der Entwick-
lungsgeschichte des Kapitels die Aussagen in Ez 34 über Gott als
kommenden Hirten seines Volkes, Verse 11–16. Herausragender Zug
bleibt, wie bei zahlreichen verwandten Texten, die angekündigte
Sammlung des Gottesvolkes durch Gott. Ez 34 scheint bereits voraus-
gesetzt zu sein in Zef 3:19, ebenso in Mi 2:12; 4:6–7. Mi 7:14 ist
in die Form einer Bitte gekleidet. Weisheitlich spricht von Gott als
einzigem Hirten Koh 12:11; von seiner Führung gegenüber allen
Menschen Sir 18:13.

Neben die Ankündigung von Gott als dem künftigen Hirten seines
Volkes tritt in der Prophetie um die Zeit der Zerstörung Jerusalems
und des Endes der Monarchie Judas (587 v. Chr.) die Verheißung

eines kommenden Hirten, der Gottes Sorge für sein Volk wahrnehmen wird.[46] In Mi 5:3 wird ein vom Weibe Geborener als kommender Hirt Israels angekündigt, in dem man eine messianisch-politische Gestalt sehen darf (die sieben Hirten in Vers 4 sind schwer deutbar). Im übrigen finden sich die wichtigsten Texte vom kommenden Hirten wieder bei Jeremia und Ezechiel. Verspricht Gott in Jer 3:15 allgemein Hirten nach seinem Herzen, ähnlich wie in 23:4, so konkretisiert sich diese Hirtensorge in der Ankündigung eines kommenden Davididen in 23:5–6 (wobei dann freilich der Hirten- durch den Königstitel ersetzt wird). Auch in Ez 34:23–4 wird die Ankündigung des kommenden einzigen Hirten vermutlich nachträglich verdeutlicht[47] durch die Identifikation mit Gottes Knecht David, der Fürst in der Mitte der Israeliten genannt wird.[48] David begegnet dann noch erneut in Ez 37:24 als der eine Hirt Israels, nachdem Gott sein Volk gesammelt, zurückgeführt und erneut geeint hat (Verse 21–3). Hier führen unmittelbare Linien hinüber zu dem 'einen Hirten' und der 'einen Herde' von Joh 10:16.

In die nachbiblische jüdische Literatur führt bereits die LXX. Die Übersetzer des Psalters denken in Ps 2:9 offenbar an einen kommenden Hirten der Völker, indem sie das 'du wirst sie zerschlagen mit eisernem Stab' wiedergeben mit 'du wirst sie weiden'.[49] Das Wort ist in dieser LXX-Fassung aufgenommen, nur in der ersten Vershälfte in die dritte Person gebracht in Offb 2:27; 19:15. An der ersten Stelle ist es vom Christen als Sieger, an der zweiten von Christus als kommendem Herrscher verstanden.[50] Vgl. PsSal 17:24 mit 40.

Von der kommenden Hirtensorge Gottes für sein Volk spricht im Anschluß an Ez 34:11–12 das erwähnte Ez-Apokryphon.[51] Heimführung der verirrten Schafe, Heilung der verwundeten sind übernommene Einzelzüge. Die Nähe Gottes zu seinem Volk wird mit der Nähe des Mantels zur Haut verglichen. Auch vom Anrufen ist die Rede: wenn die Israeliten den Herrn anrufen, wird er sie erhören. Ein messianischer Herrscher wird nicht erwähnt.

Ebenfalls an Ez 34 orientiert ist vermutlich ein Text aus der Damaskusschrift. In Spalte 13 ist ab Zeile 7 vom Aufseher (*mᵉbaqqēr*) die Rede. Er war offenbar der Vorsteher der Laienschaft in der Gemeinde von 'Damaskus'.[52] Sein Titel erinnert nach Ch. Rabin an Ez 34.[53] Dort wird die kommende Sorge Gottes als Hirten für sein Volk mit dem Verb *bqr* zum Ausdruck gebracht. Angesichts der Seltenheit des Verbs im AT[54] ist ein Zusammenhang wahrscheinlich, zumal Ch. Rabin als unverdächtiger Zeuge gelten kann. Als Funktion des 'Aufsehers' wird in Zeile 9 ausdrücklich gesagt: 'Und er soll

Erbarmen mit ihnen haben wie ein Vater mit seinen Söhnen und alle ihre Verstreuten zurück[bringen] wie ein Hirt seine Herde.' (Übersetzung Lohse. Vgl. Ez 34:12, 16)

Es ist nicht uninteressant, daß zur Abfassungszeit des Vierten Evangeliums der Hirtentitel im jüdischen Bereich auf das Gesetz und die Weisheit übertragen werden kann. Die syrische Baruchapokalypse (77:13–17) stellt fest: die Hirten Israels sind nicht mehr, doch ist dem Volk in Gesetz und Weisheit Hirt, Lampe und Quelle gegeben.[55] Eine messianische Deutung wird hier gerade nicht gegeben (vielleicht schon in Auseinandersetzung mit dem Christentum), doch wirft die Übertragung des Hirtenbildes auf Gesetz und Weisheit auch interessantes Licht auf die Verwendung des Bildes in Joh 10.

2.4.3 Der Tod des Hirten und das Heil der Schafe

Der Lebenseinsatz des Hirten für seine Schafe in Joh 10:11–18 findet in den Texten des AT vom kommenden Hirten gemeinhin keine Entsprechung. Wenn hier gelegentlich auf die Lebenshingabe des Gottesknechtes in Jes 53:12 hingewiesen wird (vgl. oben 2.3), so fehlt dort doch das Hirtenbild. Statt dessen wird der Knecht Gottes in Jes 53:7 mit dem Lamm und Schaf verglichen.

Eigenartig bleibt Sach 13:7: 'Schlag den Hirten, dann werden sich die Schafe zerstreuen'. In Mk 14:27 par. Mt 26:31 wird das Wort in einer gegenüber dem Urtext und der LXX veränderten Fassung zitiert, wobei das Schlagen des Hirten als beabsichtigte Handlung Gottes hingestellt wird. Jesus sagt voraus, daß der Vater den Hirten schlagen wird und die Schafe (Mt: der Herde) sich daraufhin zerstreuen werden. Dabei ist ein positiver Ausgang zugleich in den Blick genommen: Jesus wird den Seinen nach seiner Auferweckung nach Galiläa vorausgehen.

Es ist zumindest möglich, daß die Stelle bereits bei Sacharja einen positiven Sinn hat, indem der Tod des Hirten den Weg frei macht für eine neue Sammlung der Herde. Der Gedanke wird ermöglicht durch die anzunehmende Gleichsetzung des geschlagenen Hirten von Sach 13:7 mit dem Durchbohrten von Sach 12:10, dessen Tod die Reinigung des Volkes einleitet.[56]

Das Wort aus Sach 13:7 ist aufgegriffen in der Damaskusschrift 19:7ff. Auch hier ist es ein Gerichtswort über den Hirten, zugleich aber Überleitung zu einem Heilswort für einen Teil der Herde, hier 'die Armen der Herde' (Z. 9). Ihre Rettung und die Vernichtung der übrigen durch das Schwert wird mit dem Kommen des Gesalbten aus Aaron und Israel verbunden (Z. 10–11).[57]

Es ist wahrscheinlich, daß Sach 13:7 nicht unmittelbar auf die johanneische Hirtenrede eingewirkt hat. Dennoch ist es auffallend, daß zumindest die johanneische Redaktion in Joh 16:32 bei der Zerstreuung der Herde auf Sach 13:7 anzuspielen scheint.[58] Die Nähe der johanneischen Passionsüberlieferung zu Deuterosacharja zeigt das Zitat von Sach 12:10 in Joh 19:37: 'Sie werden auf den blicken, den sie durchbohrt haben.'[59]

2.4.4 Die Tür

Noch immer sperrt sich die doppelte Selbstbezeichnung Jesu in Joh 10:7, 9 gegen eine befriedigende traditionsgeschichtliche Erklärung. Der Sinn des Wortes dürfte, wie die Übersetzer und Ausleger zumeist annehmen,[60] in beiden Versen ein verschiedener sein: In Vers 7 bezeichnet sich Jesus (im Sinne des Bildes in Vers 1–2) als Tür 'zu den Schafen', anders als die, die sich der Herde mit Gewalt bemächtigen. In Vers 9 ist er die Tür 'für die Schafe', womit das Herausführen von Vers 3b–4 aufgegriffen wird. Die plausibelste Erklärung ist immer noch, wie schon J. Jeremias[61] gesehen hat, daß man in dem doppelten Türwort in Joh 10:7, 9 die Wiederaufnahme des Türmotivs der *Paroimia* von Vers 1–5 sieht.

Möglich bleibt die an gleicher Stelle von J. Jeremias vorgeschlagene Deutung, die sich durch fast alle Kommentare zieht, daß hier Ps 118:20 LXX eingewirkt haben könnte, wobei das messianische Verständnis dieses Psalms im Judentum in neutestamentlicher Zeit in Rechnung zu ziehen ist.[62] Doch läßt sich auch an eine neutestamentliche Weiterentwicklung der alttestamentlichen Vorstellung vom Tempelvorhang (Ex 26:31ff.) denken, wie sie sich in Hebr 10:19–21 findet: 'Als Tür zu den und für die Schafe eröffnet Jesus als der sein Leben für die Schafe hingebende gute Hirte die *prosagoge eis ton theon* ebenso wie er selbst den kommenden Gott repräsentiert.'[63] Für die Rolle der Tür in gnostischen Texten darf hier auf den Beitrag von J. D. Turner verwiesen werden.

3 Zusammenfassung

Für die traditionsgeschichtliche Erklärung der Hirtenrede in Joh 10 ist die Forschung nicht vor die Notwendigkeit gestellt, entweder ein direktes Einwirken alttestamentlicher Texte oder einen direkten Einfluß frühgnostischer Texte anzunehmen. Auch die 'pastoralen' Texte später neutestamentlicher Schriften bieten sich nicht als unabweisliches Ableitungsfeld an, wie neuerlich behauptet wurde. Es läßt sich vielmehr eine 'Entwicklungslinie' vom AT, vor allem von den Büchern Jeremia, Ezechiel und Sacharja, über alttestamentliche Apokryphe und die Damaskusschrift bis ins NT verfolgen, die den untauglichen Hirten der Vergangenheit Gottes Hirtensorge in der Endzeit gegenüberstellt. Sie wird entweder durch Gott selbst oder durch den erwarteten Messias wirksam. Freilich ist diese letztere Erwartung deutlich schwächer bezeugt. Zumindest die Möglichkeit besteht, daß auch der Tod bzw. die Lebenshingabe eines letzten Hirten bereits zu den aus dem Judentum stammenden religionsgeschichtlichen Voraussetzungen der johanneischen Hirtenrede gehört.

3

THE HISTORY OF RELIGIONS BACKGROUND OF JOHN 10

John D. Turner

In this study of the Johannine discourse on the Good Shepherd, I propose to take the text of John 10 section by section, and inquire into the possible religious and conceptual backgrounds for the major images and concepts employed by the evangelist. It is true that I implicitly endorse the observation that some dislocation has occurred in the text, as reflected in the order of treatment I adopt, 10: 19–30; 10: 1–18; and 10: 31–42. But I am not wholly convinced that this is the original order, and in any case offer no explanation for how the text came to be in its present state. Nevertheless, the order of treatment I adopt will not materially affect my treatment of the question I am trying to deal with: the background and environment of the Johannine shepherd discourse, with particular attention to the Graeco-Roman conceptual sphere and the question of possible relationships to Gnosticism.

In the course of my treatment I shall occasionally stray beyond these confines, particularly into ancient Near Eastern and OT territory, since these spheres did not exist in isolation from the more Hellenic sphere, and in any case, because I see there an important basis on which to understand the shepherd imagery of the discourse. In addition to the shepherd I shall attend particularly to the motif of the sheep's recognition of the shepherd by means of being 'his own' and by recognising his 'voice'.

I shall explore also certain possibilities for a Gnostic understanding of the text. Various features of the discourse certainly lend themselves to a Gnostic understanding, but whether it was intended as such I am reluctant to believe. Rather, I sense that such Gnostic mythological structures as may be seen residing in or behind the text are natural developments of the Hellenistic Jewish wisdom tradition, itself moving already on a trajectory leading toward classical Gnosticism at the time of the gospel's composition, but not yet definitively. Indeed, much the same could be said of several of the Gnostic texts (or the identifiable sources and traditions on which they appear to draw) that I shall adduce for purposes of comparison. Thus in general, I do feel that the comparative study of relevant Gnostic literature is useful for the understanding of the shepherd discourse as for the gospel as a whole. But whether the discourse is Gnostic in any explicit sense is a definitional issue, and I am not inclined to believe that any important points are to be scored by branding the discourse as either Gnostic or not. So far as I can see, it does display a transcendental mythological structure, one that likely has roots in the Jewish wisdom tradition. But that only raises the further issue, which I shall not deal with here, of the extent to which that tradition was already gnosticised by the time it was received by the evangelist.

1. 10:19–21 and chapter 9

I agree with many commentators that this section was originally the conclusion to the story of the healing of the blind man in chapter 9 and has somehow been displaced, and thus we omit it from consideration.

2. 10:22–6: plain versus hidden revelation

As many commentators agree, 10:22–6 may be the original beginning and setting of the discourse on the shepherd in chapter 10. In accord with the evangelist's theory of hidden versus open revelation (cf. 16: 25, 29), the question of the 'Jews' in 10:24 presupposes that they have perceived Jesus' teaching and activity as obscure and ambiguous; the 'signs' of his identity which he has performed to reveal his glory do not conform to their literal-minded expectations.

For example, in the previous chapter, Jesus has restored the sight of a man born blind, and all the Pharisees were able to see is that Jesus performed this act illegally on the Sabbath; they cannot even see and admit the obvious fact that the blind man was born blind and now sees, but instead concern themselves with matters such as the method by which and the legality of the conditions under which Jesus acted, thus demonstrating their own blindness (inability to read the signs or to recognise the revealer). Indeed, the blindness of the 'Jews' may be used by the evangelist to indicate the insufficiency of the signs alone as the way to faith and insight.

At the end of chapter 9, the 'Jews' claim to be able to see, but are in fact blind. According to 10:20, 26–7, they hear Jesus' words, but are in fact deaf to them because they do not belong to Jesus' sheep, who alone can hear his voice. Blind to the light and deaf to the voice of the revealer, they can neither believe in him nor in the works the Father does through him (10:37–8).

The ensuing discourse on the shepherd, which the evangelist considers to be a riddle (παροιμία), will not, of course, provide the necessary insight for the 'Jews', since even Jesus' 'own' (= his 'sheep') to whom he really delivers the discourse, will not perceive the significance of any of his discourses plainly until 16:25–30, when he tells them that he came from the Father into the world and is now to leave the world and return to the Father. Reception of this insight represents the shift from the obscure revelation of the earthly Jesus to the clear and plain revelation of himself as he really is, the revealer sent from God who will lead his own into the truth and light and eternal life. Of course it is to be noted that the evangelist locates this shift at a point in the narrative before Easter, unlike most of the Gnostic revelations, indeed before his death, as does Mark. Yet it remains that only those who are Jesus' 'own', to whom he came (1:11–12), have the possibility of recognising the revealer, even in spite of the signs that he performs in the Father's name and which in fact bear witness that he is the revealer.

3. 10:27–30: sheep and shepherds

In the older Hellenic sphere, among Dorians and Ionians, the term πρόβατον ('sheep') generally designates four-footed, grazing domestic animals often intended to be slaughtered either for food or for sacrifice, while in Attic prose and comedy (but never in tragedy), it refers almost always to sheep.[1] The term is frequently used metaphorically of human beings as helpless and unable to care for themselves.

In this sense, the shepherd (ποιμήν) is classically a leader of flocks of goats, sheep and cattle, and so by extension, he figures as a leader of men. In Homer, this metaphor refers particularly to the Greek military leaders (in distinction from the soldiers) at Troy. Plato employs a long conceit on humans as sheep who in the Golden Age of Cronus were completely nurtured and provided for by a heavenly daemon as shepherd, but when God let go of the cosmic tiller and the universe began to devolve at the beginning of the age of Zeus, 'bereft of the guardian care of the daemon who had governed and reared us up, we had become weak and helpless, and we began to be ravaged by wild beasts'; because of this we need another shepherd to 'nurture the herd', a human statesman who will be called a 'shepherd for the people'.[2] Still later, we find a Stoic use of the term πρόβατον to designate persons of a lower worth or intelligence who must be guided by the wise man.[3]

Among Greek deities that were identified with shepherds, one should consider carefully the figures of Hermes and Apollo. Simply perusing M. P. Nilsson's *Geschichte der Griechischen Religion*,[4] and L. Farnell's *The Cults of the Greek States*[5] in their respective sections on Hermes and Apollo, one finds features of these gods, especially Hermes, similar to those attributed to Jesus in the Johannine discourse on the good shepherd.

For example, according to Homer, *Iliad* 14.490, Hermes loved the Trojan Phorbas, rich in herds (πολύμηλος), whose daughter Polymele bore Hermes his son Eudoros (*Iliad* 16.179). According to the Homeric Hymn to Pan, another of Hermes' sons is Pan, the shepherd god. For Hesiod (*Theogony* 5.444), Hermes is the increaser of herds, including those of sheep. According to the conclusion to the Homeric Hymn to Hermes (5.567), Hermes is given the special task of caring for various domestic animals, including sheep, and of ruling over herds of goats and sheep as well as being the messenger in the underworld. In this sense he often receives the epithet ἐπιμήλιος ('shepherd', e.g. Pausan. 9.22.2) which is reflected in typical scenes that depict him as Kriophoros, or lamb-bearer. His status as master herdsman and master thief is amply portrayed in the well-known myth about his theft of the cattle of Apollo. Among Hermes' functions was also that of gatekeeper, especially of temples and sanctuaries: 'Rufus, priest of Zeus, set up [a statue of] Hermes the gatekeeper (θυραῖον) as a guard and defender of the temple'. In the shepherd discourse, Jesus also implies his role as gatekeeper.[6]

Probably owing to his early association with the stone cairns that marked the site of graves, Hermes was given the function of leading the souls resident therein to the underworld. Homer (*Odyssey* 24.1ff.) has Hermes conduct the souls of the fallen suitors of Penelope, squeaking like bats, past the streams of Oceanus, the Leucadic Rock, past the gates of the Sun and the land of dreams, to the asphodel meadows. The tragedians call him 'the great κῆρυξ [herald] of things above and below' and apply the epithets πομπαῖος and πομπός to him as 'escorter' (Aesch. *Choephoroi* 5.1.124; Soph. *Oed. Col.* 5.1548). Hermes also acquired the epithet ψυχοπομπός (Diodor. 1.96; Cornutus, *Theol.* 16, p. 22 Lang). In this role he is later associated with celestial immortality, as in Diogenes Laertius' life of Pythagoras (*Vitae* 8.33): 'Hermes is the steward of souls, and for that reason is called πομπαῖος, πυλαῖος and χθόνιος, since it is he who brings in the souls from their bodies at land and at sea; the pure are taken to the uppermost region, but the impure ... are bound by the Furies in unbreakable bonds.' In this regard, Hermes has a role much like that of Jesus in the present discourse when he implies that the shepherd leads his sheep forth from the sheepfold.

Likewise, Apollo is also a great shepherd god. Nilsson cites Macrobius 1.17.45[7] as well as Pindar, *Pyth*. IX, 5.64 for the epithet ὀπάωνα μηλῶν ('attendant of sheep') and Clement of Alexandria *Protr*. 2.28 for the epithet νόμιος ('pastoral'). One recalls also the episode of his enforced service as shepherd to Admetus, Eumelus and Laomedon and his role in Hermes' theft of his cattle. Nilsson suspects that another of Apollo's epithets, Κάρνειος ('ram-like'), was originally a shepherd god in his own right.

Like Hermes, Apollo was also associated with doors or gates, as suggested by his epithet 'Αγυιεύς ('door-keeper', i.e. one who averts evil from entering the gates of the city). Nilsson supposes that the stone battlements, the sacred pillars of Apollo Agyieus, which stood before the gates of the Homeric Troy were the distinctive symbols of Apollo; other such sacred stones of Apollo were at Megara (Apollo Karinos), Malea (Apollo Lithēsios) and of course the more well-known Omphalos at Delphi.

While it does not seem possible to trace any genealogical connections between these understandings of Hermes and Apollo and the functions of Jesus as shepherd and door (if ἡ θύρα be the correct reading of John 10:7 and 9) in the Johannine shepherd discourse, one ought to bear in mind this interesting collocation of functions in the case of two famous Greek deities when considering precedents for these epithets of Jesus. This is so particularly in the case of Hermes, who has to do with the leading of souls to their post-mortem destination in the asphodel meadows, much as the Johannine shepherd calls his sheep by name and leads them out to pasture. Just as the Johannine Jesus calls himself 'the way (ὁδός), the truth and the life', so also Hermes was called ὅδιος (guardian of roads) according to Hesychius' list of his epithets, explained by a scholiast on Plato's *Phaedrus* 107C as: 'Hermes, the unexpected gain from the first fruits placed along the roads.' As door, Jesus certainly constitutes the way to the Father, and as shepherd, he certainly leads his sheep to the Father's pasture.

Although it seems that the oriental, especially OT, imagery of the shepherd likely stands closer to the Fourth evangelist, there is no reason a priori to exclude any influence of these traditional and popular understandings of Hermes upon the evangelist either. Certainly the figure of Hermes loomed large in the movement associated with Hermes Trismegistus, which may well have been contemporaneous with, even though perhaps geographically removed from, the activity of the evangelist. And, although the etymology 'Shepherd of men' for Hermes in the Hermetic treatise *Poimandres* may be historically false, it doubtless would have occurred to those familiar with the traditional pre-Hermetic epithets for the revealing deity of this movement.

The image of shepherd together with flocks (goats, sheep, cattle) is even more profuse and frequent in oriental than in Greek literature. Everywhere one finds the shepherd's crook as the emblem of royal authority. In the Egyptian Pyramid texts, the image of the shepherd is applied to the ruler of the world to come (usually Osiris or the dead pharaoh), who protects his subjects even in the underworld; in the Middle Kingdom the image is frequently applied to the reigning king or even to a god such as Amun.[8] In ancient Mesopotamia, the king is frequently referred to as shepherd: fifth in the line of antediluvian kings in the Sumerian King List is the 'shepherd Dumuzi'; the office of 'shepherdship' is ranked eighth, between 'the exalted throne' and 'kingship', in a list of one hundred elements of civilised life in the Sumerian poem 'Innana and Enki: The Transfer of Civilised Arts from Eridu to Erech'; in the 'Hymn to Enlil, the All Beneficent', Enlil is called shepherd (line 84).[9]

In the OT, the shepherd image is used to represent Yahweh's care for and rulership over the people.[10] The motif of the people following the shepherd (as distinct from the other gods) is found mostly within the Deuteronomic sphere.[11] Close to the image of the shepherd in John 10 is the idea that the shepherd is the one who leads the flock out and brings them in, as applied to Joshua in Num. 27:17 and to Moses in Deut. 31:1. Oddly enough, there is no reference to a ruling Israelite king as 'shepherd', yet the term is applied to Yahweh's future appointed one, the Davidic Messiah (esp. Ezek. 34—7), or the stricken shepherd of Zech. 13:7.[12] In later Judaism, both within Pharasaic Judaism and the Qumran community, following OT precedent, God continues to be referred to as shepherd, as are faithful leaders and teachers of Israel including Moses and David, while the occupation of common shepherd becomes viewed in an increasingly pejorative light by Pharisees who regarded these loose, nomadic people as robbers and cheats. Philo also follows OT precedent, but supplements it by the frequent image of the human νοῦς as the shepherd of the irrational powers of the soul, or of the divine λόγος as the nourisher of the world.[13]

Despite the role of real shepherds in the nativity story of Luke 2:8–20, one finds the metaphorical application of the shepherd image to God only in the parables of Jesus (Luke 15:4–7 par.; Matt. 18:12–14; Gos. Thos. 107), perhaps, as Jeremias suggests,[14] because its frequent application to Jesus pre-empted the older use. Among Jesus' sayings one finds the metaphor of sheep being applied to those who are lost with no one to provide for them (Mark 6:34; Matt. 9:36; 10:6; 15:24; Luke 12:32 and 19:10 [which alludes to the image of Ezek. 34]), whose shepherd will be struck down (Mark 14:27–8 par.; Matt. 26:31–2 alluding to Zech. 13:7), as well as the image of the Son of Man, who like a shepherd will separate the sheep from the goats at the last judgement (Matt. 25:32). Elsewhere in the NT one finds the term shepherd applied to Christ as the chief overseer of the flock (= the Church; 1 Pet. 2:25; 5:4; Heb. 13:10), while in Rev. 7:17 (cf. 14:4), the victorious shepherd is said to be the Lamb who leads those who survive the tribulation to the springs of Living Water.[15]

4. The origins of the shepherd metaphor

Whence comes this ancient image or metaphor of the shepherd as leader and saviour of the people as his flock, and how can it illumine the application of this image to the Jesus of the Fourth Gospel?

In a thoughtful essay on 'Pastoral Origins and the Ancient Near East',[16] David Halperin suggests that in dealing with the ancient figure of the shepherd, one ought to distinguish between the herdsman who is part of the economic enterprise of the city-state and lives in the countryside just outside of town, and the pastoral nomad who shepherds his flock through uninhabited areas in the company of his non-agrarian fellow tribesmen. Ancient Mesopotamians and Egyptians alike had a steady confidence in the value of city life as the one and only form of social organisation, and little desire to escape it, while on the other hand the ancient Israelites, to judge from the OT, viewed the city as a source of luxury, corruption and social inequity, and nostalgically saw the prospect of a return to a nomadic existence in the desert as spiritually advantageous.

An interesting exception to this general rule is the figure of Enkidu in the Akkadian Epic of Gilgamesh. The point of Enkidu's transition from wild to civilised life occurs, of all places, at a shepherd's hut, where he is introduced to the intoxicating effect of strong drink produced from the products of the city's grainfields. This seems to reflect a historical situation wherein the shepherd existed on the border between the agrarian sphere dependent on the sophisticated irrigation systems only supportable by the city, and the arid area beyond, where animals could graze outside the areas of intense cultivation. In this sense, one may consider the shepherd as a *liminal* figure, oscillating between two worlds, between the isolation of the wilderness and the hustle and bustle of the settled communities. Enkidu is thus integrated into human society at the shepherd's hut as a sort of halfway house between nature and culture.

The physical isolation of the herdsman from village life seems to have suggested to the ancients a withdrawal from human culture. Insertion into the world and forces of nature meant the corresponding possibility of freer intercourse with the divine: it was while Paris was shepherding his flocks on Mount Ida that he judged between the three goddesses; Hesiod encountered the Muses while shepherding on Mount Helicon; Aphrodite approached Anchises shepherding on Mount Ida. In the OT, Moses heard the voice of God from the burning bush only after he had inherited a flock from his father-in-law Jethro and had led it to the wilderness. Later, God altogether ignores the more civilised urban candidates and instead settles on the shepherd boy David to be king over his people; perhaps removal from the city suggested a greater degree of innocence or moral rectitude, such that the kingship, a corrupt political institution modelled on that of Israel's heathen neighbours, could be purified by drawing on more rural stock than the house of Saul. Even the prophet Amos is called a *noqēd*, a lowly sort of shepherd.

It seems, then, that thanks to his liminal social position and concomitant increased exposure to divinity, the figure of the shepherd in oriental and Hellenic speculation would easily lend itself to being an apt designation for the mediator between the divine sphere and the luxurious, seductive sphere of civilised existence. The shepherd is one who moves back and forth between the untrammelled wilderness inhabited by the divine and the worldliness of the city and marketplace so full of conflicting voices and claims. Divine figures such as Jesus no less than Hermes qualify eminently for such a role.

Thus, although it is a fact that the shepherd at all times has separated his own sheep from others by calling them by name, and they respond to his voice and not that of strangers, it is probably not this pastoral commonplace that is in view in John 10. Rather the voice the sheep hear and respond to is the voice of their true shepherd who calls them out of the 'mixture' of the world. That is, the sheep uniquely recognise their shepherd's voice not on the grounds of habit, but because they are the shepherd's 'own'; they share some affinity with the shepherd that enables them to recognise his voice above all others. Jesus' own hear his voice as do all those who are of the truth (18:37; cf. 5:25; 10:4–5, 16), but outsiders, the 'Jews', do not (5:37; cf. 3:8). Jesus is represented as speaking with the divine *voice* of revelation, which by tradition was not always perceived as articulate, in contrast with the divine *word* that was regarded as clear. In 12:28–32 the divine voice that glorifies Jesus' name is perceived as thunder or the voice of an angel. In chapter 1, Jesus is the fully articulate Word in contrast to John the Baptist, who is only a voice of one crying in the wilderness.

O. Betz characterises the significance of the term 'voice' for the fourth evangelist as follows:[17]

> For him the voice of God is uttered in the present with the witness of the Spirit and special stress is laid on hearing the voice of Jesus, 5:25, 28; 10:3, 16, 27; 18:37 ... Only he who is of the elect can hear the voice of Jesus and in faith and obedience receive it as the eschatological Word of grace and truth ... Πᾶς ὁ ὢν ἐκ τῆς ἀληθείας ἀκούει μου τῆς φωνῆς, 18:37. One must stand in the realm of truth and not see oneself in the light of the world's reality if one is able to hear God speaking in the voice of Jesus, 8:47, cf. 3:3, 21. John 3:8 also has in view the voice of the Revealer. Here the metaphor of the wind is used for the inconceivable miracle of regeneration by the Spirit: τὸ πνεῦμα ὅπου θέλει πνεῖ, καὶ τὴν φωνὴν αὐτοῦ ἀκούεις, ἀλλ᾽ οὐκ οἶδας πόθεν ἔρχεται καὶ ποῦ ὑπάγει. The Logos belongs to the world of the Spirit and the Jews do not know whence He comes or whither He goes (8:14); they do not hear his φωνή.

The basic idea here, that Jesus' own can alone hear his voice, suggests a certain affinity, sympathy, even identity or consubstantiality between the saviour and those to whom he comes; both are 'of the truth'. Such an idea is more typical of Gnosticism than of any other religious stance of the period, although traces of it can be found in the wisdom literature. Nowhere is there to be found a better parallel to the concept of the revealing voice in the Fourth Gospel than in the Gnostic treatise, the *Trimorphic Protennoia* (NHC XIII, *1*).[18]

This treatise presents one with a sort of theology of revelation, in which the First Thought of the Invisible Spirit reveals itself throughout history in increasing degrees of articulateness: first, a pure, but not fully articulate Voice, which in some sense empowers Protennoias' members; second, a more articulate Speech which gives them shape, i.e. 'informs' them; and third, the fully articulate Logos who appears in their own, human, shape. Interpreted in light of the Sethian salvation history of *The Apocryphon of John*, the First Thought's appearance as Voice occurs with the revelation of the shape of the 'Father', the divine Adamas, in whose image the earthly Adam is made; her second appearance as the Speech of the Voice occurs as Mother, in the form of the spiritual Eve, who reveals to Adam his spiritual origins, his true 'shape' or 'form'; and third, she appears as Son, in the form of the Logos, which grants full enlightenment, and which, at least in *The Gospel of the Egyptians*, manifests itself in the eschatological advent of Seth disguised as Jesus, revealing the Five Seals, the Sethian baptismal ritual that brings final enlightenment.

One may compare this with the Fourth Gospel, in which God reveals himself directly through the inarticulate sound that can be taken for thunder (12:37), through the person of John the Baptist, who is 'the voice of one crying in the wilderness' (1:23) and who in turn is the witnessing precursor to Jesus, himself appearing as the Logos. Yet, in the scheme of the Fourth Gospel, the shift from obscure to clear does not rest so much on this theory of increasingly articulate revelatory media as it does on the key event of the crucifixion; Jesus as revealer speaks in riddles until the point of his glorification on the cross, at which point it becomes clear to the disciples that not only has he come from the Father, but he is also going back to the Father (16:25–30; see section 2 above for details). Nevertheless, both the Fourth Gospel and the *Trimorphic Protennoia* clearly associate the Logos with the final, definitive stage of revelation. Also, both understand the Logos in terms of a Wisdom-like figure.[19]

This is most evident in the thought-world of the Fourth Gospel and its understanding of Jesus as the manifestation of the divine Wisdom in the masculine form of Logos, and who speaks with the divine Voice. In the Hellenistic Jewish Wisdom tradition, Wisdom is the fountain or spring (Sir 24; Philo, *De fuga* 109) from which comes the Word like a river (Philo, *De fuga* 97) and out of which men may drink instruction (Sir 24; John 4:13–14). This conception is taken up into the gnostic portrayal of the bearer of salvation through enlightenment; it is not by itself Gnostic, but rather invites Gnostic interpretation, as in the *Trimorphic Protennoia* and to a lesser extent in the Fourth Gospel. In fact, it is very tempting to regard such wisdom theology in the Fourth Gospel and in the passages quoted from the *Trimorphic Protennoia* as sharing a common position in the religious background of the first century, one which, while not explicitly Gnostic, is nevertheless on the road to Gnosticism.

5. 10:1–6: the shepherd and the sheepfold

The imagery of this passage has been explained in three basic ways: 1) it derives from the OT imagery of God or the Israelite king as shepherd of his flock Israel, especially as depicted in Ezek. 34,[20] 2) it derives from or is a parable of Jesus,[21] or 3) it derives from a Gnostic portrayal of the saviour such as is found in the Mandaean Right Ginza V, 2 (M. Lidzbarski, ed., *Ginza* (Göttingen, 1925), 180, 5ff.) and Book of John (Lidzbarski, ed., *Das Johannesbuch der Mandäer II* (Gießen, 1915), 44,25–51,4; 51,4–54,5), even though these sources are ostensibly later than the Fourth Gospel.[22]

1) It is true that many components of the imagery derive from the OT; for example, Ezek. 34:13–16: 'I shall lead them out of the peoples, and gather them from the countries, and will bring them into their own land ... I will feed them with good pasture ... I myself will be the shepherd of my sheep, and I will make them lie down, says the Lord God. I will seek the lost.' Further, in Psalm 100 one finds much of the vocabulary of our passage: 'Know that the Lord is God! It is he that made us and not we; we are *his* people, and *the sheep* of his *pasture*. Enter his *gates* with thanksgiving, and his *courts* with praise!' Many more passages could be adduced, but while there is no gainsaying that such OT imagery is certainly part of the background of our passage, nowhere can one find the motif of the sheep recognising the model shepherd who gains welcome entrance to the sheepfold through the door as opposed to the thief and robber who steals into the sheepfold by another, illegitimate way and calls the sheep with a strange voice.

2) Again, while one finds the imagery of shepherd and sheep in some of the sayings of Jesus, this passage cannot be an example of

a parable of the Kingdom, unless it has been reworked so as to be all but unrecognisable. To use the categories of J. D. Crossan,[23] the passage in John 10: 1−5 lacks the characteristic features of Jesus' parables of the Kingdom: the elements of seeking, finding, discovery, surprise and mystery surrounding the advent of the Kingdom with its implied radical reversal of established values and perceptions. Clearly the passage has not to do with the unexpected and surprising advent of the Kingdom or a token thereof, but with the advent of a habitually recognised *figure* through the *expected* or proper entrance.

Clearly, as Bultmann recognised,[24] the conceptions of this passage are either original with the evangelist, or derive from other quarters than the known parables of Jesus.

3) The suggestion of Bultmann[25] is that the image of the shepherd was taken from the Gnostic tradition and is most clearly evident in the Mandaean tradition, namely the Right Ginza V, 2 and Book of John.[26]

More recently, Karl Martin Fischer[27] has taken up the question of the Gnostic background of the Johannine shepherd discourse. On John 10: 1−5 he says:

> Only he is the Redeemer who comes out of the light-world through the gate, which is located between the world of light and the world of darkness, into this world (i.e. αὐλή) in which the soul is caught. But he who comes from elsewhere (namely from the world of darkness), is a thief and robber. He who comes through this door is the (real) shepherd of the sheep.

For Fischer, this world is the sheepfold[28] in which the human soul is trapped, and therefore into which is sent a revelation from the divine world in the form of a redeemer figure or in the form of a divine voice or message in order to awaken the soul to its present condition and restore it to its true home from which it has fallen. Therefore the figure of the shepherd is to be understood, on the model of Bultmann, as a Gnostic redeemer and the souls to be redeemed as sheep.[29] On this basis, one might hypothesise that the figure of the door-keeper could have represented for the author of the discourse something like the Valentinian Horos, or boundary between the Pleroma and the lower created order, through which (as Cross) the Saviour must descend and through which the redeemed souls must eventually ascend. Or perhaps the door-keeper might represent something negative, such as the various cosmic powers which the Saviour must pass by and deceive on his incognito descent to impart revelation to his fallen kinsmen below, as in the *Trimorphic Protennoia* (NHC XIII, *1* 47,13–49,20). For the motif of calling the sheep by name, Fischer refers to *Gos. Tr.* (NHC I,*3*: 21,25–34): 'Those whose name he knew in advance were called at the end, so that the one who has knowledge is the one whose name the Father has uttered. For he whose name has not been spoken is ignorant. Indeed, how is one to hear if his name has not been uttered?' In like manner, the leading forth of the sheep who follow the shepherd is the saving ascent of the redeemer with the redeemed, a motif so frequent in Gnostic texts as not to require citation beyond a few references.[30] The thieves and robbers that enter from elsewhere, which the Johannine passage seems to identify with strangers whose voice the sheep do not recognise, are identified by Fischer with the hostile spiritual powers or Archons of Gnostic mythology.[31]

It is clear that Fischer can find no single passage in the extant Gnostic literature (other than the presumably late Mandaean passages Bultmann had already cited) that clearly presents the Gnostic saviour under the image of shepherd. Instead, one finds only occasional references to the shepherd figure, mostly in the Nag Hammadi treatise, *Authoritative Teaching* (NHC VI,*3*). This lack is not fatal for Fischer's interpretation, however, since what is important to him is the mythological *structure* of the passage, not just the individual images or metaphors of which it is composed. Fischer actually has in mind a reconstructed form of a hypothetical Gnostic mythological archetype (*Urmodelle*) or, as structuralist critics might put it, a mythical 'deep structure' from which the later, more complex versions of this basic Gnostic myth derive, namely the notion of the fall into this world of a feminine being who must be redeemed by a masculine redeemer figure. He sees such a primal form of the myth in the Nag Hammadi treatise *The Exegesis on the Soul* (NHC II,*6*):

> A feminine being is separated from her consort and falls into this world. The Archons seize her and commit every outrage against her and introduce her to the body (a whorehouse, as it were), so that she can no longer return. Now she mourns and repents and bids the Father to help. At her cry the Father shows mercy and again sends her her consort, the Monogenēs, who unites with her. She recognizes him and follows him into the bridechamber where she is purified from the pollutions of this world. Then follows her reconciliation, and the soul

rejoices: 'This is the true resurrection from the dead; this is the redemption from captivity; this is the ascent to go to heaven; this is the way to go to the Father.' First the advent of the redeemer frees her from her dubious situation. All who had come before are criminals, adulterers who only feign love for the soul, but are untrustworthy and abandon the soul as a 'poor lonesome widow'.

Despite the absence of the assignment of opposite genders to the redeemer and the object of his redemption, the doctrine of consorts and the bridechamber, and the denigration of the world as a whorehouse, all this is very close to the structure of the Johannine shepherd discourse, indeed to the mythological structure of the Fourth Gospel as a whole. This structure reminds one very much of the story of the divine wisdom who descends to the world to find a home among men, except that in the Fourth Gospel the condition of that world is one of blindness and lack of perception or recognition, while in the Gnostic myth the soul is actually said to fall into a world which is itself actively antagonistic and beguiling, not simply blind.

6. 10:7—10: Jesus as the door of the sheep

Clearly these verses are meant to be a commentary on the preceding passage, 10:1—5. In 10:7—10, Jesus now presents himself as the door for or to the sheep, instead of as the shepherd who enters through the door. That is, Jesus as the door is not here the one who comes, but instead he to whom others come and through whom they enter. The thieves and robbers are no longer those who enter the sheepfold from elsewhere (10:1) but are now equated with the strangers whose voice the sheep do not recognise (10:5). The *lectio difficilior*, πάντες ὅσοι ἦλθον of 10:8, if original, is extremely ambiguous; would it be a gnomic aorist, 'all who come', or a simple aorist, 'all who came'? In any case, they are no longer the deceptive and illegitimate competitors of Jesus as they were in 10:1—5, since now Jesus is the door whom they presumably approach. The πρὸ ἐμοῦ certainly qualifies the absoluteness of the phrase, but even so a door cannot be said to *come* after thieves and robbers. Perhaps the passage merely means to say that all those who came before [the door], that is, 'up to' the door, are deceivers, but then why not use the expected πρός? As the passage stands, 10:8 clearly relates not to the door, but again to the shepherd, conceived as the revealer who is superior to all his predecessors who are deceivers, as Bultmann noted.[32] Perhaps we are to understand these predecessors as representatives of the un-believing world symbolised elsewhere by the 'Jews'; perhaps they are Jewish teachers or prophets, or perhaps they are representatives of the spiritual movement from which the Johannine community sprang, for example the disciples of John the Baptist (not, of course, John himself, who is a witness to the light who comes after him).

On the other hand, the image of the door makes sense in 10:9, especially as an entrance. It may well be that one has to do here with the influence of Num. 27:17, where Moses is commanded to appoint Joshua as 'a man over the congregation who will go out before them and come in before them, who shall lead them out and bring them out and bring them in, that the congregation of Yahweh may not be as sheep without a shepherd'. Perhaps, if we follow Fischer's inter-pretation of this passage in light of the Gnostic myth, the going in and out of the sheep implies also their original entrance into the world, perhaps a sort of elementary 'fall' of souls into the world. Even if one assumes that the image of the sheepfold is a metaphor for the Johannine community, which is experiencing the hostility of op-ponents who are regarded as thieves and robbers, it is still difficult to account for the motif of both the entrance and exit of the sheep (i.e. members). Perhaps in this case the implication is that 'sheep' enter the sheepfold by joining the Johannine community from which they then go out, as it were, to find 'pasture' in the 'light', that is, experience the higher insight to which the Johannine church thought it had access. In view of the larger text of the gospel, it is perfectly comprehensible why Jesus should be called the door: 'I am the way, the truth and the life; no one comes to the Father, but by me' (14:6).

7. 10:11–15: the good shepherd versus the hireling

This passage introduces yet another image to be considered, that of the hireling who cares nothing for the sheep and abandons them to the wolf, in contrast to the good shepherd who knows the sheep and lays down or risks his life for the sheep. Fischer interprets the hireling as that with which the good shepherd is actually contrasted, rather than the thieves and robbers with which the discourse begins. The image of the shepherd as concerned leader in John 10 is thus directly related to that use in the OT, and Fischer calls attention to *Exeg. Soul* (NHC II, 6: 129, 6–22), where Jer. 3:1–4 is quoted to the effect that just as the people of Israel prostituted themselves and submitted to many shepherds, so also the soul has been misled by many false rulers during its journey in the world. In this sense, the hireling would be a ruler figure, perhaps an Archon in the Gnostic sense. *Auth. Teach.* (NHC VI, *3*: 32, 9–33, 3) likewise employs the image of (bad) shepherds who enslave the soul by nourishing it through the bodily appetites in contrast to the 'true shepherd' who nourishes it with knowledge.[33]

Although Fischer suggests no mythological identification for the wolf, it seems that if the sheep are here an image for the soul, then the wolf functions as a metaphor for the distracting and enslaving bodily appetites to which the hireling, the false shepherd, abandons the soul. Elsewhere in the NT, the image of the wolf appears to refer to the enemies of the disciple's mission (Matt. 10: 16) or of the church (Acts 20: 28–9, 1 Pet. 2: 25; 5: 1–2); the latter seems to be the implication of the wolf in verse 12c ('and the wolf snatches them and scatters them'). The theme of scattering does not fit the logic of the rest of the discourse (which has in view much more the hostile action of snatching, 10: 12 and 28) and seems to relate to the multiple (i.e. scattered?) folds which the shepherd assembles into a single flock in v. 16.[34] Indeed, it may be a redactional echo of Mark 14: 27 pars. (= Zech. 13: 7; cf. John 16: 32).

Nevertheless, the distinguishing characteristic of the good shepherd in 10: 11–18 is that he lays down his life or soul for the sheep. Of course this idea too has its echoes within the (especially Valentinian) Gnostic sphere, in the sense that the Gnostic saviour must take on a psychic body in his descent in order to deceive the cosmic rulers, but he must also put off the psychic body in order to re-enter the world of light on completion of his mission (Irenaeus, *Haer.* 1.5.1–7.5). In the Fourth Gospel it is said that the saviour first lays down his soul in order to take it up again, and that he does this freely, yet at the same time he is also commanded to do so by the Father. A thorough-going Gnostic interpretation of this act would be that the saviour discards the psychic body with which he descends, in order to receive it again in the form of the souls he has come to rescue, but Bultmann (*The Gospel of John*, pp. 384–5) is more likely correct in relating it in its present context to the Johannine conception of the death of Jesus on the cross as his exaltation.

8. 10:31–42: the 'Jews' continue to disbelieve

The concluding verses of chapter 10 seem to add little to the imagery of the shepherd discourse, but rather serve to link the discourse with what precedes it by again stressing the failure of the 'Jews' to believe in either the signs or words of the revealer, and with what follows it by the notice that there were some who believed in him not on the basis of signs, but on the basis of John's testimony. Of course, true belief in Jesus rests neither on such signs nor on testimony, but on hearing Jesus' voice and seeing that he does the Father's works, is one with the Father, and is the Son of God. This section derives from the free hand of the evangelist rather than from any specific inherited tradition, except perhaps for the somewhat rabbinically flavoured argument from less to greater in verses 34–6, based on a citation from Psalm 82:6. Curiously, Jesus' understanding of the charge of blasphemy, namely that he called himself the Son of God, differs in phrasing from the charge of the 'Jews' that Jesus has made himself equal to God, a charge that seems to rise directly from the discourse itself at the point where Jesus says that he and the Father are one.

9. Conclusion

The main points made about the history of religions background of the Johannine shepherd discourse in this essay are the following:

1. The image of the shepherd was widespread in antiquity. The image lent itself aptly to designate a figure mediating between the purity of the divine world and the confusion and corruption of the human world by virtue of the liminal position of the shepherd in ancient society as inhabiting and passing back and forth between the wild and civilized worlds.
2. The imagery of the shepherd in this discourse seems to owe much to concepts found in OT texts, especially Num. 27:17 and Ezek. 34. It seems that the evangelist meant to present Jesus as the appropriate leader of the community in contrast to the Jewish authorities to whom the discourse is addressed. He even may have had in mind the question of the legitimate post-Easter leader or shepherd of the Johannine churches, mainly on the grounds that the discourse is formulated in the concepts of following and protection from external threat, and that Jesus is portrayed as possessing unique character- istics of leadership, mainly knowing his own and laying down

his life for the sheep. At any rate, such leadership seems to be the dominant thrust of the discourse.

On the other hand, the section 10:7–10, on Jesus as the door, whose secondary character some have suspected on textual grounds, seems to have a much more otherworldly cast, and constitutes, I suspect, one of the main grounds why a commentator such as Bultmann sees the figure of the shepherd more as a revealer than as a leader of an earthly community, in which case one will see the shepherd's leadership less in terms of the regal character of the OT shepherd imagery and more in terms of the role of the psychopomp or Gnostic redeemer who leads fallen souls heavenward by means of a saving revelation. And certainly the motifs of the mutual recognition of sheep and shepherd, the recognition by the sheep of the shepherd's voice, and the granting of eternal life, which are important motifs throughout the gospel, make one think of the revelatory function of the shepherd.

3. Insofar as the shepherd functions as the revealer, the shepherd manifests characteristics of the divine wisdom found in the Jewish wisdom tradition. Study of a multitude of Gnostic texts reveals how fundamental the myth of Sophia is to the Gnostic soteriologies. In fact, there is not much in the Gnostic texts quoted in this essay that could not be easily derived from interpretation of various Jewish wisdom books. Yet, to my knowledge, lady Wisdom is nowhere called a shepherd or a door (to salvation) and certainly does not lay her life down for those who love her, no matter how eager she is to make known to them her secrets. Certainly also the myth of the pre-existent divine wisdom descending from the divine world in search of her own underlies much, and perhaps most, of the Fourth Gospel, not only its prologue.

4. There are Gnostic texts that contain motifs and mythological structures in the light of which the shepherd discourse can be intelligibly, perhaps even profitably, read. There is a certain parallelism between the shepherd and the Gnostic revealer, the sheepfold and this world, the pasture and the divine world, the door and the entrance to the divine world, the thieves and robbers and the hostile archons, the wolves and the bodily passions, the shepherd's voice and the Gnostic call to awakening, leading out to pasture and the ascent to the

divine world, and the shepherd's laying down his soul and
the Gnostic redeemer's stripping off his psychic body on
return to the divine world. There is a sense in which the axis
of movement in the discourse is vertical, from above to below
and from below to above, rather than merely horizontal, in
and out between a this-worldly sheepfold and pasture, or
between outside society and the inside world of the Johannine
community. In fact, the Fourth Gospel as a whole invites this
sort of reading, which Gnostic texts also invite. The entire
discourse is bitterly hostile towards the worldly authorities,
who are viewed as thieves, robbers and hirelings, blind and
deaf to the words and deeds of the shepherd. Perhaps one
has here something of the Gnostic emnity towards the world,
or of Wisdom's disappointment at human blindness to the
evidence of the divine presence in the world, or of the aliena-
tion of a sectarian community of insiders at an unbelieving
world. I should say that probably all of these possibilities are
to some extent correct.

5. One of the more puzzling discoveries of this essay is the
   extraordinary parallels between the Johannine shepherd and
   the popular estimation of the god Hermes and, to a lesser
   extent, Apollo. Hermes was a son of god the Father (Zeus),
   a divine shepherd, guardian of doors and access ways, and
   the divine psychopomp who led the souls of the dead not
   only in the classical sense to the underworld, but also in
   later times to the supernal heights. At least in the Egyptian
   Hermetic community, probably active at the time of the
   fourth evangelist, Hermes thrice-greatest, alias Poimandres,
   was a principal revealer figure as well. And it is no accident
   that Dodd was able to examine a multitude of parallels
   between the Hermetic literature and the Fourth Gospel in his
   The Bible and the Greeks and *The Interpretation of the
   Fourth Gospel.*[35] If the shepherd discourse were written
   with a Hermes figure in view, then certain points would be
   scored over Hermes, since Jesus was more than Hermes: not
   only a divine shepherd, but *the* true shepherd who gives his
   life for the sheep; not only a guardian and shower of ways,
   but *the* very way, truth and life themselves; not only the
   keeper of sacred doors, but *the* very door itself; not only the
   leader of souls to their post-mortem destination, but *the*
   grantor of eternal life; not only a son of god, but *the* Son

of God. Since, however, we found it not possible to establish a genealogical trajectory between the figure of Hermes and that of the Johannine shepherd and thus develop a more vivid dependence of the latter on the former, we can at present only be suspicious of some connection between the two.

4

TRADITION, HISTORY AND INTERPRETATION IN JOHN 10
John Painter

John 10 is a complex chapter. Problems arise for the interpreter because of questions about the relation of the chapter to the rest of the Gospel as well as doubts about the order of the chapter itself. Special features, such as the ἀμήν-sayings, the παροιμία and the ἐγώ εἰμι-sayings, also complicate the task of interpretation.

Chapters 5–10 form an important section of the gospel in which the great debates and disputes take place. These chapters focus on conflict with 'the Jews'. The first reference to the persecution of Jesus (5:16) is followed by the first account of an attempt to kill him (5:18). Persecution was a consequence of his having broken the Sabbath, and the attempt to kill him followed because he justified his action (*work*, ἔργον) by appeal to his relation to the Father (5:17–18), a theme taken up in 10:14–18, 29–39,[1] where another attempt to kill (stone) Jesus is described. Attempts to arrest or kill Jesus run through these chapters (5:16, 18; 7:19, 20, 25, 32, 44; 8:20, 59; 10:31–3, 39). The implicit charge against Jesus in 5:18 is explicitly spelt out as blasphemy in 10:33.[2] But in chapter 10 Jesus' appeal to his *works* is made to justify his claimed relation with the Father (10:25, 37–8) whereas, in chapter 5, his appeal to his relation to the Father justifies his *work* (5:17). Thus, in typical Johannine fashion, the claimed relation is used to justify the *work* and the *works* are used to justify the claim.[3]

The Sabbath controversy is introduced as an afterthought in 5:9 and 9:14, suggesting that the miracle stories of chapters 5 and 9 were not transmitted in the context of Sabbath controversy, but have been placed there by the evangelist as a basis for his dialogues. In the controversy, Sabbath-breaking proved, to the Jewish authorities, that Jesus is a law-breaker, a sinner (5:16; 9:16). For Jesus' opponents the miracle of healing is disregarded except as a proof that Jesus broke the law. For others the *healing*, rather than the emphasis on a Sabbath-breaking *work*, is crucial (9:16; 10:21).[4] Chapters 5 and 10 form an *inclusio* on the theme of conflict. From a formal point of view chapter 5 introduces the first of a series of signs (miracle stories) which are used as the basis of a set of dialogues or a lengthy discourse.[5] The interlocking themes of these chapters are all related to the conflict with 'the Jews'[6] and recognition of this provides a key for interpreting John 10.[7]

John 10, like chapter 15, with which it shares a number of characteristics, follows a chapter that appears to have concluded its theme, yet the new chapter does not signal a new beginning. There is no note indicating a new time, place, or audience for the discourse. Chapter 10 opens with a characteristic Johannine double ἀμήν-saying.[8] Most of these sayings have an introductory quotation-formula such as, 'Jesus said to them.' In six instances the ἀμήν-saying is a continuation of Jesus' discourse and does not require a quotation formula. Thus 10:1, being without introductory formula, is formally a continuation of the words of Jesus begun in 9:41. The tension between the formal continuity of chapters 9 and 10 and the apparent change of subject in the παροιμία has led to a widely held view that the text of chapter 10 has been disrupted. This is supported by the view that the σχίσμα[9] caused by the words of Jesus (10:19–21) fits well as the conclusion to 9:39–41, especially as 10:21 refers back to the healing of the blind man. John 10:22–9 is then seen as the introduction to the new section, providing a temporal and geographical note, to the effect that the incident about to be narrated took place in Solomon's porch in the Temple, during the feast of Dedication in mid-winter. In this situation 'the Jews' were provoked to demand that Jesus tell them plainly whether or not he is the Christ. Verses 1–18 would then follow 10:22–9. The order suggested by Bernard, and followed by others, is 10:19–21, 22–9, 1–18, 30–42. But there are problems with this suggestion quite apart from the lack of textual evidence for the disruption. The schism of 10:19–21 does not fit the unbelieving Pharisees of 9:40–1 but implies a broader group such as is referred to in 9:16. The words of Jesus in 10:26–30[10] presuppose at least the παροιμία of 10:1–5. Consequently this case for rearrangement breaks down.

An alternative to a disruption theory, for which, as we have seen, there is no textual evidence, no convincing explanatory hypothesis or textual reconstruction, can be developed on the basis of the hypothesis that the gospel was not written at a single sitting. Without denying that the evangelist made use of sources or that his work might have been subjected to later redaction, the evidence suggests that the evangelist's compositional work was a process taking place over a number of years.[11] It is sometimes possible to discern the tradition with which the evangelist was working and to uncover layers of interpretation applicable to various stages of the history of the Johannine Christians. This evidence is consistent with a process of composition and need not imply that a different hand was responsible for each layer.

1 The παροιμία (10:1−5)

John 10:1−18 can fruitfully be compared with 15:1−11. These passages recount what, for John, most closely resemble the parables and allegories of the Synoptics. In John there are other short parabolic sayings, such as John 5:19−20; 12:24, but no other extended parables or allegories. We may ask whether the isolation of such sayings puts us in touch with ancient traditions, perhaps authentic Jesus traditions. John 15:1−11 contains an allegorising interpretation (of an implied parable) in the form of an extended 'I am' saying. The παροιμία of John 10:1−5 is, however, allegorised only through the 'I am' sayings which follow in the interpretations (10:7−18).[12] In the allegories of both chapters the relation between Jesus, the Father, and believers is set out. Unlike John 15, however, chapter 10 begins with a παροιμία which is introduced by a solemn double ἀμήν-saying. This saying, and the one following in 10:7, bring this discourse into relation with the recurrent use of the formula throughout the gospel.

1.1 The double ἀμήν-sayings

This formula, peculiar to John, is always placed on the lips of Jesus. It is the equivalent of the single ἀμήν-formula of the Synoptics, there also always on the lips of Jesus.[13] It could be that the evangelist has portrayed a characteristic mode of Jesus' speech, simply doubling the ἀμήν for the sake of solemnity. It need not follow that the sayings so introduced have been drawn from the Jesus tradition. While Barnabas Lindars recognised that the double ἀμήν-formula is no part of the saying that it introduces, he argues that the evangelist has used it to signal that authentic material from the Jesus tradition follows.[14] It may be that the evangelist does sometimes introduce old and even authentic traditions with this formula, but an analysis of the twenty-five ἀμήν-sayings does not confirm Lindars's view, because many of these sayings are distinctively Johannine. Given the difficulty in distinguishing the evangelist's reinterpretation of traditional sayings from his creation of sayings using traditional themes, it is not justifiable to take the παροιμία as a traditional saying of Jesus simply because it is introduced by the ἀμήν-formula.

1.2 The παροιμία

Is the παροιμία of 10:1–5 a traditional parable of Jesus or a Johannine construction? As we have seen, nothing can be concluded from the use of the introductory double ἀμήν-saying. Nor do Synoptic parallels throw much light on the situation. The παροιμία was not derived from the Synoptic tradition, though elements of it might have been. See Mark 6:34 (= Matt. 9:36) and the Q parable of the lost sheep (Matt. 18:12–14 = Luke 15:3–7) and possibly also Mark 14:27 (= Matt. 26:31) in which Zech. 13:7 ('I will smite the shepherd and the sheep will be scattered') is quoted by Jesus to foretell the way the disciples would be scattered by his arrest and execution. On this see John 16:32. That tradition (Zech. 13:7) is not mentioned in 10:1–5. Reference to the scattering of the sheep does occur in the second interpretation (10:12, σκορπίζει) and their regathering is in view in 10:16. All of this is consistent with the evangelist's reworking of traditional themes.

There is widespread agreement that the παροιμία has been developed making use of traditions from the Old Testament[15] in which God is depicted as the shepherd of Israel[16] and the leaders of the people as true or false shepherds.[17] The question is, was the παροιμία created by Jesus, introduced into the tradition, or constructed by the evangelist? By isolating the parable in 10:1–5 and demonstrating its Synoptic-like character some scholars hope to show that the evangelist has derived it from the tradition.[18] The problem is, however, more complex because the evangelist could as well have created this parable by using traditional themes and motifs. What is needed is an overall view of the evangelist's compositional method. Is it his method to use small units of traditional material as a basis for more extended interpretative *discourses*, or has all material been thoroughly reinterpreted by the evangelist so that only traditional themes and motifs are visible? An overall view of the evangelist's compositional method can, however, only be built up by a detailed examination of each part of the gospel where the problems we have noted in 10:1–5 also appear. Only in certain *narratives* where there are Synoptic parallels – the cleansing of the Temple (2:13–22); the healing of the nobleman's son (4:46–54); the feeding miracle

(6:1–15); the walking on the water (6:16–21); and elements of the Passion Narrative – can we be certain that the evangelist is using traditional material. In all of this there is evidence of Johannine interpretation but there can be no doubt that there is underlying tradition. In some other instances – the healing of the paralytic (5.2–9a), the healing of the blind man (9:1–12) – although there is no Synoptic parallel we may feel confident that the evangelist is working with traditional stories. The situation is quite different when we turn to the discourse and sayings material.[19]

In an attempt to isolate the tradition more precisely J. A. T. Robinson argued that the παροιμία of 10:1–5 is a merging of the remnants of two independent parables.[20] In the first (10:1–3a) Jesus challenges the 'watchmen' of Israel (represented in the parable by the θυρωρὸς) to recognise his authority, while the second (10:3b–5) affirms that Jesus' authority cannot be proved by signs. The interpretation of the first parable is implausible because that would make Jesus' authority dependent on his recognition by the Jewish authorities, 'to him (the shepherd) the θυρωρὸς opens the door', and the interpretation of the second is more appropriate to the evangelist than the Jesus tradition. The double interpretation in 10:7–18 seems to imply that the duality goes back to the παροιμία of 10:1–5. But need the double interpretation imply two parables? That 10:1–5 does not provide an adequate basis for the following discourse is perhaps the strongest evidence that the evangelist was here drawing on tradition, a view supported by the Synoptic-like material of 10:1–5. But if the double interpretation manifests the underlying parables, why did the evangelist merge them? The theory of two conflated parables is, therefore, unconvincing. An alternative to this is to see 10:1–6 as a stratum of the gospel to which 10:7–18 was added later. The point of the παροιμία and to a lesser extent the first allegorical interpretation (10:7–10) was to judge the Jewish leaders by their attitude to Jesus. For this, the tradition of Ezek. 34 was important, and perhaps also Jer. 7:11. In John 10:11–18, however, the unique authority of Jesus appears to be asserted in the context of an internal conflict within the Johannine community. Probably the first interpretation (10:7–10) was slightly modified to take account of the addition of 10:11–18.[21] Consequently, it is especially the second layer of interpretation, which introduces figures not to be found in the παροιμία, that has given the impression of a double parable.

Tradition suggests an association between Jesus and the shepherd (Luke 15:1–7 = Matt. 18:1–12). But the question then is, who is the θυρωρὸς upon whose recognition the shepherd depends? In John it may be that the Baptist is thought of in this role (1:6–7, 29–34). Certainly in John 9 Jesus has acted as the shepherd. He has found the once blind man, who in turn has recognised his voice and followed him. But he would not listen to the voice of others (the Jews and the Pharisees, 9:13–34, especially verses 25, 30–3; and see 10:3b–5). Alternatively, the παροιμία can be interpreted so that Jesus is identified with the θυρωρὸς.[22] The key for the identification of the shepherd is that he is admitted by the θυρωρὸς. Those who are not so admitted are thieves and robbers.[23] From this perspective the shepherd is the leader of the Johannine community who comes to the sheep, being admitted by Jesus. Regardless of the view of the θυρωρὸς adopted, the thieves and robbers are to be identified with the Jewish leaders who rejected the once blind man (and Jesus as well as the Johannine community). John's gospel can be understood at two levels: straightforwardly it is the story of Jesus; and at the reflected level we discern the story of the Johannine community. The story of Jesus is best portrayed if the Baptist is understood as the θυρωρὸς and Jesus is the shepherd. This was probably the original Johannine meaning of the παροιμία. But the identification of Jesus with the θυρωρὸς might be suggested by the first interpretation (10:7–10) and the association of θύρα and θυρωρὸς. The authoritative role of the θυρωρὸς in the παροιμία also suggests this identification.

1.3 Clues to the history of the Johannine community

For the evangelist, 10:1 is a continuation of the words of Jesus begun in 9:41. I have argued elsewhere[24] that three strata are discernible in John 9, and that 9:39–41 belongs to the third stratum. Recognising this confirms the view that 10:1–5 is a Johannine construction making use of traditional themes and motifs. The παροιμία fits the context of the Johannine community rather than that of Jesus. At the level of the story it is addressed to the unbelieving Pharisees of 9:40–1. But its meaning is dependent also on its location in the history of the Johannine community implied by the third stratum. The three strata can be set out briefly here:

    a. *The miracle story* (9:1–3, 6–12) was a traditional story used to win members of the synagogue to faith in Jesus and implied a christology based on miracles, such as is frequently attributed to a signs source.[25]

    b. *The dialogues* (9:13–38) illustrate the disputes which took place between Jewish believers and those in authority in the synagogue. Central to the dispute is the question of Sabbath observance (9: 14 and compare 5: 9), which is no part of the story itself. In John 9, it is the once blind man who is cast out of the synagogue (9: 22, 34) because the decision had been taken to cast out anyone who confessed, 'Jesus is the Christ'. Jesus remains aloof throughout these disputes, but he does receive the man after he was cast out of the synagogue. The focus on the man and his fortunes, with Jesus standing in the background, is quite uncharacteristic of John and suggests that the man represents the Johannine Christians who have been cast out of the synagogue. While the disputes must have gone on for a lengthy period, the dialogues, in their finished form, reflect the breach from the synagogue. That would seem to imply a date around 85 and a location somewhere in the diaspora, perhaps Asia Minor.

c. *Judgement pronounced* by Jesus (9: 39–41). The words of Jesus execrate the authorities who have cast out the Johannine believers. The two groups have acrimoniously taken leave of each other. These words express the perspective of the Johannine community in the face of excommunication from the synagogue. John 9: 4–5 and 10: 1–6 also belonging to this stratum.

The words of 9: 41, and hence 10: 1–6 also, are addressed to 'those of the Pharisees' (ἐκ τῶν φαρισαίων, 9: 40, and see 9: 16). In 9: 16 it is said that certain of the Pharisees (ἐκ τῶν φαρισαίων τινές) concluded, 'This man is not from God because he does not keep the Sabbath.' But 9: 13–17 makes clear that this was not the view of all of the Pharisees. In fact, others (ἄλλοι) concentrated on the σημεῖα Jesus did. Hence there was a σχίσμα amongst the Pharisees (9: 16). The Pharisees in 9: 13–17 should be compared with the Jews of 10: 19–21, which begins with the reference to the σχίσμα amongst the Jews. The majority (πολλοὶ) accused Jesus of being mad, in theological terms, demon possessed. The minority (ἄλλοι) rejected this view, drawing attention to Jesus' work of opening the eyes of the blind. Thus there is no distinction in John's use of 'Pharisees' and 'Jews' in John 9–10. Indeed, he refers alternatively to the Jews and Pharisees in John 9: 1–10: 21. In both groups there is a σχίσμα because of Jesus' words and actions. It is the unbelieving 'Jews' who cast out the man from the synagogue (9: 22, 34), and it is upon the unbelieving Pharisees that Jesus pronounced judgement (9: 39, 41; 10: 1–5).

1.4 On recognising true and false shepherds

In the παροιμία of 10:1−5 the authority of the recognized shepherds of Israel is challenged. They have not come into the sheepfold by the door. They are thieves and robbers. The sheep (the Johannine community) do not listen to them. In chapter 9 action is taken against those who confess Jesus to be the Christ, not against Jesus himself as in John 5; 7; 8 and later in chapter 10. This clue suggests that the conflict with the false shepherds (10:1−5) does not directly involve Jesus, but the Johannine community (represented by the once blind man) and the unbelieving Jewish leaders in the synagogue who had cast them out. In the παροιμία the position of the believers is authenticated by the evidence that they hear the shepherd's voice and follow him (10:3b−5). The theme is characteristic of a sect, which justifies its rejection and lack of recognition by those outside in such terms. In condemning the leaders of the synagogue the evangelist intended to reassure the members of his own community, the readers or hearers of his Gospel, that they were in the right and to ground this reassurance in his appeal to the evidence that listening to his voice proved they were genuine members of the flock.

2. The interpretation of the παροιμία (10:7−18)

The παροιμία of 10:1−5 shares certain features with the parable of 'the soils' in Mark 4. Both follow a series of conflicts with the Jews. In each case an editorial note follows, indicating that the hearers did not understand (Mark 4:10−12; John 10:6).[26] An explanation of the parable to 'the twelve' then follows in Mark 4:10, 13−20. In John 10:7−18 there is no indication of a change of audience,[27] though the introduction of the editorial note in 10:6 might imply such a change if it were thought that Mark 4 influenced John at this point. Rudolf Schnackenburg argues that in 10:7 there is 'With πάλιν the beginning of a fresh discourse by Jesus (cf. 8:12, 21)', which is addressed neither to the Pharisees of 9:40 nor the Jews of 10:19, but to the believing readers.[28] Indeed, the whole gospel is addressed to believing readers, but the words spoken by the actors in the drama imply an audience within the narrative of the gospel. The case is different in a few situations where the words of the actor fade into the words of the narrator. Two good examples of this appear in John 3 where the words of Jesus to Nicodemus fade into the words of the narrator somewhere in 3:13−21 and the words of the Baptist fade into the words of the narrator in 3:31−6. Those instances differ from 10:7−18 because here we are told that Jesus is the speaker and his words presuppose the same audience as 10:6, which can only be the unbelieving Pharisees. On the other hand, 10:19−21 indicates a broader audience, including, alongside the majority which rejected Jesus, a minority which was impressed by the opening of the eyes of the blind. This is the audience of the preceding verses. But is the implied audience of 10:6−7 the same as that of 10:19−21 and is 10:7−18 a single stratum of tradition?

John 10:7−18 contains four 'I am' sayings,[29] the first being introduced by an ἀμήν-saying with quotation formula, indicating some sort of new beginning after the editorial note. The use of the ἀμήν-saying in 10:7−10 repeats and takes up the double ἀμήν of the introduction to the παροιμία in 10:1.[30] The 'I am' sayings are characteristically Johannine, and the identification of Jesus with the door in verses 7−10 almost fits the context of the παροιμία (if Jesus is there thought to be the θυρωρός). Verses 11−18 appear to be a later stratum of interpretation which does not fit the παροιμία. The addition of this section probably led to minor modifications of verses 7−10. It is then 10:11−18 which presupposes the audience of 10:19−21. The words of Jesus in 10:11−18 make an appeal to the hearers of a broader audience, whereas the παροιμία and 10:7−10 condemn the false shepherds whom Jesus addresses in 9:41. Naturally, in reality the evangelist was addressing the members of his own community. Consequently, the other side, implied by the words of condemnation, is the assurance to the members of the community that they have found life, salvation. It is confirmed to them in that they recognise the shepherd's voice (10:4−5, 8), and is emphasised in the interpretation of Jesus as the door to salvation (10:7−10).

2.1 First interpretation (10:7−10)

While the general theme of 10:7−10 arises from the παροιμία of 10:1−5, surprising new ideas are also introduced. The 'I am' saying of verse 7 surprisingly identifies Jesus with the door not the θυρωρός or the shepherd, and with the door '*of* the sheep' not *to* the sheep, as might be expected on the basis of the παροιμία, implying that it is the sheep, not the shepherd, who are to enter, as confirmed by verse 9. This modification may have been influenced by the evangelist's characteristic christocentric treatment of a theme from the gospel tradition (Q, Luke 13:24 = Matt. 7:13−14) concerning entering the door to life/salvation,[31] a development reflected in John 14:6, which may have influenced the interpretation of Jesus as the door in 10:7, 9. The declaration of verse 8, that 'all who came before me are thieves and robbers', almost fits the παροιμία, although this also has been modified in the light of the claim, about to be made, that Jesus alone is the good shepherd. When it is said that, 'all who came *before me* are thieves and robbers', the contrast of the shepherd with thieves and robbers is taken up implying that Jesus is the shepherd. The παροιμία itself assumed only that the shepherd should enter by the door. While in verse 9 the 'I am' straightforwardly identifies Jesus with the door, what follows shows that it is the sheep who go in and out, not the shepherd. Verse 10 fits the παροιμία in filling out in a little detail what thieves do, but goes beyond it in the direction of the identification of Jesus with the shepherd by having him affirm his life-giving purpose. Thus, what originally identified Jesus with the shepherd, hence showing the self-styled shepherds of Israel to be thieves and robbers, was subsequently modified to present Jesus as the door to life and to prepare the way for the presentation of Jesus as the good shepherd. This interpretation, though formally addressed to the unbelieving Pharisees, was aimed at waverers in the synagogue, affirming that only by facing excommunication and entering the Johannine community could they have life. Naturally it was also addressed to the Johannine community to assure them that they had eternal life.

2.2 Second interpretation (10:11−18)

Whereas the contrast in the παροιμία (and 10:7−10) was between the shepherd and thieves and robbers, in 10:11−18 two new figures are introduced, the μισθωτός and the λύκος. The basic contrast is now between the shepherd, now designated as ὁ ποιμὴν ὁ καλός,[32] with whom Jesus identified himself, and the 'hireling'. The exclusiveness of the door in 10:7−10 is now matched by the exclusive role of the good shepherd, a role already implied in 10:3b−5, 8, 10, which is now spelt out in the contrast with the 'hireling'. The shepherd is the one to whom the sheep belong[33] and he gives his life for the sheep. The sheep do not belong to the hireling, who flees in the time of danger. Since the figure of the hireling has been introduced into the discourse, without any basis in the παροιμία, we are probably right in seeing the figure as representative of a problem in the life of the Johannine Christians.[34] What clues has the evangelist left to help us identify the figure?

The insistence that Jesus alone is the good shepherd suggests that the figure of the hireling[35] is representative of the claim of some other to be the legitimate shepherd. The claim is not identified with the problem of the thieves and robbers, that is, the unbelieving Jewish authorities. The hireling has a legitimate role, though it is relativised by comparison with the shepherd, to whom the sheep belong. Hence it seems likely that 10:11−18 reflects an internal Jewish Christian conflict concerning leadership in the community. The evangelist argued that no leader in the community replaced Jesus. In support of this he set out the differing behaviour, in the face of danger, of the shepherd and the hireling. The good shepherd gives his life for the sheep.[36] On the other hand, the hireling flees in the face of danger. In Mark 14:27−31 (and parallels) Jesus predicts the scattering of the sheep, quoting Zech. 13:7, 'I will smite the shepherd and the sheep will be scattered (διασκορπισθήσονται).' In what follows Peter argued this would not be true of him and Jesus predicted his threefold denial. The tradition was known to John (see 13:36−8 and 21:15−19). Indeed, in John 21 Peter's reinstatement is portrayed in terms suggesting the role of an hireling. The point is made after each of Peter's affirmations of devotion, when Jesus calls on him to 'feed *my* sheep'. In each case it is clear that the sheep are the flock of Jesus.[37]

The scattering of the flock (referred to in Mark 14:27, from Zech. 13:7) strikes a chord with the description of what happens when the hireling flees before the wolf (John 10:12). The wolf ravages the flock and scatters (σκορπίζει) it. This happens because the hireling does not care for the sheep. In the New Testament λύκος is used only six times, of which two are in John 10:12, and two from the Q mission charge (Matt. 10:16 = Luke 10:3). But perhaps the most important reference is in Paul's farewell address to the Ephesian church leaders in Acts 20:28. They are called on to shepherd (ποιμαίνειν) the flock (ποιμνίῳ),[38] the church of God, and are warned of the coming of ravening *wolves*. The wolves here represent those who bring heresy and schism within the flock, and it is said that some of the leaders present will do this. Also important is the portrayal of the 'false prophets' as 'ravening wolves' (λύκοι ἅρπαγες) in Matt. 7:15 (compare John 10:28−9). Such false prophets shatter the unity of the community. Their appearance in the Johannine community is referred to in 1 John 4:1. They caused a schism in the community (1 John 2:19), and there is a good case for seeing the wolf in John 10 as representative of those who have rent the community by their false teaching.

The wolf takes his opportunity in the neglect of the hireling. Once the situation of confusion has arisen, the hireling, claiming to be the shepherd, seeks to assert his authority. The evangelist, however, argues that the scattering of the flock is a result of the flight of the hireling and that the confusion cannot be remedied by an appeal to authority.

The use of Peter as a representative figure, as the hireling, needs further clarification. Naturally it is not Peter himself who is in view. He had long been dead by the time of this crisis in the Johannine community. John 10:11−13 appears to have been formed in the internal struggle within the Johannine community, which the evangelist thinks was a result of the appearance of heretical teachers. In that crisis appeal is made for the recognition of a more formal institutional authority, such as Peter represents. While the evangelist recognizes the need of leadership within the community, he does not accept the claim that the leaders hold an institutionalised authority over the community. Absolute authority belongs to the shepherd, the leaders are hirelings.[39]

John 10:14−18 further develops the role of the good shepherd. Initially this is rooted in the παροιμία, where it is said that the shepherd knows his sheep by name and they know his voice. This is now expressed, in words placed on the lips of Jesus, in a mutuality formula which is extended christologically to express not only Jesus' relation to his own but also his relation to the Father. 'I am the good shepherd, and I know mine and mine know me, even as the Father knows me and I know the Father' (14−15a). While this relation is implicit throughout the gospel, the expression of it in these terms is unique and, according to Bultmann, signals the influence of a mystical tradition such as occurs in the Gnostic literature,[40] where it describes 'the mutual determination of the elements which have been combined together into a single whole'. It is true that the formula admirably fits the Gnostic schema. Alternatively, it can be seen as an expression of sectarian consciousness.[41] It is helpful to see the evangelist's image of the community as the mirror image of his christology. It should also be seen in relation to the Q tradition (Matt. 11:25−7 = Luke 10:21−2). Here again we find that one of the most distinctive of Johannine themes has roots going back into the Synoptic tradition. Of course it also needs to be noted that this particular Q passage is quite unique in the Synoptics. It is not part of a common Synoptic theme, though it could be seen as an elaboration of the Father/Son relation in the Synoptic tradition, along lines that were taken up more systematically by John.

The clue to what the evangelist means by this mutual knowledge is to be found in the παροιμία, as far as the relation between Jesus and his own is concerned, and in 10:15b, as far as his relation with the Father is concerned. Jesus, as the good shepherd, knows his sheep, he calls them by name. The sheep know him and his voice and they follow him. Jesus' relation to the Father is expressed in laying down his life for the sheep and taking it again (10:15b, 17–18). This he does at the command of the Father. Hence the Father's knowledge of the Son is expressed in sending him, commanding him, and the Son's knowledge of the Father is expressed in obedient fulfilment of the Father's will. Because of this they are one. The Son's knowledge of his own is expressed in calling them, and that call is expressed in his giving of his life for them, while their knowledge of him is expressed in obedience to his call.[42]

In both of the 'I am' sayings of 10:11–13 and 10:14–18 the role of the good shepherd is spelt out in terms of his giving his life for 'the sheep'. It is given for '*the* sheep', not '*my* sheep', which might have been expected in 10:15, following the mutuality formula.[43] In the first saying his life-giving action is contrasted with the action of the hireling. In the second it is portrayed as the appropriate action expressing the mutuality of knowledge (10:14–15). In it he fulfills the will of the Father. Consequently it is important to stress the voluntary nature of the act (10:17–18). He has the authority and responsibility to give his life and take it up again. Thus the image of the good shepherd goes beyond that of the door because it is interpreted in terms of Jesus' death, and also, to some extent, in terms of his resurrection. 1 John also focusses attention on the significance of Jesus' death, perhaps in opposition to those who saw him only as the way of initiation into knowledge.[44] Against such teachers the evangelist asserts that Jesus is the good shepherd who gives his life for the sheep.

The shepherd also looks to the task of bringing other sheep, not of the Johannine community (τῆς αὐλῆς ταύτης), to constitute one flock under one shepherd (10:16). It could be that this is the counterstrategy of the evangelist against the attempt to bring the Johannine community under the authority of the one he designates a hireling. Those who are scattered need to be united in one flock under the one shepherd, Jesus. His authority depends on the sheep hearing his voice, and the evangelist conceives of his gospel as the means by which the voice of Jesus would call his sheep into one flock. More likely than the view that the Gentiles are intended is the suggestion that the evangelist has other Jewish Christians in mind, or perhaps the re-gathering of his own community, scattered through the emergence of rival teachers and false teachings evidenced in 1 John (compare especially 1 John 4:1 and Matt. 7:15).[45]

3. The response (10:19–21)

With these words (verses 19–21) the narrative context of the life of Jesus returns to the surface. The evangelist announces the σχίσμα among 'the Jews' as a result of hearing the words[46] of Jesus. It is said that a σχίσμα occurred *again*,[47] referring to 7:43. There (in 7:37–9) the σχίσμα is also a consequence of hearing Jesus' words (τῶν λόγων τούτων), and, as in 9:16, a variety of views is expressed before con-cluding that there was a σχίσμα. In 10:19 the schism is first stated, before indicating the variety of views in response to Jesus' revelation of himself as the good shepherd in which he predicted his passion and resurrection.[48] Yet there is no specific reference to this discourse by either side in the schism. The majority (πολλοί) conclude that Jesus has a demon and is raving,[49] and this might be intended as a reference to the content of the discourse. The minority (ἄλλοι) reject this view, appealing to Jesus' work of opening the eyes of the blind.[50] The majority demand of them, 'Why do you hear him?' The defence does not appeal to Jesus' words, but defends them by appeal to his works, in this case the healing of the blind (10:20). This prepares the way for the subsequent charge of blasphemy against which Jesus defends his words by appeal to his works (10:31–9). It is the words of Jesus, explicitly christological, that caused the schism.

Verses 19–21 are the evangelist's summary. Unlike 9:16, which is also a summary statement, 10:19–21 is appended to the preceding section. It is not an integral part of it as is 9:16 in the dialogues of that chapter. In this regard it is more like 7:40–4, to which πάλιν (of 10:19) refers. Given that 10:19–21 is a loose addition, what are we to make of it in the context of the gospel? In chapter 9, the deci-sion of 'the Jews' to cast out from the synagogue anyone who confessed that Jesus is the Christ was executed on the healed man, and at the end of the chapter Jesus pronounced judgement on the unbelieving Pharisees. The situation of broken relations is also presupposed by 10:1–18. But such a situation implies that Jesus no longer walks freely amongst 'the Jews'. Yet in the narrative of the gospel Jesus' final conflict with 'the Jews' remains in the future, and this summary state-ment brings the reader back to that perspective. Naturally the schism within the Jewish community can also be read at a second level, to indicate the schism within the Christian community over the question of leadership. In the narrative of the gospel, however, 10:19–21 reintroduces the situation of disputation, not now between the healed man and 'the Jews', but between Jesus and the Jews directly, thus preparing the way for what is to follow.

4. The disputation (10:22–39)

The disputation has direct links with the situation of chapter 5 (and 7). It is largely the composition of the evangelist using a few traditional themes and motifs. In both chapters 5 and 10 Jesus' words concerning his relation to the Father and his *works* are closely related, and the reported attempts to kill him in chapter 5 lead well into chapters 7–10. In this context it might seem that chapter 6 is something of a diversion, not only geographically, but also thematically. This view does not sufficiently note the disputational character of chapter 6 and the way it concludes by noting that Jesus knew that not all of the disciples were true believers and which of them was about to betray him (6: 60–71).[51] In this situation (in: 7:1) the narrator indicates that Jesus could not move openly in Judaea 'because the Jews sought to kill him'. This is at the time of the feast of Tabernacles. He does subsequently go up to Jerusalem and reveal himself in the middle of the feast (7:14). From that point onwards there is an open disputation with the Jews seeking to arrest (πιάσαι, 7:30, 32, 44; 8:20, 10:39; 11:57) or to kill Jesus (7:19, 20, 25; 8:59; 10:31, 33; 11:49–50). Only chapter 9 breaks this pattern. There the action is directed against the man rather than against Jesus himself. It is also notable that there is no indication of time and place in chapter 9. That lack is now supplied in 10:22.

It is now mid-winter, some two months after the last reference to time in 7:2, 14, 37. The occasion is the feast of Dedication, celebrating the purification of the Temple after its profanation by Antiochus Epiphanes. That Jesus should be walking in the Temple at the feast of Dedication is quite fitting, but perhaps surprising in the light of earlier attempts to arrest or stone him and reports of his own evasive action. Indeed, the narrative seems to presuppose a situation prior to any decision to take action against Jesus or his followers. 'The Jews' are however, presented as cohesively hostile (10:24), unlike the divided 'Jews' of 10:19–21. That hostility is indicated by the way they surrounded (ἐκύκλωσαν) Jesus, and by the nature of the question and its apparent tone. The question is really a demand that Jesus should tell them plainly if he is the Christ. It ignores the fact that, according to the dialogues of John 9, there are already those who confess 'Jesus is the Christ', and that the decision had been made to cast them out of the synagogue (9:22). The tone of the demand in 10:24 reflects the evangelist's return to the situation of the story of Jesus.

There is, however, another perspective which impinges on the demand for an answer. In the traditional narrative of the trial of Jesus, the demand was made that he should answer whether or not he is the Christ (Mark 14:61 and parallels). In Mark 14:62, as in John 10:24–5, an unequivocal answer is given. This detail, absent from John's trial scene, has been introduced at this point because, in John, Jesus' christological claims are made openly, almost from the beginning of the gospel. All of the evangelists set their accounts of Jesus' life in the context of such claims, but only John places these claims directly on the lips of Jesus, for example, in the great 'I am' sayings. Hence it is fitting that this question should be put to him prior to his trial. It is also important for the evangelist that Jesus himself should defend the christology proclaimed in his gospel because it involves a reinterpretation of traditional messianic categories. There is, in these disputations, a defence, not only against the Jewish charge of ditheism, but also against the charge laid by Christian Jews that this christology is not true to Jesus' messianic status and role.[52]

The defence is given in the words of Jesus (10:25–30), making the following points: a) He has already told them what they desire to know but they will not believe his words; b) His works, done in his Father's name, support his claim; c) They do not believe because they are not his sheep; d) His sheep hear his voice and follow him; e) He gives his own (sheep) eternal life: they will never perish; none can snatch (ἁρπάσει) them from him; f) The Father, who has given them to him, is greater: none can snatch (ἁρπάζειν) them from him; g) The climax is reached in the assertion, 'I and the Father are one'.

The theme of a) and b) is taken up again in 10:37–8. Here it is clear that the question of whether Jesus is the Christ has been answered in the affirmative but interpreted in terms of the Johannine understanding of Son of God (see also John 20:31). The disputation is not, then, about a Jewish concept of messiahship, but about its Johannine interpretation. In c), d), and e) we find the expression of a sectarian consciousness, which explains why the mass of people do not believe and reassures the few of the correctness and security of their position. That security is dependent on the relation of Jesus to the Father, which is expressed in f) and g).

Central to the expression of these points is a dependence on the παροιμία and its interpretations in 10:1–18, where the relation of the shepherd to his sheep is developed, and the role of the wolf is described using the verb ἁρπάζει (10:12, and see 10:28, 29, and λύκοι ἅρπαγες in Matt. 7:14). None can snatch (ἁρπάσει) the sheep from Jesus' hand nor from the Father's. If the wolf is the symbol of the false teachers, these words are a guarantee to the faithful that they are safe against such onslaughts. What guarantees their safety is Jesus' hand which guards them. He guards them because the Father has given them to him.

Now comes the paradox that is essential to the Johannine christology. The Father is greater than the Son and his hand also protects the sheep. But there are not two protecting hands, because the Son and the Father are one. Here we find, in enigmatic form, the argument based on the relation of the Son to the Father that was set out in 5:17, 19–30. The truth is that Jesus does the will and work of God, which he was sent to do, so that what he does the Father does. There can be no distinction between the two agents in the action. Yet the Son is not the Father, who is greater than the Son, though the Son has come to make the Father known and to do his work. In the language of the emissary, applied to Jesus, and the affirmation that the Father is greater, we find evidence of subordination. But in the Father/Son relation and the language of unity (and equality, 5:18) there is evidence of an ontological equality. Perhaps the closest we can get to the formulation of John's view is that he proposed an ontological equality and a functional subordination, because, if Jesus did not do the Father's will he could not make the Father known.

This christology was developed in the conflict with the synagogue; and the charge of blasphemy, which follows in 10:31–9, was a natural response to it, with the indication that the Jews again (πάλιν) took up stones to stone Jesus.[53] Jesus' appeal to the many good works[54] which he had shown them from (ἐκ) the Father[55] (10:32 and see 10:25), like the appeals in 9:16 and 10:21, is a generalised appeal to works, though he then asks which of these works is the basis for their decision to stone him. Here there is an emphasis on the good works (ἔργα καλὰ) not made in 9:16 and 10:21, though it may be implied in the reference to such signs (τοιαῦτα σημεῖα), and in the assumption that opening the eyes of the blind (plural) is a good act. Here no room is left for ambiguity. Jesus asserts the goodness of his works. This is not contested. It is now, however, allowed (by 'the Jews') to have a bearing on the dispute. The reference to works (ἔργα), with the dispute which follows, indicates that we have returned to the theme of chapter 5, especially 5:16–30. Indeed, it may be that the charge of working on the Sabbath suggested the appropriateness of the term 'works' at this point.

In 5:17 Jesus justified his action on the Sabbath by appeal to the accepted view that God works on the Sabbath. In itself that was no justification for his own action. It would only justify him it he could show the identity of his action and the action of God. That is the way 'the Jews' understood his argument in 5:17. Calling God his own (ἴδιον) Father, in this context, was making himself equal (ἴσον)[56] to God. In what follows in chapter 5 it is argued that equality does not imply independence but dependence. Only because the Son does the Father's will can he make the Father known, so that there is an identity of action. In chapter 10 the same logic is followed by the 'Jews' as they had expressed in chapter 5. Jesus' speaking of God as his Father is now formally called blasphemy because it is understood in terms of a man claiming to be God (10:33).

Jesus' defence here, unlike in chapter 5, takes the form of an appeal to the Jewish Torah.[57] The logic is simple and follows the pattern of rabbinic argument. If, in the Torah, those to whom the word of God came are called gods, how much more appropriate is the term for the one whom the Father sanctified and sent into the world. The precedent in scripture justifies the ascription of the title 'God' or 'Son of God' to the emissary of God.[58]

At the level of the language the ascription of the title 'son of God' is said to be justified in that Jesus is demonstrably the emissary of God. The works are the evidence. The language of sonship and the works form a unity. This emissary christology has its roots in the Synoptic tradition, for example in the Q passage found in Matt. 10:40 and Luke 10:16 and in Mark 9:37 and parallels. There Jesus says that the disciples stand in the same relation to him as he does to the one who sent him (ἀποστείλαντά με), a saying which should be compared with John 13:20, except that there the verb πέμπω is used (τὸν πέμψαντά με). Given that, in John, the two verbs are used more or less synonymously (of the sending of Jesus, and the disciples) the use of different verbs does not appear to be theologically significant. John, however, does not use ἀποστέλλω as an active participle with the article. In this form he uses only πέμπω.[59] The language in John, comparable to the Synoptics, is suggestive of a functional relationship. This, with the similarity of argument used to justify the language, suggests that the evangelist is drawing on tradition.

Given that both Jesus and his disciples are portrayed as sent we might expect them also to be called sons (υἱοὶ) of God. This is not the case. The evangelist restricts the term 'Son' to Jesus, using the term children (τέκνα) of God of believers. If it is suggested that this is because Jesus himself was sent by God, but the sending of the disciples was mediated through him, it must be noted that the gospel portrays the Baptist too as 'a man sent from God', and there is no suggestion that the title 'Son of God' should be ascribed to him. There are peculiar Johannine nuances which indicate that the language, when used of Jesus, implies more than an emissary christology. Characteristically, the evangelist has Jesus speak, not only of 'the one who sent me', but of 'the Father who sent me' (ὁ πέμψας με πατήρ). The emissary is not only sent, he is the one 'whom the *Father* sanctified and sent into the world' (ὃν ὁ πατὴρ ἡγίασεν καὶ ἀπέστειλεν εἰς τὸν κόσμον, 10:36). The Father/Son relation is an essential ingredient, and the notion of being sent *into the world* implies more than an emissary christology. It implies that the emissary is not merely a human messenger but comes from the divine side of reality into the world. With the combination of functional and ontological sonship we find the distinctive Johannine christology, which is the result of a reinterpretation of the tradition.

The argument concludes (10:37−8) with an appeal to take account of the works. Perhaps that implies that even the provisional acceptance of emissary status is an acceptable beginning, though Jesus' own words call for the acceptance of an ontological sonship. The argument that follows shows that beginning with the works will lead on to understanding the ontological sonship of Jesus since, 'the Father is in me and I in the Father' (10:38), which is a variation on the theme expressed in 10:30, 'I and the Father are one'. The form of the argument seems as much, and perhaps more, aimed at those who already acknowledge Jesus, as at outright Jewish opponents. It is likely that the Johannine christology appeared as blasphemy to early Christian Jews. What the evangelist does is to show the implications of believing that Jesus does the works of God and to argue that recognition of Jesus as a messenger of God implies recognising him as Son of God, one with God, in whom God is present and acting. The consequence of the argument is that 'the Jews' again (πάλιν) sought to arrest (πιάσαι) Jesus, but he evaded them (10:39).

5. Transitional summary (10:40−2)

The transitional note, appropriately following 10:39, indicates Jesus' return to the place where John was first baptising, and provides the context for the final contrast between John and Jesus (10:41). The role of John as witness is reiterated and, in denying that he performed any signs, the evangelist cleverly draws attention to the signs of Jesus and the many who believed because of them, suggesting that 10:40−2 might have been part of the original conclusion to the signs material and originally followed by 20:30−1. Alternatively, the reference to the Baptist might have originally followed the παροιμία, to draw out for the reader the identification of the Baptist as the θυρωρός. The emphasis on Jesus' signs continues the theme from chapter 10 while reaffirming the legitimacy of the Baptist as a witness to Jesus. The probability is that this material is developed on the basis of tradition,[60] though it has been thoroughly reworked by the evangelist. Reference is made to the signs (σημεῖα), not to the works (ἔργα), which would have been more in keeping with the language and theme of chapter 10. But it would be a mistake to attribute this to the influence of a source because it is the Johannine Jesus who speaks of his works while the narrator indicates that the masses believe on the basis of the signs (2:23; 3:2; 6:2, 14; 11:45, 47−8; 12:18, 37, 42). The contrast of 10:41 implies that Jesus did many signs and that this is the basis of the belief of the many mentioned in 10:42, and this is not unrelated to the witness of the Baptist.

In this place Jesus stayed (ἔμεινεν),[61] and many came to him. Here, no doubt the account is to be understood at the level of the story of Jesus. Whatever opposition he may have faced from the institutional leadership of 'the Jews', his popularity amongst 'the masses' (πολλοί) seems clear. Consequently it is indicated that 'many (πολλοί) believed in him there'.[62] It is interesting and important to note that the evangelist does not put in question the faith of the masses, as he does, for example, in 2:23 and 12:42. He is not so opposed to the signs as is sometimes supposed. Rather, it was his opinion that belief on the basis of signs alone did not go far enough in deducing the implications of the signs/works in developing christology.

6. Concluding remarks

In plotting the course of the history of Johannine christology the following points can tentatively be made: a) Signs were used, in the early stages of Johannine history, to demonstrate Jesus' messianic status in the debate with the synagogue, and it could be that, in relation to Baptist loyalists, the aim was to show that Jesus, not John, was the Messiah. b) In the debate with the synagogue, where Jesus' opposition to Moses and the Torah was stressed, the evangelist emphasised Jesus' status and role as the emissary from God. Here he was able to use traditional material which suited his purpose. c) Given the logic of the evangelist's argument, Jesus' mission from God implies an ontological relation to God. Hence the traditional language is reinterpreted to develop a christology of functional and ontological sonship, an emissary and incarnational christology.

On the basis of our analysis of the παροιμία in John 10: 1–5, and its subsequent interpretations, certain conclusions can be drawn about history and tradition in that chapter: a) The basic contrast drawn in the παροιμία is between the shepherd and the thieves and robbers. It appears that (in the παροιμία) Jesus is to be identified with the shepherd and that the Baptist is the θυρωρός. b) Only in the interpretation that follows (10:7–10) is he identified with the door to salvation. In the first interpretation, as in the παροιμία, the thieves and robbers are identified with the Jewish leaders who have rejected Jesus and his followers. c) In the παροιμία the shepherd can only represent Jesus or, at a secondary level, the leader (the evangelist) or leaders of the Johannine community. It is possible that 10: 1–5 is a traditional parable, though it is more likely a composition of the evangelist, using traditional themes and motifs. d) In the second interpretation (10: 11–18), Jesus is the good shepherd. The theme of recognising his voice, which dominates the παροιμία (verses 3b–5), and is important in chapter 9 (verses 35–8), is now muted. In its place is the emphasis on the good shepherd laying down his life and taking it again, for which the παροιμία has not prepared the reader. The thieves and robbers have disappeared, and with them, it seems, the conflict with the synagogue. In their place we find two figures who have not appeared in the παροιμία, the 'hireling' and the 'wolf'. The focus on the 'hireling' reflects a leadership struggle within the community. The evangelist appeals to the direct relationship between the good shepherd and those who respond to his voice. The treatment of the denial and restoration of Peter suggests that we have here a reflection of a struggle with Petrine Christianity. That struggle might well have developed after the Johannine community was ravaged by a schism caused by what the evangelist perceived as false teaching.[63] The false teachers are portrayed as ravening wolves that scatter the flock. The shepherd's aim was to re-gather the flock. It is interesting that, in 1 John and in John 10: 11 – 18, focus falls on the significance of Jesus' giving his life, something which 'the opponents' in 1 John either ignore or deny. Consequently, a case can be made for seeing the later strata of the gospel as more or less contemporary with 1 John, though probably prior to the hardening of the schism of 1 John 2: 19.

5

JOHN 10 AND ITS RELATIONSHIP TO THE SYNOPTIC GOSPELS

M. Sabbe

On the hypothesis of a direct dependence upon the Synoptists and in continuity with the approach used in our previous examination of some pericopes, such as the arrest of Jesus and the footwashing of the disciples, we examine John 10 in the hope that the results will be equally fruitful and convergent.[1] Although the hypothesis of direct dependence upon the Synoptists was generally denied in the last half-century, for centuries it was the general consensus and it has gained its protagonists within the last twenty-five years. It is in that light that we will examine the text to see how familiar John, whose view was certainly retrospective, could have been with the Synoptic material and even with the gospels themselves.

1. A trial of Jesus by 'the Jews' (John 10:22–39)

Since a sound point of departure is to proceed from the clear to the more obscure, we shall start with the second half of chapter 10, i.e. with verses 24–39, which to a certain extent may be considered an anticipation of the Passion Narrative of Jesus as we know it from the Synoptic Gospels. Here we observe several elements which normally belong to such a narrative: the enemies of Jesus are quoted and there is a sort of arrest of Jesus (verses 24a, 31, 39), followed by a trial consisting of an interrogation about his Messiahship (verse 24b), a self-defence of Jesus which mainly coincides with a Messianic self-proclamation of his divine sonship (vv. 25–30, 32, 34–8) and a condemnation to death on the basis of blasphemy (verse 33) with an attempt at stoning him. One may not overlook John 11:47–53, where the same plot of the high priests (and Caiaphas) to kill Jesus is reported immediately before the anointing at Bethany as in Mark and Matthew, a passage which already belongs to the context of the effective Passion Narrative itself.

1.1 The narrative Framework (verses 24a, 31, 39)

1. *'The Jews' as the hostile opponents of Jesus* are twice mentioned as such (verses 24 and 31). In the Fourth Gospel they are normally referred to as the hostile religious authorities of Jerusalem, and this is usually understood as a Johannine simplification.

2. It is possible to interpret the role of 'the Jews' in the three different transitional narrative verses 24a, 31 and 39 of the pericope as *a kind of anticipation of his actual arrest*? The first element 24a – ἐκύκλωσαν οὖν αὐτὸν οἱ Ἰουδαῖοι can be given a dual interpretation: 'The Jews gathered around Jesus/ they surrounded him.' Comparable situations are those of John 1:26; 20:19, 26; Luke 2:46; 22:27; 24:36; Mark 14:60; Matt. 18:2; Acts 1:15; 17:22; 27:21. Considering that all these references are based on the term μέσος, it may be better to look at the expression of Mark 3:34 where Jesus addresses 'those who sat about him' (περιβλεψάμενος τοὺς περὶ αὐτὸν κύκλῳ καθημένους λέγει) and of Rev. 7:11 ('all the angels stood round the throne saying' – εἰστήκεισαν κύκλῳ τοῦ θρόνου ... λέγοντες).

Rather than suggesting such a neutral attitude of curiosity or of sympathy, the saying of verse 24a seems to purport threat and hostility: 'The Jews encircled Jesus', introducing the ominous interrogation: 'How long are you going to keep us in suspense?' So, the expression corresponds to the pejorative use (only four times in the NT) of the verb κυκλόω as in Luke 21:20 and in Heb. 11:30. A favourable meaning of the verb can be distinguished in Acts 14:20. A positive meaning is obviously absent in John 10:24 where 'the Jews' play a role similar to that of the high priests, the elders and the scribes or even the whole Sanhedrin in the trial scene of the Synoptists. The verb κυκλόω used in our case is indeed apropos to a gathering of that sort.[2]

The way 'the Jews' are acting in verse 31 fits within the framework of a persecution and Passion Narrative. Threatening Jesus with death through stoning – absent in all other Passion Narratives – is a feature again referred to in John 11:8; it appears already in 8:59a combined with Jesus' escape. 'The Jews' seek to arrest Jesus or to stone him but Jesus escapes from their hands.

Jesus' persecution by 'the Jews' is a motif that appears almost throughout the whole gospel, having its starting point in John 5:16, 18, after the healing at the pool, because Jesus did this on the Sabbath. This starting point is particularly interesting since most probably for this pericope the author of the gospel was inspired by Mark 2:1 – 3:6, concluding with the Pharisees taking counsel with the Herodians as to how they might destroy Jesus.

It is not surprising to find that a general attempt to kill Jesus has become a reference to stoning him. In John 18:31−2, it is evidently understood as the normal death penalty consequent upon a Jewish trial. We may even accept Luke 4:29 as bearing this interpretation. Some influence by latter text may not be excluded,[3] all the more since the escape of Jesus as mentioned in Luke 4:30 (αὐτὸς δὲ διελθὼν διὰ μέσου αὐτῶν ἐπορεύετο) has been influential on diverse variants of John 8:59 (καὶ διελθὼν διὰ μέσου αὐτῶν ἐπορεύετο) as a prolongation of the usually accepted reading, 'Jesus hid himself and went out of the temple' (see also John 12:36 and cf. 19:38). The other Johannine parallel of Jesus' escaping after a stoning attempt, in John 10:39 (καὶ ἐξῆλθεν ἐκ τῆς χειρὸς αὐτῶν) is no different. It is comparable to John 7:30 and 7:44. The verb ἐξέρχομαι, as used here in 10:39, surely means 'to escape', a sense which is obviously confirmed by the further specification 'from their hands' and which is also applied in 8:59. The use of the verb ἐξέρχομαι in John 8:59 and 10:39 can be considered a kind of synthetic reference to the description of Luke 4:30.

1.2 Are you the Christ? (verses 24b−30)

1. The narrative framework (verses 24a, 31, 39) is itself already a kind of anticipated or duplicated version of the Passion Narrative. Here the fact that *the trial of Jesus before 'the Jews'* (verses 24b−30, 32−8) is anticipated in the whole of the Johannine composition of the gospel need not surprise us. It is often acknowledged that the scene in John 18:19−24 cannot really be considered a trial of Jesus. It is not even a summary but only a formal substitute and a rather 'Johannine' refusal of Jesus to answer and to reveal himself here to 'the Jews'. His real confrontation with them, Jesus' open proclamation to them, and so to the world (John 18:20; see also 17:4, 6 and cf. 12:36b), has been anticipated and spread over the first part of the gospel.[4] All that was related in the Synoptists' Sanhedrin session of the trial of Jesus has already previously been treated in the Johannine gospel: the temple logion comes in 2:19; Jesus has already revealed himself as Messiah and Son of God in 4:25−6; 5:17−18; 8:58; 10:30−8; the Jews have repeatedly tried to arrest or to kill him in 7:32; 5:18; 8:59; 10:31, and an official condemnation to death has occurred in 11:47−53.[5]

In the Markan narrative of the trial of Jesus before the Sanhedrin — after seeking testimony against Jesus and with the focus on his criticism of the temple and the temple saying — the high priest interrogates Jesus with a double question: σὺ εἶ ὁ Χριστὸς ὁ υἱὸς τοῦ εὐλογητοῦ; (14:61). The Matthean narrative (26:63) has a slightly different version: 'I adjure you by the living God ἵνα ἡμῖν εἴπῃς εἰ σὺ εἶ ὁ Χριστὸς ὁ υἱὸς τοῦ θεοῦ.' Luke, in turn, dropping the whole introductory search for testimonies (see, however, Luke 22:71 = Mark 14:65, Matt. 26:65) as well as Jesus' temple criticism, emphasises Jesus' double self-proclamation by splitting the original Markan question of the high priest into a double interrogation proceeding from the whole assembly of the elders of the people, both chief priests and scribes: λέγοντες εἰ σὺ εἶ ὁ Χριστὸς εἰπὸν ἡμῖν (verse 67) and again εἶπαν δὲ πάντες· σὺ οὖν εἶ ὁ υἱὸς τοῦ θεοῦ; (verse 70).

John has already anticipated the temple logion in 2:19 and he will substitute the high priests' questioning within the trial by a general interrogation in 18:19.[6] Here in 10:24–38, which is undeniably inspired by the Lukan account, brings Jesus before the Jews: καὶ ἔλεγον αὐτῷ (οἱ Ἰουδαῖοι) ... εἰ σὺ εἶ ὁ Χριστός, εἰπὲ ἡμῖν παρρησίᾳ (verse 24), the second element of Jesus' proclamation being found in verse 36: ὅτι εἶπον, Υἱὸς τοῦ θεοῦ εἰμι.

2. In *John 10:24* 'the Jews' as the adversaries of Jesus function perfectly as a general reference to the group mentioned in Luke 22:66. (One must not overlook the reference to the Sanhedrin in this Lukan verse; together with John 11:47, these are the only places in Luke and John where συνέδριον is mentioned and in an identical context.) The *verbum dicendi* (καὶ ἔλεγον αὐτῷ) used in verse 24 (as well as in 11:47) seems to echo the plural λέγοντες of Luke 22:67, which differs from the singular in Matt. 26:63 (εἶπεν αὐτῷ) and Mark 14:61 (ἐπηρώτα αὐτὸν καὶ λέγει αὐτῷ). Both places, however, express the addressee with αὐτῷ, as in John 10:24. Although the question as formulated in Luke (εἰ σὺ εἶ ὁ χριστός) is based upon the text of Mark, it is identical to that of John, and in both gospels it is somehow separated from the second question. Even the way Jesus is invited in Luke 22:67 to give an answer (εἰπὸν ἡμῖν) is almost identical to that of John (εἰπὲ ἡμῖν). Both Luke's invitation, which is identical with that of Luke 20:2 (another Lukan redaction, cf. also Luke 20:3), and the more pressing adjuration of Matt. 26:63 can be interpreted as an accidental parallel interpretation of the Markan question. But John's text is very close to Luke's, the only difference being the

the element παρρησίᾳ. The latter is a typical Johannine characteristic of style; tell us 'plainly' is used again, not accidentally, in 18:20.[7] It underscores what is already expected in Mark 14:61 and expressed more clearly in Luke: a public proclamation of Jesus' Messiahship.[8]

The sentence in verse 24b (ἕως πότε τὴν ψυχὴν ἡμῖν αἴρεις) can hardly be understood as a friendly, open question: 'Please tell us finally who you are; we are eager to know it. How long will you keep us in suspense?' In line with the hostile ambience of the whole context, it rather suggests impatience and a clear will to bring the whole story to an end: 'Do not wait any longer to come out with a clear statement about your Messianic pretensions so that we can judge you. How long will you trouble, annoy in this way?' Compare ἕως πότε, tinged with a similar bitterness and haughtiness on the part of Jesus himself in Mark 9:19(bis)(= Matt. 17:17 and Luke 9:41). The verb αἴρω is often used in John, and as it appears in the expression οὐδεὶς αἴρει αὐτὴν (τὴν ψυχήν) ἀπ' ἐμοῦ in the same chapter 10 (verse 18), it has a similar—evidently pejorative—meaning.

3. *Jesus' answer in verse 25* seems to be a paraphrase of his reply in the Lukan account of the trial (Luke 22:67):

verse 25 ἀπεκρίθη αὐτοῖς ὁ Ἰησοῦς	verse 67 εἶπεν δὲ αὐτοῖς
εἶπον ὑμῖν	ἐὰν ὑμῖν εἴπω
καὶ οὐ πιστεύετε	οὐ μὴ πιστεύσητε

As was the case with the preceding questioning, the parallel with the Lukan text continues. Rather than explaining this as Luke's dependence upon a separate source which follows a tradition more closely related to the (core) report found in the Fourth Gospel,[9] we have the impression that the Lukan account is a redactional elaboration of the text of Mark (showing some accidental minor agreements with the Matthean version) and that the author of the Fourth Gospel was more closely inspired by Luke.

Already the introductory lemma (ἀπεκίθη αὐτοῖς ὁ Ἰησοῦς) resembles that of Luke (εἶπεν δὲ αὐτοὺς); in both gospels the addressees are in the plural form. The use of the favourite Johannine word ἀποκρίνομαι, not followed by the verb λέγω,[10] and with an explicit mention of the subject (as is generally done in the combination with this verb in John) − here of the name of Jesus, as in Mark 14:68 = Matt. 26:64, emphasises the sayings of Jesus in this important moment of self-proclamation and defence.

Ἐῖπον ὑμῖν καὶ οὐ πιστεύετε is a slight transposition of the Lukan text and, as in Luke is a perfect reply to the question as it was put.

In John, Jesus' response is more assertive: he seems to refer to former less overt proclamations about his Messianic identity; yet, at times he even spoke openly. Or perhaps he tries to avoid a direct use of the ambiguous Χριστός title, comparable to a similar situation in the Synoptic Gospels (see for instance Mark 8:29–30 and pars., and even in the trial before 'the Jews'). We would have to think of moments like 4:26; 5:17, 18; 6:35, 41, 51; 7:26 (ἴδε παρρησίᾳ λαλεῖ ... ὅτι οὗτός ἐστιν ὁ Χριστός) or would we perhaps be allowed to accept that, in a sense, a reference to the Synoptic trial scene of Jesus before 'the Jews' and his Messianic proclamation is implied?[11] The sense of Jesus' answer clearly indicates that despite his repeated proclamation about his Messiahship, there is no response, there is no faith.[12]

It is obvious that Jesus' argument in verse 25b embodies two typically Johannine motives: 'the works he does in the name of the Father' and 'the giving of testimony to Jesus'. The most striking parallel for the combined use of both elements is undoubtedly 5:36: τὰ γὰρ ἔργα ἃ δέδωκέν μοι ὁ πατὴρ ἵνα τελειώσω αὐτά, αὐτὰ τὰ ἔργα ἃ ποιῶ, μαρτυρεῖ περὶ ἐμοῦ. One can, however, hardly be unaware of the fact that in the Synoptic trial before the Sanhedrin an important occupation has been to find witnesses against Jesus.[13] May we not discern in the text of John a redactional elaboration upon the Synoptic trial narrative in which he opposes his favourable (and true) witnesses to the contradictory (and false) ones of the Synoptic account?

4. *The idea of unbelief*, which in the preceding verse 25 has been taken over from the Lukan account, is repeated redundantly in verse 26 with an emphasis in both places on those addressed put in the second person plural. Faith should be expected as a valuable response not only to the revealing activity of Jesus (verse 25a) but also to the works done in the name of the Father which give testimony to Jesus (verses 25b–26a). These verses 25b–26a are in continuity with verse 25a and show a parallelism with it.

In the light of the already-mentioned parallelism between the scene in 18:19–24, wherein Jesus is questioned by the High Priest, and that of 10:24b–38, where Jesus is questioned by the Jews, it is possible to discover some similarity in the argumentation and in the composition of both scenes. Jesus refuses to give further explanation, pointing to his disciples or to his works as evidence; they know it, and they give witness.

A further reason for their unbelief is given in verse 26b: because they do not belong to his sheep. So this self-defence and self-proclamation of Jesus in the temple is linked to the preceding discourse of Jesus on the theme of the shepherd and the sheep. This specific relation between the shepherd and the sheep (verse 27) seems to be the primordial basis for the possibility of faith.[14] His sheep hear his voice and follow him (cf. 10:3, 4, 16 and 10:4, 5). Jesus knows them (cf. 10:14) and looks with favour upon them, not as in 2:23–5, where he criticises the people of Jerusalem who believed because of the signs which he performed – 'for Jesus knew all men and what was in man.'

5. The application in the following verses 28–9 of a typically Johannine theme of the salvation and protection which Jesus extends to his disciples,[15] by its clear parallelism,[16] stresses particularly the *union between Jesus and his Father*, thus preparing perfectly for the fhigh christological statement of verse 30 (ἐγὼ καὶ ὁ πατὴρ ἕν ἐσμεν). Can we not say that this Johannine statement interprets nothing more than the Lukan redaction of Jesus' answer given at the trial before the Jews (Luke 22:69)? In this Lukan version of the saying of Jesus the reference to the Son of Man title is understood not so much in its eschatological meaning but as an assertion of the present glorified divine status of Jesus sitting at the right hand of the power of God.[17] After this response of Jesus, in Luke the high priests and the scribes by way of conclusion ask him σὺ οὖν εἶ ὁ υἱὸς τοῦ θεοῦ; – a proclamation which is also discussed in the following verses of John.

1.3 I am the Son of God (verses 32–8)

The threat of death through stoning (verse 31) interrupts the narrative of the questioning of Jesus and his self-revealing critical answer. This not only fits in a Passion Narrative but also broadens the separation which already in Luke 22:67–70 had split the twofold question concerning his Messiahship: 'Are you the Christ?' (verse 67) and 'Thus you are the Son of God?' (verse 70), the latter being the culminating point. In fact, the dialogue of John 10:32–8 deals mainly with Jesus' *self-revealing statement, 'I am the Son of God.'* It is difficult to see in ὅτι εἶπον, υἱὸς τοῦ θεοῦ εἰμι, a repetition of a saying of Jesus previously related in the gospel of John. There is no such self-proclamation of Jesus mentioned in the Fourth Gospel, although an implicit reference to the preceding statement of verse 30 can be understood. If any formal *Rückverweisung*[18] has to be thought of, why not consider Luke 22:70 and see in the text of John a synthesis of 'Thus you are the Son of God?' and 'You say that I am' (slightly different from Mark 14:61−2).[19] Of course, there is also a striking similarity and parallel with Ps. 82:6 quoted in verse 34 (ὅτι ἐγὼ εἶπα, θεοί ἐστε), but the primary passage in mind is undoubtedly the word of Jesus quoted in verse 36, the quotation of the psalm (note also the differences) being adduced only as a midrash for Jesus' arguing in defence of his assertion.

This probable reference to the Lukan trial of Jesus before 'the Jews' is further confirmed by the *allegation of blasphemy* on the part of Jesus (verses 33, 36). Whereas John, as we have observed, was up to now regularly more inspired by the text of the trial in Luke, here differing from Luke, who drops the element of blasphemy[20] (and also that of the condemnation to death), he goes back to the text of Mark and above all to that of Matthew with the double mention of blasphemy. Moreover, the Johannine form (λέγετε ὅτι βλασφημεῖς) seems to be very close to that of Matt. 26:65a, meanwhile adapting it perfectly to the new content. The verb λέγω is put into the plural form referring to the group of Sanhedrists, as in Luke and as understood in John (instead of to the high priest alone, as in Matthew) and the verb βλασφημέω is put in the second person, as addressed now directly to Jesus.

2. Now that we have clarified the Synoptic background of the central statement (verse 36) of this second half of Jesus' anticipated trial before the Jews (verses 31−9), let us investigate how the other elements fit in the discussion.

It is not surprising that in verse 33b, while giving the motivation for the stoning, 'the Jews' clearly formulate their *accusation against Jesus*. It is an anticipated duplication of the statement mentioned in verse 36b: an accusation of blasphemy and its grounds, 'because you, being a man, make yourself God'. The latter (ὅτι σὺ ἄνθρωπος ὢν ποιεῖς σεαυτὸν θεόν) is a Johannine elaboration of the Synoptic statement of verse 36 (ὅτι εἶπον, υἱὸς τοῦ θεοῦ εἰμι). It is also repeated as the accusation of the Jews against Jesus in their answer to Pilate in John 19:7 (see also 18:29),[21] but with the use of the Son of God title: ὅτι υἱὸν θεοῦ ἑαυτὸν ἐποίησεν. Both passages are paraphrased of John 5:18 (ὅτι ... πατέρα ἴδιον ἔλεγεν τὸν θεόν, ἴσον ἑαυτὸν ποιῶν τῷ θεῷ).[22] In all these instances a reference to the required death penalty is included (John 5:18; 10:33, 19:7). Verse 33b thus seems to serve the purpose of the trial form of the pericope.

The text of verses 34−6a can be considered a Johannine theological *apology of Jesus* of a midrash genre, enclosed within a twofold accusation of blasphemy and of pretended divine origin (33b and 36b).

As we have seen in the first part of the questioning concerning his Christ title, so too with respect to the Son of God title in the second part, Jesus' self-defence is expanded. The Johannine interest for dialogues and expanded discourses of Jesus has obviously influenced the elaboration of the sayings of Jesus.

The reasoning of the fourth evangelist's Jesus in verses 34–6 is not so transparent. Obviously, he makes use of two Biblical texts: an explicit quotation of Ps. 82:6 and an allusion or implicit reference to Jer. 1:4, 5, 7.

The argumentation of the text of John is pregnant with meaning: an antithesis between the judges whom God has called gods and Jesus, who said of himself 'I am the Son of God.' If that one statement, the saying of God of Ps. 82, is true, the same applies *a fortiori* to the other, that of Jesus' self-revelation about his divine Sonship. The sending of Jesus into the world by his Father is a Johannine theme (see also John 3:17; 17:18, 21, 23, 25) combined here as also in 17:19 (self-consecration of Jesus) with the consecration by the Father. This idea is seemingly inspired by the Jeremiah text and linked with the oneness of the Father and the Son (in 10:38 as in 17:21) in the further perspective of a similar consecration, sending and oneness of the disciples (John 17:17–23).

3. *Looking back at our trajectory through the second half of John 10*, we may assume that the approach has been fruitful. At first, the reader of this pericope may have the impression of being confronted with Johannine gospel material, foreign to the Synoptic tradition, going from topographical and chronological topics to theological themes such as: faith, bearing witness, bestowing eternal life, sending into the world, knowing, works done in the Name of the Father, Jesus as Christ and the Son of God and his oneness with the Father.

However, upon closer examination of the text one discovers a great number of similarities with the Synoptic Gospels: Jesus was walking in the temple of Jerusalem (verse 23), as in Mark 11:27, where already after the cleansing of the temple, his adversaries the chief priest, the scribes and the elders came to question him about his authority – an incident which developed into a sharp dispute (comparable to John 2:18–20) – just as 'the Jews' did in verse 24a. They encircled Jesus as if they were about to arrest him, threatening him with stoning (see also verses 31, 39), thus anticipating the scene of the arrest. The feature of a duplicated Passion Narrative becomes all the more obvious as we see that verses 24–30 in fact are nothing but a

Johannine redactional elaboration of the Lukan report of the trial of Jesus before the Jews, explaining why Jesus refuses to answer the questions of the high priest in John 18:19–21. Here in John 10: 24–30, on the contrary, when the group of the Jews is questioning him about his Messiahship in terms almost identical to those they use in the Lukan redaction of it (Luke 22:67), Jesus gives an answer also similar to that given in Luke criticising their unbelief (cf. Luke 22:67b, 68), openly revealing his Messiahship and his divine Sonship (cf. Luke 22:69). Even the Synoptic motif of witness (cf. Luke 22:71 = Mark 14:55–7; Matt. 26:59–60) is applied, but in its proper Johannine form.

In the following section (verses 32–8) of the pericope, which we have called a trial scene of Jesus before the Jews, a second kind of dispute is developed. It is separated from the first interrogation in a similar but more emphatic way than in Luke 22:70a. The dialogue is now concentrated on the self-revealing statement of Jesus, 'I am the Son of God' (cf. Luke 22:70), which is duplicated in a Johannine form in verse 33c and expanded in a midrash argumentation in verses 34–6. Besides the themes of faith and unbelief, of the works from the Father as in the previous section, it incorporates also Synoptic elements such as the accusation of blasphemy (verses 33, 36; cf. Mark 14:64; Matt. 26:65), and the perspective of death penalty (verses 31–3a) which is more formally retained in the condemnation to death of John 11:47–53 (cf. Mark 14:64; Matt. 26:66; 27:1).

One may not overlook the Johannine structure and elaboration of the second half of John 10,[23] but the weight of the Synoptic similarities is so important that a literary relation with the Synoptic Gospels, and more particularly with Luke, seems undeniable. Of course, the evaluation of such data will be appreciated differently by various critics. Some will see in it some echo of Johannine tradition or pre-Johannine documents which have influenced diversely both the gospel of Luke and that of John. Others will rather accept an influence of the gospel of Luke (and of Matthew and Mark, respectively) upon a previous stage of the redactional evolution of the Fourth Gospel or upon a pre-Johannine source dependent upon the Synoptic Gospels.[24] I am rather inclined to accept a direct relation between the Synoptic Gospels and the gospel of John, which in this case has been basically inspired by the gospel of Luke which John has redactionally and creatively elaborated into his own Johannine perspective and christology. Much depends, of course, upon the state of conformity, the degree of agreement with the Synoptics, for instance, with the specific redactional aspect of the Lukan text, but also upon the convergence with the most probable interpretation of other pericopes of the Gospel of John which are related to the Synoptic Gospels. In my opinion, our analysis of the Johannine text has sufficiently indicated that the hypothesis of a direct dependence, which is probable for many other sections of the Fourth Gospel, is also valid for this pericope.

2. The discourse of the shepherd and the sheep (John 10: 1–21)

In the light of our findings in the second part of John 10, let us now examine the first part. Could we not discover in the preceding discourse of Jesus on the shepherd, the sheep and the sheepfold some similar inspiration from the Synoptic Gospels? Different motifs, among them the motif of knowing, the relation between the Father and Jesus, the giving of one's life, appear in both parts of the chapter, with at least one direct link between them: Jesus' reference, in his apology before 'the Jews', to his sheep (verse 26). Let us, therefore, first examine the theme of the shepherd and the sheep.

2.1 The shepherd and the sheep

In principle one may not deny that in applying this well-known literary topic the gospel of John shows some similarity to the way it occurs in the OT and in Jewish or in Hellenistic literature. However, one is tempted to inquire whether also here John was not inspired more directly by the Synoptic evangelists.

1. From the same literary background of the Passion Narrative of the Synoptics *one text in particular* comes to our attention. At his departure to the Mount of Olives, announcing the falling away of his disciples (πάντες – ὑμεῖς – σκανδαλισθήσεσθε) and introducing the prediction of Peter's denial, Jesus quotes a text of Zech. 13:7: πατάξω τὸν ποιμένα, καὶ τὰ πρόβατα διασκορπισθήσονται (Mark 14:27); the parallel text of Matt. 26:31 mentions even τὰ πρόβατα τῆς ποίμνης. Although the text of Zechariah is not formally referred to in John 10, it is probable that the author of the Fourth Gospel is fully aware of the Synoptic Biblical quotation. Anticipating the prediction of Peter's denial in the farewell discourses of Jesus (John 13:36–8), as Luke did (22:31–4), he has also incorporated there the falling away of the disciples: ἵνα μὴ σκανδαλισθῆτε (16:1), their scattering and the leaving alone of the shepherd (ἵνα σκορπισθῆτε

ἕκαστος εἰς τὰ ἴδια κἀμὲ μόνον ἀφῆτε – John 16:32 and Mark 14:50; Matt. 26:56). With all these elements built into the farewell discourses of Jesus, the situation is similar to that of the Lukan farewell discourse and not so different even from the departure passage connected with the Last Supper, as in Mark and Matthew; in each case we are in the immediately preceding context of the arrest of Jesus.[25]

That John, in the framework of what we consider a discourse of Jesus[25] which precedes the anticipated arrest and trial scene of John 10:23–39, could have paraphrased that specific Zechariah passage of the Synoptics or could at least have found his main inspiration in it should therefore not surprise us. This is all the more probable, seeing that in the Johannine narrative of the death of Jesus – the striking of the shepherd – (John 19:37) another Zechariah text is referred to: ὄψονται εἰς ὃν ἐξεκέντησαν (Zech. 12:10), 'they shall look on him whom they have pierced'.[27] The two verbs (πατάσσω and ἐκκεντέω – see also Rev. 1:7) are not so different in meaning, being in fact two verbs of killing either through beating, striking (with a sword in Zech. 13:7) or through piercing or stabbing. It seems that the evangelist has interpreted as one unit the oracle of Zech. 12–13, on the siege of Jerusalem with the protection of its inhabitants and their mourning for the man who was wounded and killed, thus transforming the whole situation into conversion and blessings on the day of the Lord. In this way the suffering figure (12:10; 13:7) is understood as a prophetic symbol coming to its fulfilment in the death of Jesus.

2. Having found inspiration in the Synoptic model of the Biblical quotation and in the text of Zechariah itself, the evangelist develops it creatively but not without retaining *several concrete allusions* to or transpositions of it. The scattering of the sheep (σκορπίζω) by the wolf in verse 12 could be a reminiscence of it. Observe also the parallel use of ἁρπάζω in verse 12 to that in verses 28–9: 'No one shall snatch the sheep out of my hand.'[28] The role of the shepherd, on the contrary, is to bring them together so that there shall be one flock, one shepherd. The way this is said in verse 16 (κἀκεῖνα δεῖ με ἀγαγεῖν ... καὶ γενήσονται μία ποίμνη, εἷς ποιμήν) can very well be understood as inspired by the saying of Mark 14:28; Matt. 26:32. After the shepherd had been struck down and the sheep scattered (by adding τῆς ποίμνης Matthew even stresses the dispersal of the sheep and thus the value of the shepherd),[29] the risen Jesus will go before them so as to reunite his disciples, to restore the flock

(προάξω ὑμᾶς). This gathering of the dispersed flock is also clearly suggested in John 11:51−2. The decision to put Jesus to death − the death of the shepherd in the perspective of his resurrection, as in Mark 14:28; Matt. 26:32 − as pronounced by the high priest Caiaphas has a prophetic meaning: ἵνα καὶ τὰ τέκνα τοῦ θεοῦ τὰ διεσκορπισμένα συναγάγῃ εἰς ἕν.[30] As we have already mentioned previously, this is another Johannine anticipation of the trial of Jesus before the Jews.[31]

The role of gathering the dispersed sheep is a qualification of the authentic shepherd − John 10:11, 14 calls him ὁ ποιμὴν ὁ καλός − as opposed to that of the faithless shepherd. In John 10:12−13 the latter is called ὁ μισθωτὸς καὶ οὐκ ὢν ποιμήν, whose definiiton we can read in Zech. 11:9, 15, 16−17. More particularly the description of verse 16 (τὸ διεσκορπισμένον οὐ μὴ ζητήσῃ καὶ τὸ συντετριμμένον οὐ μὴ ἰάσηται) and of verse 17 (οἱ ποιμαίνοντες ... καταλελοιπότες τὰ πρόβατα) is contrary to John 11:52 and 10:16 and very close to the literary extension of John 10:12−13 (ὁ μισθωτὸς ... ἀφίησιν τὰ πρόβατα καὶ φεύγει ... καὶ οὐ μέλει αὐτῷ περὶ τῶν προβάτων). Also the redaction of Matt. 9:36 seems to allude to these texts of Zechariah 11 (as also to Zech. 13:7) and thus to confirm our hypothesis of literary dependence: ὅτι ἦσαν ἐσκυλμένοι καὶ ἐρριμμένοι ὡσεὶ πρόβατα μὴ ἔχοντα ποιμένα (cf. also Ezek. 34, in particular verses 4, 16).

3. *Some other Synoptic sayings* on the shepherd and the sheep may have influenced the Johannine discourse. Besides the already mentioned texts of Matt. 9:36 (see Mark 6:34) and Matt. 25:32, one may also think of the Matthean τὰ πρόβατα τὰ ἀπολωλότα οἴκου Ισραήλ of Matt. 10:6 and 15:24 (cf. Ezek. 34:12−16). John 10:16 concerns 'the other sheep (ἄλλα πρόβατα) that are not of this fold', i.e. not his own sheep who are perhaps the Jewish disciples of Jesus (τὰ ἐμά, τὰ ἴδια πρόβατα − verse 14 and verse 3). Could not this text − comparable to that on the children of God who differ from the Jewish ἔθνος (11:51−2) − allude to the gathering (ἀγαγειν − verse 16) of these lost sheep of the house of Israel, but heightened now to the gathering (συνάγαγη − 11:52) of all the dispersed children of God, the Gentiles born from God?

Another close text to be considered is the Parable of the Lost Sheep (Luke 15:4−7; Matt. 18:12−14). The man of the parable leaves (Matt. verse 12 ἀφήσει, cf. John 10:12; Luke verse 4 καταλείπει, cf. Zech. 11:17) the ninety-nine sheep and goes in search of the one that went astray, that got lost (ζητεῖ of Matt. verse 12 cf. Zech. 11:16; πλανηθῇ ἕν, τὸ πλανώμενον of Matt. verse 12, differing from Luke's verse 4 and verse 6 ἀπολέσας ἕν, τὸ ἀπολωλός cf. John 10:10).[32] The text of Matt. verse 14 ('It is not the will of your Father ...[33] that one of these little ones should perish' — ἵνα ἀπόληται ἕν) can be compared with John 10:28–9: '(the sheep) οὐ μὴ ἀπόλωνται εἰς τὸν αἰῶνα' and 'no one will snatch them out of my or my Father's hand'. Substituting Jesus, who is the shepherd in John 10, for the Father of the Parable of the Lost Sheep (although in John 10 the perspective of the Father as shepherd is still retained) is not so surprising since precisely the parallel, and even the unity between the Father and Jesus, is emphasised in John 10:26–30.[34] Furthermore, in the Synoptic parable one can discover an analogous christological perspective: the behaviour of Jesus is similar to or even identified with that of God.[35] 'He lays it — the one sheep — on his shoulders' of Luke 15:5 does not seem to have directly influenced the text of the Fourth Gospel, although when we refer to the Good Shepherd it is commonly that picture that we have in mind.

2.2 Other Synoptic elements behind the discourse

1. *The willingness of the shepherd to die* for the sheep as mentioned in verses 11 and 15 — a unique feature in the Johannine picture of the shepherd[36] — may be understood as a further explanation of the stricken shepherd of Zech. 13:7 already referred to. However, the literary formula τίθημι τὴν ψυχὴν αὐτοῦ, used to express that idea, seems to have its own weight.

Formally applied in verses 11 and 15 to the Good Shepherd and his attitude toward the sheep, it seems to go beyond the imagery and in verses 17–18 to grow out as a main theme of the discourse. In view of the imminence of the arrest of Jesus, his trial before 'the Jews', the threat of death and condemnation, such a statement of Jesus concerning the sense of his approaching death is apropos. Although it expresses the Johannine interpretation of a victorious Jesus having divine power over his own life[37] — comparable to the situation of John 18:4–6; 19:10–11 and many other passages — the formula echoes perfectly the saying of Jesus in Mark 10:45 (= Matt. 20:28): 'For the Son of Man also came not to be served but to serve and to give his life as a ransom for many' (δοῦναι τὴν ψυχὴν αὐτοῦ λύτρον ἀντὶ πολλῶν).[38] Luke has interpreted the saying and incorporated it into his farewell discourse of Jesus (22:27): 'I am among you as one who serves.' These texts of Mark and Luke have inspired the

Johannine Last Supper Narrative and Farewell Discourse so as to help John develop the Narrative of the Footwashing and the elaboration of Jesus' sayings on the commandment of mutual love in imitation of Jesus' example of love and of laying down his life for his friends (John 13:34; 15:12–14).[39]

Τίθημι τὴν ψυχὴν is a Johannine literary characteristic (no. 104). It is used eight times in the gospel (five times in John 10; 15:13; 13:37, 38) and further in the NT only in 1 John 3:16. In my opinion this is a Johannine elaboration on the basis of several Synoptic texts: the perspective of Jesus' death of Mark 10:45, the prediction of Peter's denial of Mark 14:27–31; Matt. 26:31–5 and the Lukan paraphrase of Peter's readiness to go with Jesus to prison and to death (Luke 22:33).[40] The choice of the verb τίθημι (different from Mark 10:45: δίδωμι τὴν ψυχήν) is intended perhaps to distinguish from the use of δίδωμι, so characteristically applied in several sayings of John (as giving life: ζωὴν δίδωμι – no. 160).[41]

The commandment that Jesus has received from the Father (verse 18), as compared to the new commandment of love in John 13:34; 15:12, could equally be understood as a reference to the great commandment of Mark 12:28–34 par.; in practice it consists of the readiness to sacrifice oneself, to lay down one's life for others.[42]

The sheep (his own) 'follow' the shepherd, who 'goes before' them (verse 4: ἔμπροσθεν αὐτῶν πορεύεται, καὶ τὰ πρόβατα αὐτῷ ἀκολουθεῖ – cf. 10:27). This not only indicates the good care of the trustworthy shepherd leading the sheep out (maybe to pasture of verse 9?) to be with him (John 1:37–9; 12:26) but most probably also implies the disciples' readiness to die, in imitation of the shepherd who lays down his life. Such a meaning of the verb ἀκολουθέω is intended in Peter's denial pericope of John 13:36–8 (a Johannine paraphrase of Luke 22:33; Mark 14:29a, 31) as well as in his other proclamation of loyalty towards Jesus in 21:55–22, when Peter in turn is told to tend the sheep (verses 15, 16) and to follow Jesus unto death (verses 19, 22). The expression ἔμπροσθεν αὐτῶν πορεύεται could equally have been inspired by Mark 14:28; Matt. 26:32, where προάξω ὑμᾶς (cf. John 10:3: ἐξάγει αὐτά) is said of the stricken shepherd who once raised up will go before them.

2. The *motif of mutual knowledge* of the shepherd and the sheep (verse 14b) and of Jesus and the Father (verse 15a) interrupts the self-revealing statement of the Good Shepherd who lays down his life for the sheep (verses 14a, 15b). The latter is a slightly adapted form of the statement already used in verse 11. On the other hand, the

motif is partially repeated in the apology of Jesus (verse 27), thus making a link with Jesus' discourse of the shepherd and the sheep. The manner in which it appears at first in verses 14−15 − rather than being a natural literary development of the allegory of the Good Shepherd − indicates that we are dealing with an element added to the symbolic language of the shepherd and his sheep and which already by itself is complex. One has seen elements of Gnostic origin in it: through revelation of divine knowledge the soul will be redeemed and regenerated.[43] Are we not rather invited to see in this interposed revelation element of John[44] a further theological development and original elaboration made directly on a Synoptic saying of Jesus (πάντα μοι παρεδόθη ὑπὸ τοῦ πατρός μου, καὶ οὐδεὶς γινώσκει τίς ἐστιν ὁ υἱὸς εἰ μὴ ὁ πατήρ, καὶ τίς ἐστιν ὁ πατὴρ εἰ μὴ ὁ υἱὸς καὶ ᾧ ἐὰν βούληται ὁ υἱὸς ἀποκαλύψαι − Luke 10:22 = Matt. 11:27).? A certain verbal agreement is obvious (καθὼς γινώσκει με ὁ πατὴρ κἀγὼ γινώσκω τὸν πατέρα), and in virtue of his redactional creativity John has adapted it to the new context and has extended this mutual knowledge to Jesus and his disciples; their relation is analogous to Jesus' relation to his Father.[45]

3. More distant from the themes mentioned, *a number of sayings* appear in the discourse which *refer to the door* or the doorkeeper. The door of verses 1−2 as well as the doorkeeper of verse 3 (θυρωρός no. 165; see also John 18:16, 17) probably have only a subordinate function in the narrative elaboration of the parable in order to oppose the shepherd to the thief, the robber and the stranger (cf. Matt. 24:43; Mark 13:34; Luke 12:39; Joel 2:9). The 'I am' saying of Jesus of verse 7 (ἐγώ εἰμι ἡ θύρα τῶν προβάτων) and surely that of verse 9 (ἐγώ εἰμι ἡ θύρα) are more important. One is tempted to discern in this image some echo of mythic Gnostic symbolism − the redeemer as door to the world of light.[46] The image of the door, could have been more directly inspired by some Synoptic material. The door of salvation is already mentioned in Matt. 7:13−14; Luke 13:24. It is imperative to enter (εἰσέρχομαι) through the narrow door (Luke has θύρα, Matt. πύλη, gate) in order to be among those saved (οἱ σωζόμενοι − Luke verse 23). John uses the same vocabulary (θύρα ... ἐάν τις εἰσέλθῃ σωθήσεται) but now, in a typically revelatory style, he represents Jesus himself as the door of salvation: 'I am the door; if anyone enters by me, he will be saved.' He will do likewise in John 14:6 (ἐγώ εἰμι ἡ ὁδός ... 'I am the way ... and the life; no one comes to the Father, but by me'). The latter saying could equally have been inspired by the same

Synoptic text mentioning also 'the way that leads to life' (Matt. 7:14).[47]

It is interesting to observe that the sayings of Matt. 7:13–14 (= Luke 13:24) on the entering through the door (of salvation) and on the way to life are followed in Matt. 7:15 by a warning against the false prophets who come in sheep's (πρόβατα) clothing but inwardly are rapacious wolves (λύκοι ἅρπαγες, cf. Matt. 13:19; 23:25). The imagery of John 10:12–13 on the hireling who does not care for the sheep (πρόβατα) and flees, leaving them to be seized (ἁρπάζω – cf. 10:28–9) by the wolf (λύκος), seems to be an echo of it.

In Luke the image of the narrow door (13:23–4) is associated with that of the door shut by the householder (verse 25; cf. Acts 14:27). Perhaps this Lukan text – another door of salvation saying – will equally have influenced the Johannine discourse, all the more since some emphasis is put on the motif of knowledge (Luke 13:25, 27: οὐκ οἶδα ὑμᾶς πόθεν ἐστέ = Matt. 7:23: οὐδέποτε ἔγνων ὑμᾶς [cf. Matt. 25:12 οὐκ οἶδα ὑμᾶς]) comparable to the shepherd's knowledge of the sheep (John 10:14, 27).

4. In the Fourth Gospel the discourses of Jesus are generally rather extensive; the same is true for the discourse of the Good Shepherd. Usually, however, in John 10:6 Jesus' speech is qualified as παροιμία. The term (no. 316; four times in John 10:6; 16:25 [bis], 29) is an alternative of the Hebrew *mashal* (in the Septuagint only in Prov. 1:1; 25:1 and five times in Sir.) and an equivalent to the Synoptic παραβολή. The sense of Jesus' speech, at first hidden and obscure (10:6), becomes in a second moment more transparent as the parable is explained (10:7–16); it attains its greatest clarity at the moment of his glorification when Jesus will speak openly – παρρησίᾳ λαλέω, John 16:25, 29 – when the Counsellor, the Holy Spirit will be sent, all things will be taught, all that he has said will be brought to remembrance (14:26). Not only the term itself but above all the way it is used, as opposed to speaking openly, shows some close similarity to the use of παραβολή in the Synoptics and particularly in Mark 4:10–11 = Matt. 13:10–11; Luke 8:9–10 (see also Mark 4:33–4; 7:17). Compare John 10:6 (ταύτην τὴν παροιμίαν εἶπεν αὐτοῖς ... ἐκεῖνοι δὲ οὐκ ἔγνωσαν τίνα ἦν ἃ ἐλάλει αὐτοῖς) with ὑμῖν δέδοται γνῶναι ... ἐκείνοις δὲ οὐ δέδοται (Matt.) or ἐκείνοις δὲ τοῖς ἔξω ἐν παραβολαῖς (Mark). It is interesting to observe also that the text of Isa. 6:9–10 quoted in Matt. 13:13–15 (= Mark 4:12; Luke 8:10b) is implicitly referred to in John 9:39 (the immediate context of the discourse, cf. also John 10:21) and quoted in John 12:40

to explain the spiritual blindness, the unbelief of 'the Jews'. Note also the parallel function of the παροιμία of the discourse in John 10:6 and the σημεῖα of the miracles in John 12:37.[48]

5. A final remark on John 10:19–21, *the division of 'the Jews' after Jesus' discourse*, may confirm our hypothesis of the probability of John's dependence upon the Synpotics.[49] This transitional passage forms a link with the just-mentioned ending of John 9 on the blindness of the Pharisees after the miraculous healing of the blind man, constituting with it a framework for the discourse. One can hardly but see in this passage an influence of the Synoptic accusation of Jesus by 'the Jews', of being possessed by Beelzebul (βεελζεβοὺλ ἔχει: Mark 3:22) and of casting out the demons 'by the prince of demons' (ἐν τῷ ἄρχοντι τῶν δαιμονίων: Mark 3:22 par.). The allegation δαιμόνιον ἔχει (no. 84)[50] appears also in John 7:20; 8:48, 49, 52 but in 10:20–1 it is linked to the accusation of madness (μαίνεται cf. Mark 3:21: ἐξέστη). Likewise Jesus' apology in Mark 3:23b (πῶς δύναται σατανᾶς σατᾶναν ἐκβάλλειν – cf. Matt. 12:26) is very close to the favourable reaction of those saying μὴ δαιμόνιον δύναται τυφλῶν ὀφθαλμοὺς ἀνοῖξαι (John 10:21b).[51]

3. Conclusion

Our attention was first of all concentrated upon the second half of the chapter (verses 22–39) where we were able to see a Johannine narrative foreshadowing the arrest and the trial of Jesus before 'the Jews'. The similarities, especially with the Lukan report of the Jewish trial of Jesus, were so convincing that in our opinion the acceptance of a direct influence explains the duplicated dispute of Jesus with 'the Jews' (verses 24–30; 32–8) and its christological impact. Such an anticipation of the Passion Narrative has made it easier for John to reduce the trial before 'the Jews' in verse 18 and to extend, in the first part of the gospel, the confrontation of Jesus with 'the Jews', who will finally reject him. In so doing, this second half of the chapter developed into a climax of christological self-revelation of Jesus in his confession of his Sonship of God.

The discourse of the shepherd has literary links with it, and, as far as its framework is concerned, also with the preceding miraculous healing story of the blind man. Although at first sight it appears to be a purely Johannine revelation discourse, it also manifests a variety of similarities with the Synoptic Gospels – the basic one being that of the dispersal of the sheep, which is in fact a text of Zechariah quoted in Mark 14:27; Matt. 26:31 and implicitly referred to in John 16:1, 32. Together with the willingness to lay down his life, an element which is very close to Mark 10:45, it probably constitutes for the discourse a fundamental inspiration which comes from the Synoptics. As in the Synoptics, so also in John 10, it immediately precedes a (what we have called anticipated) Passion Narrative of Jesus and thus, on the basis of Zechariah, brings the whole parable and explanatory discourse within the perspective of Jesus' death. This interpretation is confirmed by the quotation of another Zechariah text in the Johannine narrative of Jesus' death (John 19:37) and maybe also by the emphasis put by John − quoting Zech. 9:9 − on the humble coming of the Messianic king in John 12.

This striking inspiration from the Synoptic Gospels, which is valid for John 10 in general, helps us to explain its compositional aspect and its theological significance.

6

A SYNTACTICAL AND NARRATOLOGICAL READING OF JOHN 10 IN COHERENCE WITH CHAPTER 9

Jan A. Du Rand

It is the purpose of this essay to take relevant snapshots of some of the recent developments in the text-linguistic and communicative fields that have been applied methodologically to a syntactical and narratological reading of John 9−10. It is challenging to a New Testament scholar to re-enter the gospel story according to John with freshly awakened interpretative theories and models. I borrow from the theoretical pluralism in the humanities, particularly from general linguistics and literary science.

1. Demarcation and co-text

From a syntactical point of view chapters 9−10 should be taken as the co-text of John 10 and from a narratological perspective, chapters 5−10. This means that chapter 10 cannot be interpreted as an isolated island in the Johannine gospel sea. The following general observations may be considered:

The introductory words in 9:1 mark a rather abrupt beginning. The phrase καὶ παράγων shows a break with the previous verse, 8:59. The scene has also shifted from the temple enclosure (8:59) to the scene of the blind man. Jesus has turned away from the temple. The logical coherence and progression in the composition of chapters 9 and 10 flow from the sign (9:1−7), conveyed by various dialogues on the same central theme. The conclusive ending of 10:42 and the start of a totally new narrative about Lazarus in 11:1 figure as a break between chapters 10 and 11.[1] The same audience, place and time indications figure in 10:1 as in chapter 9, and the example of the blind man is recalled in 10:21. Certain expressions and phrases in chapter 10 also recall previous discourses, e.g. 'son' (cf. 10:36 with 9:35); the division among the Pharisees (9:16) and 'the Jews'

(10:19−21); 'picking up stones to stone Jesus' (10:31 with 8:59). The question arises whether 10:1−21 should be read with 10:26−7 or with chapter 9, as to audience. The problem arises from the chronological placing of the feast of Dedication (10:22), three months after the feast of Tabernacles (September/October − 7:10).[2] If we accept the thesis that the gospel story of John could probably be read on two levels, that of the Jesus events and that of the community situation,[3] the order of events need not be synchronised chronologically according to the feasts. However, it should be noted that 10:1−21 serves as a hinge and points forward to the feast of Dedication, as can be seen in 10:26−7. And that makes the narratological linking up of the feast and the sheep−shepherd imagery so meaningful in this co-text.[4] The discourse on the sheep−shepherd imagery functions as a bridge between the feasts of Tabernacles (chapter 7) and Dedication (chapter 10).

It is also important to observe that the Father−Son motif binds together the prominent discourses in 10:1−18, 25b−30 and 34−8.[5] From a narratological point of view chapter 10 fits into the sequence and is in a sense a conclusion to chapters 5−10 in which the unbelief and hostility towards Jesus are mounting, especially from the religious establishment in Jerusalem (spatial framework) around the time of the mentioned feasts (cultural framework). Although one can find breaches and abrupt transitions in the sequence of thought of the present order of chapters 9−10, the same narratological line spirals through from chapter 9 to the end of 10. Therefore, the present order is taken as a working basis for the syntactical as well as the narratological analyses.[6]

2. To understand this text

Methodological shifts in Johannine exegetical approach[7] have forced the NT scholar to take a fresh look at the paradigm used. It is the aim of this essay to apply some of the shifts to the syntactical and narratological readings of John 9−10. Therefore, a comprehensive theoretical point of departure aims at the interpretation of John 9−10 as a communicative text.

As Biblical scholars we differ from one another according to the specific perspective taken on the text of investigation. A dominating psychological perspective on John 10 would for example differ from a sociological reading of the same chapter. One could say that the relationship between text and interpreter within a certain perspective of interpretation and context results as a whole in meaning. The perspective on the text determines therefore the outcome of the interpretation. John 10 can be interpreted as a linguistic or literary phenomenon; as a system of ideas like a theological system; as a norm for people, the Word of God; as an expression of historical developments in the community or of sociological processes or of psychological realities.[8] To apply these possibilities to the real exegetical situation would show that we have heavily concentrated on the systematical, normative and historical perspectives in the past. These need not necessarily be wrong but greater emphasis should also be laid on the text as a linguistic and literary phenomenon. That means that the syntactic dimension (text-internal relations among the signs themselves), the semantic dimension (relations between signs and external meaning), and the pragmatic dimension (relations between signs and recipient) are to be taken seriously. It should, however, be kept in mind that criteria of interpretation of classical texts could not and should not one-sidedly be text-internal. The historical information on the possible socio-cultural setting of the Johannine community (although hypothetical) should be linked up with the text-immanent analyses. To bind the text together, its cohesion and coherence on the surface level should be analysed to respond methodologically to the syntactic dimension. The logical and temporal relations underlying the text form the conceptual patterns of the semantic organisation of the text, and the pragmatic dimension, then, makes use of the syntactic and semantic analyses and describes the meaning to be materialised in the relation between narrator and audience.

It is useful to apply to the narratological analysis of John 9–10 aspects from the models and theories of Greimas (1971), Bremond (1977) and Genette (1980):[9] the story (*histoire*) forms the content of the narrative text (*récit*), while the act of narration (*narration*) points to the manner in which the narrated text is presented. The text cannot be a narrative unless it tells a story and it cannot be a text unless somebody tells it or writes it down. The story level as the abstract deeper structure of a narrative text is to be reconstructed from the surface structure by the narrative propositions in their chronological sequence. It means that the sequence will start with the story of Jesus and his disciples who came across a blind man (9:1–3), proceeding up to the narration of those across the Jordan who believe in Jesus (10:40–2). And after that reconstruction has been done, the actors in their relationships to the events are to be described in order to stipulate their functions or roles on the story level – the actantial model (Greimas).[10] Such a structuralistic narratological exegesis operates mainly on three levels: the syntactical manifestation level; the narrative level (the morphological syntagmatical analysis of the phenomena which brings about the meaning) and the thematic level (the deeper meaning).[11]

Another perspective from which the Johannine story in John 9–10 must be read is the narratological point of view.[12] John 9–10 comprises a series of shorter narratives which are arranged according to a narrative point of view around the protagonist Jesus. The basic idea of the author–narrator in John's story lies on the ideological level, which manifests itself on the other phraseological, topographical, temporal and psychological levels.[13]

The reader of John 9–10 is plucked into the narrated world in order that the text might communicate. He is to identify with Jesus the healer, door, shepherd, and not with the Pharisees and 'Jews' as the antagonists. The interaction of views among the healed blind man, his parents, 'the Jews', Jesus, and the narrator focuses on the identity of the protagonist Jesus as well as on that of the flock. The reader is manipulated in this understanding of John 9–10 by the ideological perspective which is told from a particular technical angle of vision. By way of transparency, that is the view on Jesus through the perspective of the community, the Jesus story is told from the post-resurrection viewpoint. This Johannine community was evidently involved in a conflict with the synagogue and Judaism.[14] The connection between the structure and the message of the text in a specific historical socio-cultural situation represents the literary tradition on a formal level.

John 9–10 will now be analysed as a text, that is, a structure of syntactical coherence and cohesion, corresponding to the syntagmatic level of the organisation of meaning which leads to the 'deeper' dimension of meaning underlying the explicit textual surface and which corresponds to the pragmatic level of communication. The text itself should be allowed to speak for itself to communicate effectively with the reader.

3. A syntactical reading

It is important to read chapters 9–10 syntactically as a unity. Due to limited space, only a summary and framework of the analyses of the structured Greek texts can be given here. On the macro level the relations of the different syntactically defined coherent units to each other are dominated primarily by the σημεῖον (9:1−7) and the παροιμίαι (10:1−6), which function here in the same semantic field as παραβόλαι. By progression and cohesion the diversity and unity in chapters 9 and 10 are understood. We find temporal progression or development as well as logical progression among the parts. Progression is, for example, carried by dialogue, concentrating on Jesus' as well as the followers' identity. The inner relatedness among narrative, commentary, and dialogue constitutes various sets of logical relations. And cohesion, which provides the unity of chapters 9 and 10, is situated in the thematic unity. To put it retrospectively, the change from physical blindness to spiritual insight in the one line and the pretence of sight but actual spiritual blindness of the Pharisees in the other line, with Jesus as the point where both lines meet, is the thematic focus. That is why the unfolding of the thematic unity on the syntactical and semantical levels is organised temporally and also logically.[15]

3.1 The syntactic structure of chapter 9 is broadly to be divided into 4 parts, verses 1−7, 8−34, 35−8, 39−41.

Verses 1−7: On the syntactical level, verse 1 has an additive con-sequential function to verses 2−7. The focus is on Jesus who 'saw' (εἶδεν) and the blindness of the man from birth (ἐκ γενετῆς). Verses 2 and 3−5 are in logical cohesion because of the relationship of the disciples' question (ἠρώτησαν) and Jesus' answer (ἀπεκρίθη). Verses 4−7 are bound together by the linear performing of the *sēmeion.* Verses 2 and 3−5 have led temporally as well as causal-logically to the description of the outcome of the scene in verses 6−7. Prominent syntactical markers in this paragraph are the semotactical 'to see' (εἶδεν − verse 1; βλέπων − verse 7; cf. ἵνα φανερωθῇ − verse 3) and 'to be blind' (τυφλόν − verses 1, 2, 6). On surface level the semotactical focus on the words used for Jesus as the one sent (τοῦ πέμψαντος − verse 4) and the explanation of the name Siloam as 'one sent' (ἀπεσταλμένος − verse 7) should be noted. The occur-rences of 'the works'/'to work' on the surface level open up the agenda for further development (cf. τὰ ἔργα [twice] and ἐργάζεσθαι [twice] in verse 3). These correspond with 10:32. The climax of the first seven verses lies in the performing of the *sēmeion.*

Verses 8−34 are demarcated as a coherent unity by the formal series of interrogations concerning the identity of the blind man healed as well as that of Jesus. It is formally defined by temporal progression and logical connections. Four dialogues in the form of questions and answers are arranged with an intensifying build-up. We note a type of progression in which various kinds of arguments of the audience are anticipated and discussed. The cohesion is obtained by the thematic unity.

Verses 8–12, the first dialogue, concentrate on the identity of the blind man healed (verses 8–12) and shift to the question on the identity of Jesus (verse 12). Verses 8–9, 10–11 and 12 form three subdivisions in this paragraph according to the syntactic pattern: question–answer (10–11, concerning the healing of his blindness), and the interrogatives in each of the three subdivisions, verses 8–9, 10–11 and 12: 'who' (οὐχ οὗτος – verse 8), 'how' (πῶς – verse 10) and 'where' (ποῦ – verse 12). Verse 12 functions as a hinge to point forward to the real answers on the identity of Jesus.

Verses 13–14 function as information, picking up the conflict with the Pharisees and mentioning the reason for the next dialogue between the Pharisees and the blind man healed. The religious institutions are represented in the terms 'the Pharisees' and 'the Sabbath'. The main focus is carried by the semotactical expressions 'who had formerly been blind' (τόν ποτε τυφλόν – verse 13) and 'opened his eyes' (ἀνέῳξεν αὐτοῦ τοὺς ὀφθαλμούς – verse 14). The introduction of the Pharisees is a noteworthy move in the progression of the text.

Verse 15–17 form the second dialogue in the series of four. It is structured on the same pattern as verses 8–12, with the emphasis this time on the identity of Jesus. Verses 15–17 divide also into three subgroups, 15, 16 and 17. The occurrence of the marker 'again' (πάλιν) in verses 15 and 17 has the effect that the answer in each case is put into relief. The word 'again' in verse 15 refers back to the first dialogue in the series of four. The last answer of the man differs from that in verse 12, where he says 'I do not know', concerning Jesus' identity. In verse 17 he says 'He is a prophet.' In all three parts of this paragraph we are semotactically reminded of the main focus, namely the healing of the blind man.

On the surface level the logical relations show a new development: among the Pharisees there is division on the issue of Jesus' identity. The function of this is an implicit appeal to the reader to make his own decision. Another remarkable phrase in verse 16, on the surface level, which will be picked up again in 10:24–31, is the remark by some of the Pharisees: 'This man is not from God.' According to the speech acts[16] the reader knows that it is a positive statement on Jesus' identity although it is used as a remark anticipating the answer.

Verses 18–21 describe the third dialogue in the series of four, very similar to the first. The Pharisees are now called 'Jews'. Most prominent in this subsection of the unit of dialogues is the occurrence of 'they did not believe' (οὐκ ἐπίστευσαν). On the surface level it refers to 'the Jews' who did not believe that the man had been blind. The semantic function of this syntactical marker will come to the foreground in verse 38 where the healed man says: 'Lord, I believe' and in 10:38 where the Pharisees are asked whether they believe.

The build-up in verses 18–21 is arranged in a parallel. In the first part 'the Jews' ask the man's parents about their son's identity and how he got healed and in the second part the parents answer about the son's identity but hesitate on how he was healed. Look at the repeated 'Is this your son/This is our son' in verses 19 and 20. This repetition (cf. also 'to see' and 'born blind') lays emphasis on the *sēmeion* by Jesus. The references to the blind man healed are remarkable: four times in the first part and three times in the parallel part.

To keep up the dramatic focus on the identity of Jesus, the end of this paragraph flows over to another dialogue by using the terms 'to ask' (ἐρωτήσατε) and 'to answer' (λαλήσει). That means the ball is in the court of the Pharisees again: the issue stays open.

Verses 22–3 could have been the conclusive part of the previous dialogue because the marker 'parents' (οἱ γονεῖς) in verse 22 is repeated in verse 23. These verses are to be taken separately because of the commentary concerning the future of believers in Jesus as the Christ. By confessing that Jesus is the Christ they will be excommunicated. This valuable piece of information is picked up again in verses 34–5 and has a causal function. The prominent markers are 'parents' (οἱ γονεῖς – in verses 22, 23) and 'Jews' (οἱ Ἰουδαῖοι). The fear of 'the Jews' ' agreement has led to the parents' attitude.

Verses 24–34, the fourth dialogue in the series, represent an intensified version of the second dialogue (verses 15–17). The structure on the surface consists of five subdivisions according to the question–answer pattern, namely verses 24–5, 26–7, 28–33, 34a and b. The first three have questions by the Pharisees and the answers by the healed blind man. Verse 34 consists of the conclusion by the Pharisees concerning the man's destiny as well as the final deed of excommunication. Prominent syntactical markers in these verses are: 'blind man' and 'blindness healed' (24, 25, 26, 30, 32); and the three expressions 'he opened the eyes' (with variations) in verses 26, 30 and 32 figure dominantly. The progression lies in repetition. The term 'to know' occurs in verses 24, 25 (twice), 29 (twice), 30 and 31. The chiastic build-up of verses 24–5 emphasises the certainty of the healed man, that he was blind but received sight (*a* – τυφλός, *b* – οἶδα ἁμαρτωλός [twice], *a* – τυφλός, hence the schema *abba*).

A new marker now comes to the foreground, namely 'disciple' (μαθητής). According to the speech strategy in verse 27 the author–narrator uses a misunderstanding to emphasise that the real acceptance of the identity of Jesus means discipleship. In verse 26 the claim is on what Jesus did (τι ἐποίησεν and πῶς ἤνοιξεν) and in verse 27 on what the Pharisees do or do not do (ἠκούσατε, θέλετε μαθηταὶ γενέσθαι). The marker 'disciples' on the surface is remarkable because it defines the difference between Moses and Jesus (verses 27 and 28). As in 9:12 (ποῦ), the term 'where' (πόθεν) in verses 29 and 30 reminds us of the identity of Jesus and the Father that will come again to the foreground in chapter 10. It shows once more that it is essential to read chapters 9 and 10 together. The progression and build-up are clear.

The focus of all four dialogues in this series is again summarised in verse 30: 'to know where Jesus is from' and the fact that 'he opened the blind man's eyes'. The progression and cohesion in verses 24–34 can be followed by the pattern question–answer (cf. 24–5, 26–7, 28–33), until the final answer by the Pharisees and the excommunication of the blind man.

The surface structure shows the tendency to link Jesus' identity to God (verses 15–17, 24–34). This is done by contrasting Moses and Jesus. The Pharisees would easily make a decision for God but not for God's revelation in his Son. The double ἔχω in verse 34c implies the schism between the hostile 'Jews' and Christianity.

By way of summary, it is essential to look at verses 8–34 as a whole with the aim to apply it to John 10. Verses 8–34 can be understood as two parallel cycles, demonstrating progression by intensifying, see fig. 1.

Figure 1

a	8–12	*Interrogation*: the man's identity
b	13–14	Information through commentary
c	15–17	*Interrogation*: Jesus' identity (division)
a¹	18–21	*Interrogation*: the man's identity
b¹	22–3	Information through commentary
c¹	24–34	*Interrogation*: Jesus' identity (division)

When we leave aside for a moment what I call the *information through commentary* in verses 13−14 and 22−3 we have the pattern a c a¹ c¹. In a¹ the interrogation concerning the man's identity is intensified by the witness of his parents and in c¹ the identity of Jesus is more than just being a prophet − 'He is from God'. It is even interesting that b¹ tells us about the active role of 'the Jews' against their passive role in b. The second circle, a¹−c¹, is an intensified repetition of the first circle, a−c, to bring about a dramatic build-up.

Verses 35−41: The climax of chapter 9 is reached when Jesus himself appears on stage in dialogue first with the healed man (verses 35−8) and then with the Pharisees (verses 39−41). This section, then, divides into two parts, according to the actors and dialogues.

The real meaning of the *sēmeion* (verses 1−7) is foregrounded in verses 35−8, structured in two parallels. On the surface level Jesus' question to the man contains prominent markers such as 'believe' and 'Son of Man' (verse 35), while the answer of the man consists of 'Sir' (κύριε) and 'believe' (verse 36). We note the irony in the man's answer, using κύριος. The pattern of verses 35−6 is *abba*, where *a* signifies the *deed of believing* and *b* the *title* of Jesus. The function of this chiastic pattern is to bring out the signified of the *sēmeion*, namely *to believe in Jesus*. It is further emphasised in verses 37−8. The marker 'see' (ἑώρακας) in verse 37 stands semotactically parallel to 'believe', so that the same message as in verses 35−6 is repeated in verses 37−8, namely to believe in Jesus the Lord.

The identity of Jesus can only be believed when one has insight. The blind man has not only received physical sight but spiritual insight. It seems to me that on the surface the last part of verse 34 in the previous section could be read together with the conclusion in verse 38 as a way of contrasting the attitude of the Pharisees to that of the healed man, see fig. 2.

Figure 2

⌐ 34c	And they (the Pharisees) cast him out
⌐ 38b	And he (the man) worshipped Him

The 'casting out' (ἐξέβαλον) of the healed man (and eventually of Jesus) stands against the 'worship' (προσεκύνησεν) of the man. The healed man is cast out from worship in the synagogue but has found community with Jesus the Lord.

In *verses 39−41* notice should be taken of the markers 'to see' (βλέπειν) and 'not to see' (to be blind). The chiastic pattern in verse 39 emphasises this division. The reader should decide whether the man or the Pharisees have sight! This division (judgement) is elaborated further in the next chapter.

Chapter 9, then, starts with a blind man and ends with the 'blind' Pharisees. The whole chapter acts as a hinge from chapters 5–8 to chapter 10. The meaning of the *sēmeion* will be the essential door to disclose the meaning of chapter 10. This is summarised schematically in fig. 3.

Figure 3

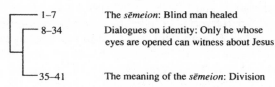

1–7	The *sēmeion*: Blind man healed
8–34	Dialogues on identity: Only he whose eyes are opened can witness about Jesus
35–41	The meaning of the *sēmeion*: Division

3.2 On the surface John 10 can be divided into three units with sub-divisions, verses 1–21, 22–39 and 40–2.

Verses 1–21, according to cohesion and progression, are to be further divided into five sections, verses 1–5, 6, 7–10, 11–18 and 19–21.

In *verses 1–5* the metaphor (parable – παροιμία) of the gate and that of the shepherd are told: verses 1–3a and 3b–5. The prominent syntactical markers are 'he who enters' (ὁ [μὴ] εἰσερχόμενος – in verses 1 and 2) and 'door', 'doorkeeper' (θύρα, θυρωρός – in verses 1, 2 and 3a). Verses 1 and 2–3a stand parallel to each other according to the coordinate and subordinate relationships in a pattern *abcacb* where *a* states the content, 'he who enters'; *b* the contrastive 'but climbs in by another way', or the result, 'to him the doorkeeper opens'; and *c* the qualification, 'to be a thief and a robber' or 'to be a shepherd'. The contrasting effect of such a build up is significant. In the second parable, verses 3b–5, the reaction of the sheep is portrayed. The syntactical markers are 'sheep' (πρόβατα, 3b, 3c, 3d, 4a, 4b, 5a, 5b, 5c – semotactical and elliptical) and 'voice', 'call' and 'to hear' (3b, 3c, 4b, 5c). In this subparagraph we find effect by contrast. The real shepherd is portrayed against the stranger, and the relationship with the sheep is portrayed by mentioning the contrasting results from the two different voices: the sheep follow or they do not follow. Therefore, the logical reason–results relationship dominates the build-up.

On the surface *verse 6* can be taken on its own, although the expression 'this parable' (ταύτην τὴν παροιμίαν) refers back to verses 1–5. The emphasis is on the expression 'they did not understand', which leads to the explanations in the following verses 7–18. In telling the parables the author–narrator uses contrastive and comparative dyadic coordinate relationships to lay the table for the explanations in verses 7–10 and 11–18. The real shepherd is contrasted with the thieves and robbers, and the Son–sheep relationship is compared to the dyadic relationship of Father and Son.

Verses 7–18 give the explanation of the parables, verses 7–10, the meaning of the gate, and 11–18, the shepherd. In verses 7–10 we note the parallel pattern aba^1b^1 in which a suggests the positive and b the negative pole. In a and a^1 (verses 7 and 9) there functions the dominant expression: 'I am the door of the sheep', and in b and b^1 (verses 8 and 10a) 'the thieves and robbers'. In the conclusive verse 10 the syntactical emphasis on the comparative and contrastive activity of the thief against Jesus should be noted in the expression 'the thief has not come' (οὐκ ἔρχεται – verse 10a) against the 'I came'. And the result of the thief's coming is sketched by the double negative, to emphasise his activity of stealing, killing, and destroying. Jesus' coming means life, abundantly.

Verses 11–18 explain the contrast between the 'good shepherd' and the 'hireling', which results in the relationship of each to the sheep. On the one hand the hireling leaves the sheep (ἀφίησιν τὰ πρόβατα) when danger comes, and on the other hand 'the good shepherd' lays down his life for the sheep (τίθησιν ... ὑπὲρ τῶν προβάτων). After the characterisation of the shepherd and the hireling in consequential coordinate relationships, with the effect of a comparison between them in verses 11–13, the next subdivision starts in verse 14 with the 'I am' saying (cf. verse 11). And in verses 14–16, the relationship between Jesus and the sheep intensifies when the parallel between Jesus and his Father is taken as basis for further comparison. On a syntactical level the transition from the comparison between the hireling and the shepherd to the substantiation of the excellence of the shepherd because of his relationship with his Father (verses 15, 17–18) lies in the marker 'to know' in verses 14–5. The prepositions ὑπέρ (of Jesus, verses 11, 15) and περί (of the hireling, verse 13) function emphatically in the comparative description of Jesus and the hireling.

Verses 17–18 sketch the basis and character of the relationship between Jesus and his Father and are chiastically organised around

'Father' (17a, 18e) and 'to lay down' (θεῖναι). The love of the Father and the function of the Son in laying down his life are emphasised. On the surface verses 17b–18d are structured in a pattern *abbaab* in which *a* suggests the marker-group 'to lay down' (θεῖναι) and *b* the term 'to take it' (λαβεῖν) and which accentuates the function of Jesus to lay down his life for the sheep. The identity of Jesus as sent by the Father is foregrounded by the syntactical emphasis on his 'power' (ἐξουσία) in verse 18cd.

In the sense of theological commentary, *verses 19–21* round off the first unit by giving the reaction to the two explanations in verses 7–10 and 11–18 in this particular co-text. Of prime importance is the first word 'division' (σχίσμα). Verse 19 functions causal–effectively. In verse 6 it was implied that the Jews did not understand the parables, but in verse 19 it has grown to a division. In verse 20 the understanding of some of them (πολλοί) is given and in verse 21 the standpoint of the others. The marker 'demon' in verses 20 and 21 points to something beyond the human sphere and which is a pointer to the real identity of Jesus (cf. 10:30–1). The dominant marker in chapter 9, 'to open the eyes of the blind', is thus used once again to round off 9:1–10:21. According to speech acts the assumption is that a demon cannot open the eyes of the blind (verse 21). In the process of thought development the author–narrator is trying to bring the idea of acceptance or rejection of the identity of Jesus to the syntactical surface.

The syntax of verses 1–21 has a hierarchical build-up which starts with the two parables in verses 1–5, followed by the static reaction, presumably of 'the Jews', in verse 6; this is followed by the two explanations of the door and the shepherd (verses 7–10 and 11–18), leading to the climactic reaction by 'the Jews' in verses 19–21. Schematically it could be illustrated as shown in fig. 4.

Figure 4

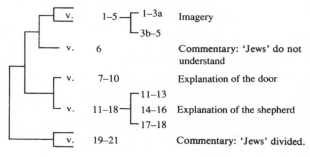

Verses 22–39: This major division starts with the mention of the feast of Dedication, only as a demarcative marker, followed by dialogues: the first one, verses 24–30, emphasises the exclusiveness of the Christian community and the second, verses 31–9, the invitation to 'the Jews' to believe in Jesus. These dialogues emphasise the two (or more) groupings among 'the Jews'.

After the setting, the time, the place, and the circumstances have been mentioned in verses 22–3, a new agendum is put forward by some of 'the Jews': 'Are you the Christ?' (verse 24). Syntactical markers in verses 22–30 have the function to remind the reader of the sheep–shepherd imagery as well as the conflict with 'the Jews' in the explanations of the imagery in verses 1–18 and 19–21. These markers serve as an intensified summary and build-up to the climax in verse 30, when Jesus says 'I and the Father are one'. In this respect we should note the following prominent syntactical markers: 'the Christ' (24c), 'I told' (εἶπον), 'I do' (ποιῶ), 'but you do not believe' (οὐ πιστεύετε – verses 25a, 28a) against 'my sheep hear my voice' (τα πρόβατα τὰ ἐμὰ τῆς φωνῆς μου ἀκούουσιν – verse 27), 'I know' (γινώσκω) and 'they follow me' (ἀκολουθοῦσιν) in verse 27. The relationship between Father and Son is sketched with reference to the relationship with the sheep. A hint at the relationship between Jesus and the Father is made in 25b, to be rounded off in verse 30. Note the syntactical parallel in verses 28c–29a and 29b–30 in the pattern *abab*, where *a* describes the same role to Jesus in 28c as to the Father in 29b

Figure 5

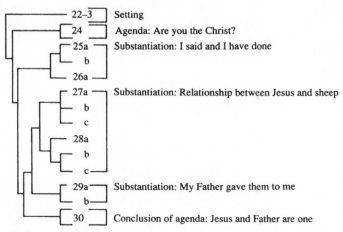

22–3	Setting
24	Agenda: Are you the Christ?
25a	Substantiation: I said and I have done
b	
26a	
27a	Substantiation: Relationship between Jesus and sheep
b	
c	
28a	
b	
c	
29a	Substantiation: My Father gave them to me
b	
30	Conclusion of agenda: Jesus and Father are one

and *b* the greatness of the Father (29a) and of Jesus (30). The outcome of the build-up in verse 30 corresponds with the agendum given in verse 24. Schematically all this is shown in fig. 5.

Verses 31−9 form the second dialogue in this series of two. The emphasis is on the reaction of 'the Jews' in verses 31 and 39, and in between is filled out by the invitation to believe in Jesus and in his works (verses 32−8). On the agenda is the accusation of blaspheming against Jesus (verses 32−3) and his answer to the Jews (verses 34−8). Verses 32−8 have a parallel build-up to verses 24−30. It also works to the climax of Jesus' words: 'the Father is in me and I am in the Father' (verse 38). The most prominent markers in this dialogue are the references to the relationship between Jesus and his Father in 32a, 33b, 36b, 37, 38b. By way of irony in 33b and 34b the author−narrator uses speech acts to influence his readers to make the right choice concerning Jesus' identity. In both instances 'the Jews' are convinced that they ought to know better. As in verses 25−6 the prominence of the marker 'to believe' (πιστεύειν) is emphasised in verses 37−8.

In contrast to the many 'Jews' who do not believe (verses 25, 26, 37−8) the fact of belief is emphasised in verses 40−2. Note the prominence of the markers 'to say' and 'to do' in verse 41. On the syntactical level the main issue of division is portrayed by the term 'to believe' (πιστεύειν).

Verses 40−2 form the conclusion of the epilogue (verses 22−39) to the sheep−shepherd imagery, illustrating Jesus as the Messiah (verses 1−21) to round off the question on Jesus' identity as seen in his work in 9:1−7.

3.3 A bird's eye view of the syntaxes of chapters 9−10, then, can schematically be illustrated as in fig. 6.

Figure 6

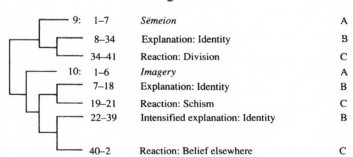

9:	1–7	*Sēmeion*	A
	8–34	Explanation: Identity	B
	34–41	Reaction: Division	C
10:	1–6	*Imagery*	A
	7–18	Explanation: Identity	B
	19–21	Reaction: Schism	C
	22–39	Intensified explanation: Identity	B
	40–2	Reaction: Belief elsewhere	C

The pattern is *ABCABCBC*, in which *A* denotes the work or word of Jesus to illustrate his identity, *B* the explanation of the meaning of the deed or word in the framework of conflict between belief and non-belief, and *C* the reaction, growing from division to a schism, to end with the firm textual marker: καὶ πολλοὶ ἐπίστευσαν εἰς αὐτὸν ἐκεῖ.

4. A narratological reading

4.1 After a reconstruction of the narrative propositions (Greimas), that is, the narrated events abstracted from their arrangement in the text according to their chronological sequence, the table is laid for further analysis. When Greimas' actantial model is applied to John 9–10 it brings to the foreground some interesting narratological observations, as shown in fig. 7.

Figure 7

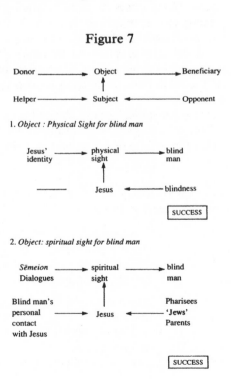

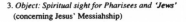

3. *Object: Spiritual sight for Pharisees and 'Jews'*
(concerning Jesus' Messiahship)

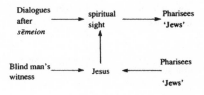

4. *Object: Belief by those across the Jordan*

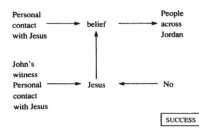

It is interesting that the disciples do not figure actantially, according to Greimas' model. On the other hand, the roles of the dialogues are very important. The object, spiritual sight for the Pharisees ('Jews') concerning Jesus' Messiahship, does not have the conclusive success of the other objects. And that is the narratological issue: spiritual sight brings real identification.

Logically the dialogue on Jesus as the good shepherd should have moved the Pharisees to believe, but that does not happen. It is interesting that according to the narrative sequence the Pharisees should have been addressed, but it seems narratologically that the dialogue is mainly with believers.

4.2 The application of Bremond's narratological model also gives useful observations. According to fig. 8 the first series of potentialities starts in 9:1 and runs through to 10:21, when a new series starts in 10:22 with a new situation. The first series begins with the potentiality of physical sight and ends with success: the blind man sees.

Figure 8

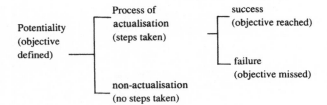

And this has led to three new series:

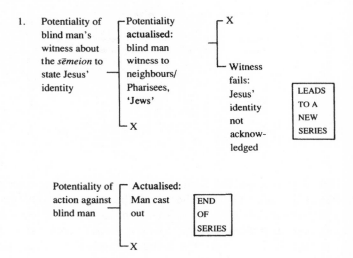

1. Potentiality of blind man's witness about the *sēmeion* to state Jesus' identity — Potentiality actualised: blind man witness to neighbours/ Pharisees, 'Jews'

    X

    — X

    Witness fails: Jesus' identity not acknow-ledged

    LEADS TO A NEW SERIES

    Potentiality of action against blind man — Actualised: Man cast out

    END OF SERIES

    — X

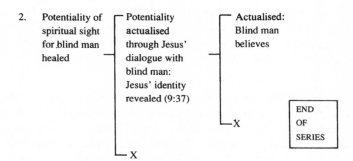

2. Potentiality of spiritual sight for blind man healed — Potentiality actualised through Jesus' dialogue with blind man: Jesus' identity revealed (9:37)

    — X

    Actualised: Blind man believes

    — X

    END OF SERIES

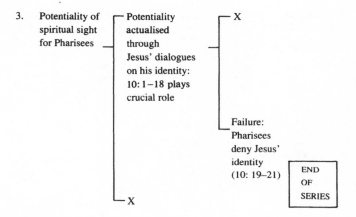

John 10: 22 starts a new series to be schematised as follows according to Bremond's model:

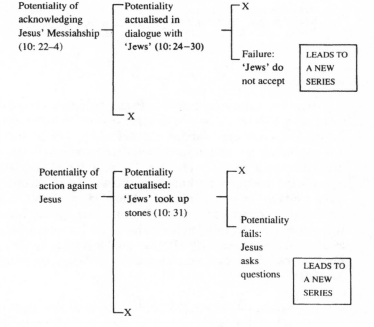

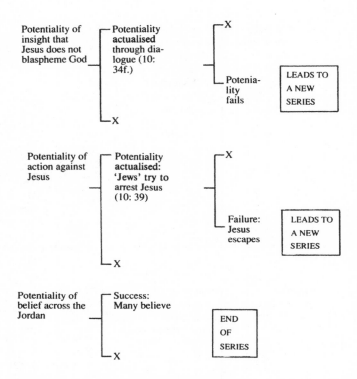

From this analysis according to Bremond's model it is clear that every series ends with a positive or negative reaction to the protagonist Jesus. And the biggest success is belief in Jesus (9:38 and 10:42). The narratological relationship between the blind man healed and the many across the Jordan is obvious. The function of the dialogues is to bring the receivers to acknowledgement of Jesus' identity. Every series leads to the potentiality of acknowledging Jesus' identity as the Son of God. And the potentiality of action against Jesus intensifies when it is actualised in the taking up of stones (10:31) and the attempt to arrest Jesus (10:39). The emphasis on belief at a distant place, across the Jordan, has definite narratological meaning for the exegesis.

4.3 It is worth taking a quick look further, at the narratological relationship of text and time. According to S. Rimmon-Kenan's distinctions,[17] when they are applied to the text, the analepses in John 9−10 function generally as an illustration of Jesus' identity (9:2, 11,

15, 25, 35; 10:6, 15, 17, 25, 29, 34, 36, 41), and the prolepses function to build up tension because they ought to happen in the reader's future. John 9:3; 10:11, 16 and 18 are examples of prolepses.

The relationship of the length of the narrative to the length of the story – the duration – in John 9–10 points to the following interesting results: John 9:1–41 describe a day or two; 10:1–18, a day, and 10:22–39, a day during Jesus' second year. The Johannine sequence consists generally of snapshots with the function of emphasising a vivid style. From 9:1 – 10:21 we find scenes, summaries and pauses, and after 10:21 an ellipse before we continue in 10:22–44 with scenes and summaries.[18]

We do not find real character development in John 9–10, only types of character in their typical development. For example, Jesus is characterised by his deeds (*sēmeion*) as well as by his own words concerning himself. He calls himself Son of Man (9:35), the light of the world (9:5), the good shepherd (10:11, 14), the Christ (indirectly – 10:24–5), one with the Father (10:30). He is also characterised by the blind man healed as the prophet (9:17) and by the Pharisees as someone who stands opposite Moses (9:28–9). The blind man is characterised through what he does, namely, witness about Jesus' *sēmeion* and about Jesus' identity, as well as through the deeds done to him: he was cast out. That shows that he was a believer in Jesus.

The Jews and Pharisees are characterised by their deeds – to cast out the blind man healed, to try to arrest Jesus – and by their disbelief. Their words also help to sketch their attitude. They say that they are disciples of Moses and that Jesus is just a human being. It is interesting that the protagonist Jesus gives relief to the roles of the antagonists, 'the Jews', and Pharisees in what he says and does, and vice versa. The blind man, his parents, and the disciples are only catalytic agents to emphasise the contrastive views of the protagonist and the antagonist on the issue of the identity of Jesus.

Even the function of the spatial indication of the pool of Siloam and the explanation that it means *sent*, and the contrasting of the temple with the region across the Jordan (the division between unbelief and belief) should not be overlooked in the message of these chapters.

4.4 The author–narrator and the protagonist have the same ideological point of view in the unfolding of the plot in these chapters, namely the identity of Jesus, the Messiah, the Son of God, but also the identity of the sheep that can see.

The author–narrator tells his story of Jesus in a certain way and from a certain angle or perspective. Therefore we should read chapters 9–10 against the background of the various perspectives, such as that between the narrator and the implied reader, the perspective between the narrator and the various angle from which the characters like the blind man, his parents, the Pharisees, and the disciples are narrated, as well as the perspective of the characters among themselves. The plan of the events, the so-called plot of the Johannine narrative, determines the arrangement of the material in narratological perspective. The reader is captivated by the sympathy or antipathy aroused by the characters as they are narrated. The fear of the parents of the blind man for 'the Jews' emphasises the contrasting role of the Pharisees as antagonists. The commentary in 9:35–41, 10:6, 19–21, 22–3 and 40–2 focuses on understanding the meaning of Jesus' role. The narrator is not impartial but influences his readers with a running challenge to an orientation that affects their faith. It is decisive to accept the 'from above' perspective of Jesus' origin and destiny as Son of God. The blind man and those across the Jordan did accept this perspective, as opposed to 'the Jews' (Pharisees) who have a 'from below' point of view. The *sēmeion* serves the 'from above' point of view to reveal Jesus as the Son of God. And this is strengthened by Jesus' dialogues with 'the Jews'.

4.5 The unfolding of the plot in chapters 9–10 is given relief against the unfolding in chapters 5–8. In chapter 5 the conflict with unbelief finds its motivation, and in chapter 6 it escalates.[19] Jesus' walking on the water has the function of an epiphany against the background of a new exodus (cf. the manna, the dating near the Passover). 'The Jews' (6:41) and even the disciples (6:60–1) murmur against this new Moses who provides the bread of life, more durable than manna. The reader doubts whether Jesus will be able to fulfil his mission successfully. And in chapter 7 the antagonists, 'the Jews', seek to kill Jesus (7:1, 19, 25). His brothers also do not believe in him (7:4–5). In 7:33–4 the protagonist says that he will be with the Pharisees for a short while and is going to Him who sent him. Even the crowds charge that Jesus has a demon (7:70; cf. 10:20–1). Jesus' opponents are full of ignorance and misunderstandings (cf. 7:27, 42, 52). In chapter 8 the conflict between the protagonist and Jesus grows harsh and hostile and leaves little hope of reconciliation. 'The Jews' argue 'from below' and cannot conceive Jesus' identity. And Jesus slips away from their attempt to kill him.

In chapter 9, Jesus who reveals his Father, gives physical sight to a man born blind. And when this man confesses Jesus as the Son of man he also receives spiritual sight. This sight stands against the spiritual blindness of the Pharisees (9:39–41). The 'true light' was not received by 'his own' but by those whom he gave power to become children of God (1:10). The narrator uses even the crowd's fear of 'the Jews' (9:22; cf. 7:13; 12:42; 16:2) to accentuate his ideological point of view. The inter-relationships among the Jewish leaders, the crowds, and Jesus are expressed by the imagery of sheep–shepherd in chapter 10. Jesus' own think as 'from above' and accept him, but the opponents are like hirelings, thieves and robbers. Jesus' functional role, to reveal his Father, is demonstrated by the *sēmeion* (9:1–7) and illustrated by the sheep–shepherd imagery (10:1–18). The blind man is sent to Siloam (the One sent) and receives spiritual sight from the One sent by the Father. The 'blind' Pharisees on the other hand do not accept Jesus as the 'Siloam' of God. Only he who has received sight (physical and spiritual) can witness to Jesus' identity. Although he was cast out of the synagogue and community with his own people he has found full community with God. The author–narrator then uses contrasts to confront the reader. The reader does not want to be led by thieves and robbers and hirelings but by someone who says that he knows and that he lays down his life for his own (10:17–18). And the guarantee for this is that Jesus and his Father are one.

The unfolding of the plot concerning Jesus' identity that can only be grasped 'from above' leads to division. On the one hand one may have spiritual sight and hear the voice of the good shepherd which leads to life, but on the other hand one may stay blind (like 'the Jews') and neglect the invitations of Jesus (10:24–6) which leads to death. The unity of Father and Son is only 'visible' for Jesus' own sheep (10:27–30). The new community that has come into existence by 'sight' is tied to Jesus, just as he is one with his Father. Acknowledgement of the true identity of Jesus, or the rejection of it, determines the reader's own position according to the narrative in John 9–10.

7

JOHANNES 10 IM KONTEXT DES VIERTEN EVANGELIUMS

Hartwig Thyen

Meinen Überlegungen zu Joh 10 schicke ich einige Vorbemerkungen voraus, die hier freilich nicht detailliert begründet werden können. Sie sind jedoch insofern unerläßlich, als mit ihnen bestimmte *Voraussetzungen* meines Umgangs mit dem Johannesevangelium zu nennen sind. Daß diese für die Lektüre und Interpretation literarischer Werke an sich selbstverständlichen Voraussetzungen hier eigens genannt werden müssen, liegt an der besonderen Lage, in der wir Bibelexegeten uns aufgrund der Forschungsgeschichte befinden. Denn im Blick auf die Masse der Literatur gesehen, verfolgen wir eher quasi archäologische Ziele, als daß wir uns darum bemühten, mit allen Mitteln der grammatischen und divinatorischen Kunst (Schleiermacher) überlieferte Texte zu interpretieren. Wir lassen die Texte nicht sie selbst sein und für sich selbst sprechen, sondern benutzen sie vorwiegend als 'Quellen' für unsere Rekonstruktionen, sei es der Geschichte des historischen Jesus oder der frühen Christenheit, sei es der 'Intentionen' des oder der ursprünglichen Autoren. Über Recht und Grenzen solchen Umgangs mit biblischen Texten soll hier nicht diskutiert werden. Ich stelle ihm vielmehr einfach einen anderen gegenüber. Dabei sind meine nun zu nennenden Voraussetzungen jedoch nicht willkürlicher Natur, sondern sie sind ihrerseits im Umgang mit dem Text des Johannesevangeliums und seiner kontroversen und komplexen Auslegungsgeschichte gewonnene – und wie ich hoffe – validierte Resultate.

1. Das überlieferte Johannesevangelium von Joh 1:1 bis zu Joh 21:25 (!) ist ein kohärenter und höchst anspruchsvoller literarischer Text. Alle seine Textteile und Teiltexte bis hinunter zur Satzebene müssen aus dem Ganzen des Evangeliums und als dessen Konstituenten begriffen werden. Mögen sie auch hier und da noch die Erfahrungen und Versuchungen früher Christen in ihrer konkreten Zeit und Geschichte reflektieren, so sind sie doch in ihrer primären und für

die Textinterpretation allein relevanten Funktion nichts als die Elemente, aus denen die inspirierende Textwelt des Evangeliums erbaut ist. Seine *Leser* (21:24: γράφας ταῦτα) zu Bewohnern (μένειν!) dieser 'Welt' und sie darin des 'ewigen Lebens' teilhaftig zu machen, wurde das Johannesevangelium geschrieben.

2. Meine eigenen ausgedehnten Wege durch das Labyrinth johanneischer 'Literarkritik', 'Quellensuche' und 'Redaktionsgeschichte' haben mich statt zu dem gesuchten 'ursprünglichen Johannesevangelium' und seinem 'Evangelisten' zu der Einsicht geführt, daß das Werk kohärent und es deshalb sinnlos ist, irgend einen anderen als den Autor von Joh 21 den 'vierten Evangelisten' zu nennen. Denn seine Spuren sind dem gesamten Werk tief und unauslöschlich eingeprägt. Er ist der Schöpfer der faszinierenden Figur des 'Jüngers, den Jesus liebte' in ihrem spannungsvollen Gegenüber zu Petrus. Alle Lieblingsjünger − und Petrustexte sind von vorneherein auf ihre Klimax und glückliche Lösung in Joh 21 angelegt, und die Korrespondenz dieses 'Epilogs' zum Prolog des Evangeliums ist absichtsvoll und vielgestaltig. Das heißt − gewiß verkürzt, aber eben dadurch unzweideutig gesagt −: Bultmanns und J. Beckers 'kirchlicher Redaktor' ist unser Johannes-Evangelist. Selbst wenn er eine, von dem möglichen Verfasser einer mutmaßlichen 'Grundschrift' zu unterscheidende Person sein sollte, so ist doch allein er der in den Strukturen seines Werkes implizite Autor und Baumeister der literarischen Welt des Johannesevangeliums, in dem alle seine vermeintlichen oder tatsächlichen 'Vorstufen' im dreifach Hegelschen Sinne des Wortes 'aufgehoben' sind.

3. Das bedeutet, daß nicht irgendeine hypothetische Vor- oder Nachgeschichte von Textteilen − sei es der mutmaßlichen 'Prologvorlage', der vermeintlichen '*Semeia-*'[1] und 'Passions-Quelle' oder 'redaktionell' beurteilter Passagen −, sondern allein ihr aktueller Gebrauch und ihre strukturelle Valeur und Differenz zu anderen Teiltexten auf der synchronen Ebene des Werksganzen über ihren Sinn und ihre Bedeutung entscheiden. Und zwar entscheidet darüber, wenn auch nach den Partituranweisungen des Autors, allein der Leser und das Abenteuer der Lektüre. Deshalb muß mit der romantischen Idee, als sei die 'Einfühlung' in den vergangenen Autor und die Erforschung seiner 'Aussageabsichten' und 'Intentionen' legitimes Ziel und Aufgabe der Interpretation, auch jeder Versuch preisgegeben werden, so etwas wie den 'objektiven Sinn' des Evangeliums ermitteln und solche

Ermittlung theoretisch rechtfertigen zu wollen.[2] Erst wenn wir erkennen, daß alle unsere Lektüren zusammen mit denen unserer Väter nur Beiträge zu dem Gespräch sind, worin sich unter der Führung des 'Parakleten' hinein in die 'ganze Wahrheit' über die Jahrhunderte bis zum Eschaton der Sinn des Johannesevangeliums vollendet, wird darin auch ein wirksamer Impfstoff gefunden sein gegen die zumal in den Anmerkungsteilen namentlich unserer deutschen neutestamentlichen Beiträge grassierende *rabies theologorum*. Die gefährliche Illusion der mit der 'Autorenintention' identischen *richtigen* Interpretation muß zerstört werden und der Einsicht weichen, daß Texte die simple Alternative von richtiger und falscher Interpretation nicht zulassen, sondern als die Klasse ihrer *möglichen* Auslegungen begriffen sein wollen. Nur negativ können aus der unbegrenzten Fülle der möglichen Interpretationen solche ausgeschlossen werden, die der Grammatik des Textes gegenüber *unmögliche* sind. Drastischer noch nennt Umberto Eco Texte 'Maschinen zur Erzeugung von Bedeutungen': 'Der Text ist da und produziert seine eigenen Sinnverbindungen ... Der Autor müßte das Zeitliche segnen, nachdem er geschrieben hat, damit er die Eigenbewegung des Textes nicht stört.'[3]

4. Als literarisches *Werk* ist das Johannesevangelium nicht das Resultat irgendeines anonymen 'traditions-' oder 'redaktionsgeschichtlich' beschreibbaren *Wachstums*, als setzten Texte wie Bäume einfach 'Jahresringe' an, sondern vielmehr das Ergebnis eines Produktionsprozesses (ποίησις), in dessen Verlauf es sowohl den ursprünglichen Intentionen seines Autors als auch den ostentativen Bezügen zur Welt seiner primären Adressaten gegenüber autonom geworden ist. Dieser poetische Charakter des Evangeliums zwingt dazu, bei seiner Auslegung die unauflösliche Korrelation und Korrespondenz von Form und Inhalt als der beiden Seiten einer und derselben Münze streng zu beachten. Denn der poetische Text ist nicht Mitteilung von *etwas*, was ihm äußerlich wäre und was auch in anderer Form gesagt werden könnte, sondern er ist dieses Mitgeteilte selbst. Wenn es bei Hölderlin heißt, 'Was bleibet aber, stiften die Dichter', so stiften sie dieses Bleibende nicht durch ihre Worte und von ihnen ablösbar, sondern als diese Worte selbst. Darum sind alle poetischen Texte − seien sie lyrischer oder epischer Art − prinzipiell unübersetzbar und erst recht nicht paraphrasierbar. Übersetzung und Paraphrase können als Übungen der Annäherung immer nur vorläufige Schritte zu dem Ziel sein, im Original selbst heimisch zu werden.

5. Im Blick auf Bultmanns Entmythologisierungs-Forderung und die ihr korrespondierende Aufgabe der 'existentialen Interpretation' kann darum jede entmythologisierende Paraphrase der mythologischen Erzählung von Geschichte und Geschick des fleischgewordenen Logos bestenfalls ein erster Schritt dahin sein, die verlorene Sprache des Mythos wiederzugewinnen; für uns Kinder der Aufklärung gewiß ein notwendiger Schritt. Aber eben nur ein erster Schritt. Denn ohne die *Form* des Mythos läßt sich der *Inhalt* des Evangeliums überhaupt nicht sagen. An die fast grenzenlose Kapazität des Mythos, vom Transzendenten zu reden, reichen alle unsere dürren Abstraktionen nicht entfernt heran. Im Anschluß an Wendungen Dantes fordert R. M. Frye in seinem stimulierenden Beitrag zur Aufgabe der Evangelieninterpretation in literaturkritischer Perspektive deshalb die Wiederaneignung der verlorenen Fähigkeit eines *vergleichenden Sich-Angleichens* ('accomodation') als die der Sprache des Mythos angemessene Verstehensweise.[4] Ohne die Entwicklung solchen Vermögens der 'accomodation' − im Englischen wohl nicht zufällig primär die Bezeichnung für 'Wohnung' − bleibt der Leser unbehaust und vermag in der unübersetzbaren Sprache des Originals nicht heimisch zu werden. Darum beklagt Frye den Verlust der 'accomodation' als 'one of the gravest calamities in the intellectual history of Christianity'.

6. Nicht nur aufgrund seines Ortes im Bibelkanon, sondern auch insofern ist Johannes der 'vierte Evangelist', als er unsere drei synoptischen Evangelien in ihrer überlieferten Gestalt voraussetzt, und nicht etwa nur ein anonymes Analogon der 'synoptischen Tradition'. Parallel dazu, daß eine der Grundvoraussetzungen der 'Formgeschichte', nämlich die Selbständigkeit und Präexistenz der 'kleinen Einheiten' und ihre 'Rahmung' durch die Evangelisten als bloße Sammler und Redaktoren, zusehends fragwürdiger wird,[5] bestätigt die jüngere Johannesforschung mehr und mehr, was E. C. Hoskyns schon 1940 schrieb: 'That the author of the Fourth Gospel had the three synoptic gospels before him when he composed his gospel is most improbable, for his relation to them is not that of an editor. But that he was familiar with the synoptic material, and even with its form, is certain. Yet it is perhaps even more important that he presumes this synoptic material to be less before the eyes of his readers than in their heads. He presumes, in fact, that it is in their hearts, so that he expects them to follow him when he moves round and round, when he alludes to it, and when he writes it down, and most particularly

when he refashions it ...'.[6] Diese enge Beziehung des Johannes zu
den Synoptikern haben in den letzten Jahren zumal die ebenso scharfsinnigen wie gründlichen Untersuchungen von F. Neirynck und M.
Sabbe[7] ans Licht gebracht. Im Blick auf die Passionserzählung des
Johannesevangeliums zeigt die Analyse von A. Dauer – übrigens
gegen die 'Intention' ihres Autors, der Johannes aus einer imaginären
'Quelle' schöpfen läßt, die aber ihrerseits von allen drei synoptischen
Evangelien gespeist sein soll! –, daß der vierte in der Tat die drei
älteren Evangelisten voraussetzt.[8] Die sorgfältige Destruktion der
komplizierten Theorie M.-E. Boismards über die Evangeliengenese –
sie ist noch weit unökonomischer als diejenige Dauers! – durch
F. Neirynck u.a.[9] zeigt das gleiche Ergebnis: Johannes kennt die
Synoptiker in ihrer überlieferten Gestalt. In diesem Zusammenhang
ist auch daran zu erinnern, daß Bultmann für seinen 'kirchlichen
Redaktor' die Kenntnis der synoptischen Evangelien und die gelegent-
lichen Bemühungen um einen Ausgleich mit deren Tradition voraussetzt. Die schon lange beobachtete besondere Affinität des Johannes
zu Lukas ist m.E. anders als durch literarische Abhängigkeit nicht
erklärbar, zumal seit durch das Obsoletgeworden-Sein der 'Western-
Non-Interpolations-Theorie' Lk 24:12 nicht mehr als Eindringling
aus dem Johannesevangelium, sondern umgekehrt nur noch als die
Quelle der Szene vom Wettlauf der beiden Jünger zum Grab Jesu
angesehen werden kann.

Das überaus subtile und oft höchst ironische Spiel des Johannes
mit synoptischen Themen und Texten zeigt im übrigen, daß seine
eigene Evangelienschriftstellerei den Synoptikern gegenüber keinesfalls unter der Devise steht, 'Alle die vor mir gekommen sind, die sind
Diebe und Räuber', wie H. Windisch meinte. Er will die Synoptiker
weder verdrängen noch ersetzen. Als ihr Interpret setzt er sie vielmehr
voraus und damit in gewisser Weise sogar in Kraft. So will das
johanneische τετέλεσται (19:30) ebenso als die andere Seite des
markinischen Schreis der Gottverlassenheit verstanden werden wie
Joh 12:27ff. vor dem Hintergrund der Gethsemane-Szene. Anders
gesagt: Indem die Kirche das Johannesevangelium als viertes dem
Kanon einfügte, hat sie dem in ihm selbst angelegten Lektüremuster
genau entsprochen.[10]

7. Aus dem Voranstehenden folgt nun aber auch, daß es verfehlt ist,
das Johannesevangelium aufgrund seiner vermeintlichen 'Sonderüber-
lieferung', seiner 'hohen Christologie', seines radikalen Dualismus,
sowie seiner pointiert prädestinatianischen Aussagen (vgl. 6:36, 44,

65; 8:43ff. u.ö.) als das Produkt einer kleinen esoterischen Sekte am Rande der 'Großkirche' zu definieren, dafür seine durch 'Rätsel und Mißverständnis' (H. Leroy) geprägte Diktion als die typische 'Sondersprache' einer weltlosen 'In-Group' in Anspruch zu nehmen und zu behaupten, hier sei an die Stelle der weltoffenen Nächsten-, ja Feindesliebe der Verkündigung Jesu die auf den eigenen Klüngel beschränkte 'Bruderliebe' getreten und das Interesse an der Erlösung der Welt von der privaten Idylle der endzeitlichen Sammlung der Erwählten in den Wohnungen des himmlischen Vaterhauses verdrängt worden.

Wer das Evangelium so zum bloßen Überbau und Reflektor der zufälligen Geschichte einer vermeintlichen urchristlichen Sondergruppe macht, der bringt es um den Ernst seines universalen und für alle Christen verbindlichen Anspruchs. Nicht so, sondern in dem Sinne will es als 'Spiegel' gelesen werden, daß der *Leser* darin sich selbst erkennt und sich verlocken läßt, aus der Finsternis ans Licht zu kommen. Gewiß ist es keine 'Missionsschrift', weder für Juden noch erst recht für Heiden, sondern ein Buch für Christen, deren angefochtenen Glauben es festigen und die es zum 'Bleiben' ermutigen will, auch wenn dessen Konsequenz der im Martyrium gipfelnde Haß der Welt sein mag. Allein dieser aktuelle Ernstfall (vgl. 16:1ff.) und nicht irgendeine sektiererische Marotte erzwingt auch die äußerste Konzentration auf die Brennpunkte von 'Christusbekenntnis' und 'Bruderliebe'.[11] Daß überhaupt nur einem spezifisch johanneischen 'Insider' die Lektüre des Evangeliums gelingen könne, ist eine zumindest höchst einseitige Behauptung. Denn wie jedes große literarische Werk schafft es sich selbst erst seine 'Insider' durch die Lektüre. Anders als die Akteure auf der *literarischen* Bühne des Dramas – wie die Jünger, die Juden oder Pilatus – durchschaut ja der durch den Prolog 'eingeweihte' (und mit der synoptischen Überlieferung vertraute) Leser deren Mißverständnisse und läßt sich von der hintergründigen Ironie des Erzählers dankbar immer tiefer in die Wahrheit führen.[12] Im übrigen bilden aber selbst die durch ihre Lektüre zu Insidern gewordenen Leser, wie der bis heute andauernde Streit um die Johannesinterpretation eindrücklich demonstriert, keine durch eine homogene Ideologie geprägte In-Group. Auch die primären Leser befinden sich dem objektiven Text gegenüber in keiner grundsätzlich anderen Lage als alle späteren. Denn 'in Wirklichkeit kann keine Theorie der hermeneutischen Legitimation legitim sein, außer durch den Prozeß des hermeneutischen Lesens. Am Ursprung der hermeneutischen Praxis steht ein Zirkel, und es ist ganz unerheblich, wie heilig oder wie vitiös er ist.'[13]

8. Im Hintergrund des Johannesevangeliums (wie der Johannesbriefe) wird eine Situation sichtbar, worin die Christen insofern zwischen alle Stühle geraten sind, als sie mit dem Synagogenausschluß nicht allein ihre soziale Heimat und ökonomische Subsistenz verloren haben, sondern damit zugleich auch den der Synagoge gewährten relativen Schutz vor den gotteslästerlichen Forderungen der Teilnahme am imperialen Kult und so den blutigen Konsequenzen seiner Verweigerung ausgesetzt sind. Insofern mag das gerade im Johannesevangelium so spezifisch ausgearbeitete Passionsdrama mit seinem ständigen Szenenwechsel zwischen den auf ihre 'Reinheit' bedachten Juden *draußen*, die von ihrem Messias so wenig wissen wollen wie von seinen Bekennern (vgl. Joh 9), und dem Angeklagten vor dem Vertreter des Imperiums *drinnen* durchaus aktuelle christliche Erfahrungen verarbeiten.[14] Auch die bei Johannes auffällig breit reflektierte Rolle des Denunzianten Judas (6:64ff.; 13:2, 11, 18ff.) und diejenige des Verleugners Petrus, der freilich umkehrt und wie ein guter Hirte zum Märtyrer wird, weisen auf ein Klima, in dem Denunziation, Bekenntnisscheu und Apostasie gedeihen. Abgesehen davon, daß das Thomasbekenntnis, 'Mein Herr und mein Gott!', zusammen mit den ersten Prologzeilen eine große Inklusio um die gesamte Geschichte des fleischgewordenen 'Gottes' bildet, entspricht dessen *Formulierung* wohl kaum zufällig der vom späten Domitian geforderten Akklamation, 'Dominus ac Deus!'. Auf diese gefährliche Versuchung weist das kryptischsubversive, 'Kindlein, hütet euch vor den *Eidola*!' am Ende des 1 Joh und wohl auch die ihm vorausgehende Erörterung der 'Sünden zum Tode' gegenüber solchen, die nicht zum Tode führen, deren Täter aber der brüderlichen Fürbitte bedürfen.[15] Vor solchem Hintergrund gewinnt endlich die gerade bei Johannes dominante messianische Königstitulatur Jesu Gewicht und Aktualität, wie davor umgekehrt der Ruf, 'Wir haben keinen König außer dem Kaiser!' (19:15), als Lästerung und Apostasie von der Hoffnung Israels auf Gott als seinen wahren König und Imperator aller Völker erscheinen soll.

Gewiß, der johanneische Jesus offenbart nur, *daß* er der Offenbarer ist (Bultmann). Gleichwohl aber geht es keineswegs nur um dieses 'bloße Daß', sondern vielmehr darum, daß eben *er* und kein anderer der offenbare Gott ist, er, der 'sein Fleisch gibt für das Leben der Welt' (6:51) und so im Sterben für die Seinen, die er damit aus Sklaven zu Freunden, aus Hörigen zu Freien macht (13:1ff.; 15:9ff.), Gottes Liebe zur Welt vollendet (3:16).[16] Insofern ist der Rückgriff des Johannes auf die Form der Historia Jesu, ist sein Spiel mit den Texten der Synoptiker theologisch notwendig.

Daß in der Welt der primären Adressaten des Johannesevangeliums das messianische Bekenntnis zur Erfahrung des sich in Entfremdung, Verfolgung und Martyrium entladenden 'Hasses der Welt' geführt und daß dann wiederum gerade diese Erfahrung die spezifische Zeichnung und das besondere Profil des evangelischen Bildes Jesu als des *Fremden* schlechthin mitgeprägt hat, ist sicher richtig.[17] Gerade darum aber ist es notwendig, hier Entdeckungs- und Begründungszusammenhang sorgfältig zu unterscheiden und nicht Ursache und Wirkung zu verwechseln.[18] Vor allem aber gilt es, nicht hinter die Erkenntnis des auctorialen Ranges und der Kohärenz des Evangeliums als eines literarischen *Werkes* zurückzufallen, um dann Spannungen und Aporien im Text vorschnell auf dessen Genese als Spiegel der spezifischen Geschichte einer 'johanneischen Sondergemeinde' zurückzuführen,[19] statt sie als Signale an den Leser und Ausdruck realer Aporien zu begreifen.

Zur Textabgrenzung, Gliederung und Einheit von Joh 10

1. Die grammatische Verbindung von Joh 10:1ff. mit Kapitel 9, insbesondere mit 9:40–1 ist derart eng und unmittelbar, daß das neue zehnte Kapitel fast besser mit 9:40 begönne. Denn ohne Jesus als Subjekt der folgenden Rede erneut explizit einzuführen (zumal vor dem mit dem doppelten 'Amen, Amen' eingeleiteten Satz von 10:1!), läßt der Erzähler auch das pronominale ὑμῖν die 9:40 genannten οἱ ἐκ τῶν Φαρισαίων vertreten, so daß zwischen 9:41 und 10:1 kein Einschnitt ist. Die 'Pharisäer' agieren hier wie öfter auf der literarischen Bühne als Repräsentanten der im Hintergrund bleibenden Ἰουδαῖοι. Haben diese nach 9:22 den Synagogenausschluß aller Christusbekenner beschlossen, so wird der an dem sehend gewordenen Blindgeborenen dann von den blinden Pharisäern exekutiert (9:34).

2. Am Ende von Kapitel 10 zieht sich Jesus vor der seit Joh 7 ständig eskalierten Steinigungs- und Verhaftungsdrohung der Juden (10:24, 31, 39) aus dem feindlichen Judäa zurück auf peräisches Gebiet in Transjordanien (10:40–2). Der Erzähler markiert unüberhörbar: εἰς τὸν τόπον ὅπου ἦν Ἰωάννης τὸ πρῶτον βαπτίζων, καὶ ἔμεινεν ἐκεῖ, und nimmt so deutlich 1:28 wieder auf: ταῦτα ἐν Βηθανίᾳ ἐγένετο πέραν τοῦ Ἰορδάνου, ὅπου ἦν ὁ Ἰωάννης βαπτίζων. Jesus ist damit an den Ausgangspunkt seines öffentlichen Wirkens ins peräische Bethanien zurückgekehrt. Wie hier einst auf die Martyria des Johannes hin die ersten Jünger zu ihm kamen, bei ihm 'bleiben'

(1:35ff.) und dann im galiläischen Kana seine Herrlichkeit sahen und an ihn glaubten (2:11), so 'kommen' hier nun wieder viele zu ihm und glauben an ihn (10:41−2). Mit dieser abschließenden Nennung des Täufers und der nachdrücklichen Bestätigung der vollen Wahrheit seines Zeugnisses ist der dem Prolog folgende erste große Teil des Evangeliums im Sinne einer Ringkomposition zuende geführt. Wenn dabei im Vergangenheitstempus gesagt wird, πάντα ὅσα εἶπεν Ἰωάννης περὶ τούτου ἀληθῆ ἦν, so wird damit sein Tod in Erinnerung gerufen und dem unerschrockenen Bekenner (1:19ff.) nahe am Ort seines Martyriums gleichsam ein Epitaph errichtet.

3. Daß wir im Johannesevangelium neben der alles beherrschenden apologetischen Polemik gegen das von den Pharisäern geführte 'Judentum' (= οἱ Ἰουδαῖοι), das als solches geradezu durch sein Nein zu Jesus und seinen messianischen Bekennern definiert ist, noch mit einer akuten Auseinandersetzung mit einer 'Täufersekte' zu rechnen haben, ist mir wenig wahrscheinlich. Die alte, von mir selbst einst im Anschluß an Bultmann verfochtene These, die vermeintliche 'Vorlage' des Prologs sei ein ursprünglich täuferisches Lied, in dem die 'Johannesjünger' ihren Meister als präexistenten und fleischgewordenen Logos besungen hätten, ist doch allzu phantastisch.[20] Zumal sich das Benedictus des Zacharias (Lk 1:68−79) schwerlich einer analogen messianischen Täufertradition zuschreiben läßt, sondern sich als durch und durch lukanische Komposition erweist, fehlt der Prologhypothese jegliche externe Stütze. Das durchaus positive Zeugnis über Johannes den Täufer bei Josephus und dessen gleichzeitiges Schweigen über Jesus (Ant 18:116ff.) könnte dagegen ein Hinweis sein auf das Recht der Erwägung W. Wredes, daß nämlich die Juden 'den Täufer gegen Jesus ausgespielt haben. Dann hätte man diese (sc. vermeintlich antitäuferischen) Züge − und das wäre der große Vorteil dieser Ansicht − in die sonstige Polemik des Evangeliums einfach einzurechnen. Man sagte etwa auf jüdischer Seite, Johannes sei doch ein ganz anderer Mann als Jesus gewesen, er sei viel eher ein Prophet zu nennen; die Taufe habe er gebracht, nicht Jesus; er habe ja auch Jesus selbst getauft, sei folglich der Größere, Jesus dagegen sei der Taufe bedürftig gewesen, und dergleichen.'[21]

4. Innerhalb des ersten großen Evangelienteils (1:19 − 10:42), der so von der Täufermartyria gerahmt wird, gehört unser zehntes Kapitel zum letzten seiner *drei* Unterteile. In einer an scharfsinnigen Beobachtungen reichen, jedoch vielleicht allzu konstruierten Untersuchung

glaubt M. Rissi in den jeweils in Galiläa zentrierten und in Judäa/ Jerusalem ihr Ziel erreichenden *Reisen* Jesu das Gliederungsprinzip des Evangeliums entdeckt zu haben.[22] Die erste dieser Jesusreisen (1:19 – 3:36) beginnt in Peräa, führt dann nach Kana in Galiläa und endet im feindlichen Jerusalem, dessen Bewohnern Jesus sich nicht anvertraut, weil er sie alle kennt (2:24). Die zweite Reise beginnt für Rissi mit 4:1 im verachteten Samaria, führt dann abermals in das Galiläa des Glaubens (4:46–54) und endet unter offenkundigen Mordplänen (5:18) wiederum in Jerusalem mit 5:47. Endlich soll der Abschnitt 6:1 – 10:42 Jesu dritte Reise beschreiben: Ausgehend vom transjordanischen Ostufer des Sees von Tiberias führe sie wiederum nach Galiläa, wo aus dem Munde des Petrus das Bekenntnis der Jünger laut wird (6:66ff.), und ende unter sich steigernden Mordplänen und -anschlägen wieder in Jerusalem. Da bisher Jesu 'Stunde' aber noch nicht gekommen ist, entzieht er sich stets seinen Feinden. So entweicht er auch am Ende dieser dritten Reise ihnen, und zwar nun an den Ort seines Anfangs und der ersten Täufermartyria.

Rissi selbst macht darauf aufmerksam, daß der Erzähler am eigentlichen Vorgang der Reisen kaum Interesse zeige: 'Im Gegenteil, Ortsveränderungen Jesu werden im vierten Evangelium regelmäßig mit äußerst knappen Strichen angedeutet. Mit wenigen Worten wird Jesus jeweils über die größten Distanzen hinweggesetzt' ('Aufbau', 48). Auch wenn Rissi zurecht darauf aufmerksam macht, daß dem Evangelisten aber die Orte selbst und ihre Folge wichtig und von tiefer symbolischer Bedeutung seien, fragt man sich, ob dieser Reiseschematismus wirklich als Gliederungsprinzip taugt. So beginnt die erste Reise ja gar nicht in 1:19ff., sondern doch wohl 1:43ff., und eher als die Reise markiert die Wiederaufnahme der Täufermartyria den Abschluß von 1:19 – 3:36.[23] Im zweiten Teil ist die Verbindung des fünften mit dem sechsten Kapitel, das den Erweis dafür liefert, daß und wie Mose von Jesus geschrieben hat (5:46), derart eng und dagegen die durch 7:1ff. gesetzte Zäsur so auffällig, daß man als abgegrenzten zweiten Teil wohl nur 4:1 – 6:71 ansehen kann, zumal ja angesichts von 6:1 auch nicht von transjordanischem Gebiet als Ausgangsort einer Reise Jesu die Rede sein kann.[24] Endlich kann es ja keine Frage sein, daß narratologisch die Kapitel 7–10 (und nicht etwa 6–10!) eine große dritte Einheit bilden.

5. Die Zäsur zwischen 10:42 und 11:1 ist so stark, daß mit dem elften Kapitel fraglos ein ganz neuer Evangelienteil einsetzt. Da in der Lazaruserweckung – wie oft beobachtet wurde – Jesu eigene

Auferstehung vorabgebildet ist, ist ihre Erzählung zusammen mit den Ostergeschichten von Joh 20—1 als die große Inklusio des zweiten Evangelienteils zu begreifen.[25] Mit 11:1ff. beginnt der Weg Jesu in seine Passion und damit die Stunde seiner Verherrlichung. Entgegen der Warnung seiner Jünger zieht Jesus nun ohne Furcht vor den 'Wölfen' als der 'gute Hirte' mit der Vollmacht, sein Leben hinzugeben und es wieder an sich zu nehmen (10:18), aus dem freundlichen peräischen ins feindliche judäische Bethanien. Thomas spricht illusionslos aus, was die Stunde geschlagen hat: 'Laßt uns mit ihm ziehen, damit wir mit ihm sterben' (11:16). Der gute Hirte kennt seine Schafe mit Namen. Und Lazarus hört seine Stimme und kommt aus dem Tode ins Leben. Die ganze Lazarusgeschichte liest sich wie eine Dramatisierung von Lk 8:40—2, 49—56 und Lk 16:27—31: Da sie nicht auf Mose und die Propheten hören, lassen die Brüder des reichen Mannes sich auch dadurch nicht überzeugen, daß Lazarus zu ihrer Warnung von den Toten zu ihnen kommt. Ja, im Gegenteil! 'Weil viele Juden um seinetwillen hingingen und an Jesus glaubten' (12:10—11), beschließen sie, nun auch Lazarus zu töten.

Nach der Erweckung des Lazarus fällt dann das Synhedrium in offizieller Versammlung in Abwesenheit des Angeklagten (!) das Todesurteil über Jesus (11:46ff.). Das nach der Tora notwendige Verhör des Angeklagten findet im Johannesevangelium nicht statt, weshalb Jesus als Verurteilter bei seiner Gefangennahme im Garten auch sogleich gefesselt wird. Daß und wie Johannes aber gleichwohl die synoptische Verhörszene gerade in unserem zehnten Kapitel verarbeitet hat, zeigt der schöne Beitrag von M. Sabbe in diesem Bande.[26]

Liegt aber die eigentliche Zäsur im Evangelium einem fast überwältigenden Konsensus seiner Ausleger gegenüber gar nicht zwischen den Kapiteln 12 und 13, sondern mit der Rückkehr Jesu an seinen Ausgangsort von 1:19ff. und der Inklusion des ganzen ersten Teils in die Martyria Johannes des Täufers hier am Ende von Kapitel 10, das damit als Resümee alles Vorausgegangenen und Exposition des Folgenden in eine ganz zentrale Stellung einrückt, so hat das gewiß Konsequenzen für die Auslegung, die bedacht werden müssen. Die herrschende Gliederung des Evangeliums, die die Kapitel 1—12 mit 'Die Offenbarung der Doxa Jesu vor dem Kosmos' und die Kapitel 13—20 mit 'Die Offenbarung der Doxa Jesu vor der Gemeinde' überschreibt (Kapitel 21 gilt ihr in der Regel als 'sekundärer Nachtrag'), läßt sich ohnehin nicht ohne Gewaltsamkeiten durchführen. Bultmann vermag sie nur mit Hilfe zahlreicher und komplizierter

Textumstellungen und -ausscheidungen plausibel zu machen. Vor allem muß er dazu die 'Scheidung im Jüngerkreis' (6:60—71) aus dem sechsten an das Ende des zwölften Kapitels versetzen. Und noch dann bleiben die Aporien. Denn nach dem esoterischen Intermezzo von letztem Mahl mit Fußwaschung, Abschiedsreden und Gebet Jesu für die Seinen (13—17) setzt sich ja mit der Passion Jesu im engeren Sinne die Offenbarung seiner Doxa vor dem Kosmos potenziert fort und erreicht ihre Klimax erst in der Kreuzigung (vgl. zumal den dreisprachigen Kreuzes-Titulus!). Diese Zweiaktigkeit des Dramas, dessen zweiter Akt durch ein auf die Zeit danach vorausweisendes esoterisches Zwischen spiel unterbrochen ist, wird oft nur dadurch überspielt, daß die johanneische Passionsgeschichte als bloßes Traditionsrudiment und notwendiges Ausstattungsstück eines 'Evangeliums' gilt, das ansonsten aber von einem 'naiven Doketismus' beherrscht sein soll (Käsemann). Dabei ist gerade das Johannesevangelium von Anfang an und programmatisch nicht mehr 'Passionsgeschichte mit ausführlicher Einleitung' (M. Kähler). Wie die Stellung der 'Tempelreinigung' schon im zweiten Kapitel und zumal der Passarahmen des gesamten Werkes zeigen,[27] ist bei Johannes vielmehr Jesu *Passion* als seine göttliche *Aktion* zum durchgehenden Darstellungsprinzip geworden.

Setzt aber mit der Lazaruserzählung wirklich ein ganz neuer Evangelienteil ein, dann ist zu überlegen, ob statt der Stichworte 'Offenbarung', 'Welt' und 'Gemeinde' nicht eher die spezifisch johanneischen Termini κατάβασις und ἀνάβασις geeignet wären, das jeweilige Thema der beiden Teile zu formulieren (vgl. Joh 3:12—13 und 6:60ff.). Unter dieser Perspektive verdienen auch die von einzelnen Autoren immer einmal wieder vorgetragenen Überlegungen, ob nach dem Täufer nun nicht mit Lazarus der neue und wahrhaftige Zeuge der ἀνάβασις Jesu eingeführt werden soll, ob also nicht Lazarus, den Jesus liebte (ὃν φιλεῖς 11:3; ἠγάπα δὲ ὁ 'Ιησοῦς ... καὶ τὸν Λάζαρον 11:5), und der als Glaubender lebt, selbst wenn er stirbt (11:25—6; 21:20ff.), jener 'Jünger' ist, 'den Jesus liebte', neue Beachtung. Selbst wenn der hochsymbolische Charakter sowohl der Lazaruserzählung als auch der Lieblingsjüngertexte einer platten Identifikation beider Figuren widerrät, ist doch ihre Nähe kaum zufällig.[28] Zwar klingt mir das Urteil: 'Von daher dürfte sich die Suche nach einer johanneischen Grundschrift als überflüssig erweisen: Diese "Grundschrift" sind die Synoptiker in ihrer heutigen Gestalt. Johannes ist die älteste Synoptikerharmonie mit Überbietungsabsicht als die Evangelienmeditation des Lazarus [sic!]. Nicht umsonst wird noch Joh 20:7, 9 erinnernd der Leser auf 11:24f., 44 zurückverwiesen: Selbst die Ekbasis des Offenbarungsmittlers ist nichts ohne die Anabasis des Offenbarers',[29] allzu sicher. Doch ist es anregend und nötigt zu neuer Diskussion in dieser Sache.

Wie der erste Evangelienteil umgriffen ist von Sendung und Martyria des Täufers, so wäre dann auch der zweite Teil gerahmt von der Auferweckung und Berufung des toten Freundes, den Jesus liebte, und der Frage des auferstandenen Jesus nach der Liebe des Petrus, sowie dem bleibenden Zeugnis des 'Jüngers, den Jesus liebte' (21:15ff.). Dazu würde trefflich stimmen, daß die letzte Woche Jesu genau wie seine erste in ein Schema ausdrücklich gezählter Tage eingefügt wird: Wie nämlich mit dem Auftreten des von Gott gesandten Mannes, Johannes, in 1:19ff. die Tage bis zur Offenbarung der Doxa Jesu vor seinen Jüngern in der Kanahochzeit am sechsten Tag deutlich markiert sind, so beginnt Jesu letzte Woche mit dem Mahl im Hause des Lazarus 'sechs Tage vor dem Passa' (12:1), wegen des 'Dienens' der Martha wohl am Abend nach Ende des Sabbat. Jesu Einzug in Jerusalem (12:12ff.) wäre dann am (Palm-) Sonntag erfolgt, und die Offenbarung seiner Doxa am sechsten Tage, nämlich am Freitag vor Anbruch des Sabbat.[30] Möglicherweise ist auch noch die Lazaruserzählung selbst (vgl. 11:6 und 17!) in ein Sechs-Tage-Schema eingezeichnet. Wegen des nachdrücklichen Hinweises auf die 'Stunde Jesu' in 2:4 muß die Weinspende bei der Kanahochzeit im Zusammenhang mit der lebenstiftenden Spende von Blut und Wasser aus der durchbohrten Seite Jesu bei seiner Kreuzigung gesehen werden.

Bemerkungen zur inneren Gliederung und Auslegung von Johannes 10

1. Da O. Kiefer die innere Kohärenz und Logik des Aufbaus von Joh 9:41 – 10:42 sehr schön aufgewiesen[31] und U. Busse die Zusammengehörigkeit der gesamten beiden Kapitel 9 und 10 in ihrer überlieferten Gestalt klar sichtbar gemacht hat,[32] erübrigen sich alle Umstellungsversuche ebenso wie die verschiedenen Zuweisungen von Partien des Kapitels an eine 'nachjohanneische Redaktion' und deren vermeintlich andersartige 'Theologie'. 10:21 ist die bei Johannes beliebte Figur der 'Wiederaufnahme' des Erzählfadens (Plot) und kein Signal für die Lizenz zur Literarkritik. Nicht einen besseren Text zu konstruieren, sondern den überlieferten zu interpretieren, ist die Aufgabe des Exegeten.

2. Zum textkritischen Problem von 10:7 − hier liest p[75] mit einigen Ägyptern ὁ ποιμήν statt des sonst durchweg bezeugten ἡ θύρα − scheint mir Metzger's Kommentar ausreichend: 'The reading ὁ ποιμήν ... is an early alleviation of the text, introduced by copyists who found the expression "the door of the sheep" too difficult.'[33] Denn abgesehen von der 'lectio-difficilior-Regel' verlangt auch der Aufbau des Diskurses an dieser Stelle ἡ θύρα.[34] Der Einwand, diese Lesart erzwinge gegen den Duktus des gesamten Textes eine 'ekklesiologische Deutung', wonach die christlichen Gemeindeleiter durch Jesus als die 'Tür' zu den Schafen gelangten, scheint mir wenig stichhaltig, denn er verwechselt den hier vorliegenden *symbolischen* mit einem *allegorischen Modus* des Diskurses.[35] Vor allem aber ist die Lesart 'Tür' mit der dem nominalistischen Gottesbegriff Haenchens entsprechenden subordinatianischen Christologie aufgrund von Vers 8 natürlich inkompatibel.

3. Die bekannten Schwierigkeiten bei der Auslegung der Hirtenrede bestehen neben der Frage nach der Identität von 'Dieb', 'Räuber', 'Wolf', 'Fremdem' und 'Mietling' vor allem darin, daß einmal Jesus als der gute Hirte *zugleich* auch die Tür ist, und zum andern, daß diese Tür als der Zugang zu den Schafen *zugleich* auch die Tür als Ein- und Ausgang *für* die Schafe ist. Gegenüber vielerlei ebenso phantasievollen wie überflüssigen Hypothesen[36] hatte dazu schon H. Odeberg 1929 wegweisend bemerkt:

> The difficulties of interpretation are insurmountable as long as the exact identity of the Fold and of the Flock remain undefined or incorrectly defined. The usual identification of the Flock with the Christian Church, or with the specific community behind the Fourth Gospel, does not enable us to explain the sequence of ideas or the coherence of Jesus' sayings. Instead of having recourse to the hypothesis that John has taken over an allegorical discourse, the original elements of which he has not been able to fit in with his own purpose, or similar theories, the correct method is attempting to find an identification that is in keeping with the Johannine spheres of ideas in general and gives unity and coherence to the discourse.
>
> This truth once admitted, it appears that such an attempt need not move within mere guess-work or arbitrary hypotheses. One has only to admit that Jesus in every

self-predicatory utterance speaks of one and the same subject, viz. the spiritual reality, in order to realize that also in 10: 1–18 the subject is: the Divine-spiritual world and Jesus as the all-inclusive centre of that world by virtue of his unity with His Father.[37]

Noch längst vor allen textlinguistischen Überlegungen ist damit gesagt, daß jeder voreilige Schluß aus bestimmten Einzelzügen des Diskurses auf Gegenstände oder Sachverhalte der mutmaßlichen realen 'Außenwelt' in der Regel ein Kurzschluß ist. Und Kurzschlüsse wirken nie erhellend; oft führen sie gar zum Totalausfall des Lichts. Gerade durch die Zerstörung aller unmittelbar ostentativen Züge der Rede auf die Außenwelt und durch ihre neue Indienstnahme als Referenzen auf Züge der jener äußeren entgegengesetzten *Textwelt* wird das literarische Werk überhaupt erst konstituiert. Deshalb muß in geduldigem Eingehen auf ihre Zeichen und Strukturen zunächst diese geheime 'Gegenwelt' rekonstruiert werden, ehe sie dann als *ganze* zur realen Lebenswelt der Leser in Beziehung gesetzt und zur Entdeckung von deren Defiziten wirksam werden kann.

Das alles bestimmende Thema der Hirtenrede ist Jesus als der 'gute Hirte'. Die Reaktion seiner jüdischen Zuhörer zeigt sehr genau, daß sie begreifen, was hier geschieht: Nämlich nichts weniger als eine neue Vertextung der alten *Gottesrede* 'Wider die Hirten Israels' (Ez 34; Jer 23; Sach 11). Darum ist allen Versuchen gegenüber, 'Dieb', 'Räuber', 'Wolf' oder 'Mietling' mit irgendwelchen Figuren der Zeitgeschichte und die 'Herde' mit einer 'johanneischen Gemeinde' identifizieren zu wollen, äußerste Skepsis geboten. Abgesehen davon, daß sich Jesu aktuelle Zuhörer auf der literarischen Bühne, deren wölfisches Wesen der Leser ja gerade an ihrem Umgang mit dem Blindgeborenen und seinen Eltern erkennen konnte, diesen Schuh natürlich anziehen sollen, dienen alle in der Rede neben dem guten Hirten genannten Aktanten einzig dazu, ihn unverwechselbar zu profilieren. 'Das Material, mit dem das Verhalten des Hirten beschrieben wird, (ist) deutlich einem Anschauungskomplex entnommen, den die Mischna (Schebuot 8 und Baba Mezia 7) bietet. Da treffen wir unter den vier Arten von Hütern ... den Lohnhüter ... Da wird darüber verhandelt, ob es ein Zwangsunfall ist, wenn ein Wolf kommt, d.h. ob der Hüter schadenersatzpflichtig ist, wenn der Wolf ein Schaf raubt ... Da erscheint der Dieb, der stiehlt und schlachtet, und der Räuber, der im Gegensatz zum Dieb bewaffnet ist ... Im Gegensatz zum feigen Lohnhüter, der sogar wegläuft wenn *ein* Wolf kommt, obwohl er ihn abzuwehren verpflichtet ist, wagt der gute Hirte für seine Schafe das Leben. Im Gegensatz zum schwachen Lohnhüter, dem der stärkere Räuber das Schaf entreißt, ist Jesus der Hirte, aus dessen Hand niemand und nichts die Schafe reißen kann. — Es ist deutlich, daß hinter den Worten des Evangelisten der in der Mischna vorliegende Anschauungskomplex als Voraussetzung liegt.'[38]

Darauf, daß die Rede von einem *guten* Hirten einzig rabbinisch und nirgends sonst zu belegen ist, hat unter Verweis auf Billerbeck (II/536ff.) schon früh P. Fiebig hingewiesen.[39] Die johanneische Pointe besteht, wie Odeberg zutreffend betont,[40] freilich nicht in der durch die Hirtenrede aufgebauten Qualifikation Jesu als eines *guten* Hirten, so daß der bestimmte Artikel ὁ ποιμὴν ὁ καλός in den Versen 11 und 14 generisch zu verstehen wäre, sondern in ihrer Ausschließlichkeit. Der bestimmte Artikel vertritt also eine particula exclusiva. In der jüdischen Überlieferung gelten zumal Mose und David als gute Hirten der Herde Israels.[41] Daß gerade um die Rolle Moses die Auseinandersetzung im Johannesevangelium geführt wird, indiziert schon der Prolog (1:17; vgl. 3:14; 5:45–6; 6:32; 7:22–3; 9:28–9).[42] Die wegen ihrer signifikanten Verknüpfung der Metaphern von der 'Tür' und vom 'Hirten', sowie des 'Hirten' mit Gott nächste Parallele zu Joh 10, nämlich Mekhilta 13b. 14a, hat Odeberg (*Fourth Gospel*, 138–9) vollständig zitiert.

4. Die nachdrückliche zeitliche Zäsur in 10:22 mit der Nennung des winterlichen Tempelweihfestes und Jesu erneutem Auftreten im *Tempel* (vgl. 2:14ff. und 8:12ff.) gliedert Joh 9:39–10:42 in zwei große, wenn auch untereinander vielfach und eng verbundene Abschnitte, nämlich 9:39–10:21 und 10:22–42. Natürlich ist ἐγκαίνια (10:22) jedem kundigen Leser des Johannesevangeliums mehr als bloße Zeitangabe. Er weiß seit 2:21, daß Jesus, der hier in der 'Halle Salomos' wandelt, in Person der wahre Tempel, Gottes Wohnen bei seinem Volk ist, und daß mit Jesu Verherrlichung die definitive ἐγκαίνια bevorsteht, auf die die alte nur hinweisendes Zeichen sein kann. Darum spielt denn auch die Tempelzerstörung im Jahre 70 bei Johannes keine Rolle (vgl. aber immerhin 11:48!).

Der erste große Abschnitt (9:39–10:21) läßt sich folgendermaßen gliedern: I. Die *Paroimia* von der Tür und vom Hirten (9:39–10:6) — II. Die Deutung der *Paroimia* durch Jesu Selbstidentifikation mit ihren leitenden Metaphern 'Tür' (10:7–10) und 'Hirte' (10:11–18) — III. Erneutes 'Schisma' (vgl. 7:43 und 9:16) unter den Juden als

Reaktion (10:19—21). Hinter der *Paroimia* und ihrer Deutung (9:39 — 10:18) dürfte Mk 4:1ff.; Mt 13:3ff. stehen. Und zwar nicht allein schon deshalb, weil da einer Parabel ihre *Deutung* folgt, sondern vor allem wegen Mk 4:10—13; Mt 13:10ff. vor dem Hintergrund von Jes 6:9—10. Denn in unüberhörbarem Anklang an den Jesajatext ist die *Paroimia* gerahmt von Jesu Betonung der *bleibenden Sünde* der sich *sehend* wähnenden *blinden* Pharisäer und dem Kommentar des Erzählers, daß sie *nicht verstehen*, was Jesus ihnen durch die *Paroimia* sagen wollte (10:6). Im übrigen hat Johannes genauer als Matthäus die Pointe der markinischen Parabel verstanden und daß das μυστήριον τῆς βασιλείας Jesus selbst in Person ist (vgl. Mk 8:14—21 und dazu Joh 6!), verstanden. Darum muß er — wie in Kapitel 6 das Brot — hier den 'Logos' der markinischen Parabeldeutung mit dem ἐγώ Jesu identifizieren.

Das nach 7:43 und 9:19 erneute 'Schisma' im Umkreis des Laubhüttenfestes, das Jesu Rede unter seinen jüdischen Zuhörern bewirkt (10:19—21), zeigt neben deutlichen Anklängen an Mk 3:21—2 einerseits die Erinnerung an die Blindenheilung von Kapitel 9, andererseits aber durch die absichtsvoll pluralische Formulierung τυφλῶν ὀφθαλμοὺς ἀνοῖξαι (10:21) einen Rückbezug auf das erste Rahmenstück (9:39—41): Das 'Schisma' zeigt, einige der Pharisäer sind ihrer Blindheit innegeworden und damit im Begriff, Sehende zu werden.

Daß und wie in dem zweiten großen Abschnitt, der Szene am Tempelweihfest (10:22—42), u.a. das synoptische Verhör Jesu vor dem Synhedrium verarbeitet ist, hat M. Sabbe eindrucksvoll gezeigt.[43] Schauplatz dafür ist nicht zufällig der Tempel. Sagt Jesus doch in dem fast privaten Gespräch mit Hannas,[44] das bei Johannes an die Stelle des offiziellen Verhörs getreten ist, nachdrücklich: ἐγὼ παρρησίᾳ λελάληκα τῷ κόσμῳ, ἐγὼ πάντοτε ἐδίδαξα ἐν συναγωγῇ (vgl. 6:26ff.) καὶ ἐν τῷ ἱερῷ (vgl. 2:14ff.; 5:14; 7:14ff.; 8:12ff. und 10:22ff.), ὅπου πάντες οἱ Ἰουδαῖοι συνέρχονται, καὶ ἐν κρυπτῷ ἐλάλησα οὐδέν (18:20; vgl. Lk 21:37—8).

Auch dieser zweite Teil hat drei Glieder: I. das 'Verhör Jesu' (22—9) — II. Die Versuche, ihn zu steinigen (31) und zu verhaften (39), rahmen die erneute Apologie seines göttlichen Wesens unter Rückgriff auf die Schrift (31—9). — III. Jesus entzieht sich seinen Verfolgern und begibt sich an den Ort der ersten Täufermartyria ins peräische Bethanien, wo viele an ihn glaubten (40—2).[45] Das Spiel mit der Differenz zwischen erzählter Zeit und Erzählzeit erlaubt die Wiederaufnahme und Weiterführung der Hirtenmetaphorik (26ff.).

Die in den Augen der Juden blasphemische Konklusion Jesu: ἐγὼ καὶ ὁ πατὴρ ἕν ἐσμεν (30), erfordert als ihren 'Witz' die Parallelität der Verse 28 und 29. Darum ist in Vers 29 an den beiden strittigen Stellen das Maskulinum zu lesen, also ὅς und μείζων, und als Objekt des Satzes ist das αὐτά aus Vers 28 zu ergänzen.[46]

Das sich in der Steinigungsabsicht und dem Vorwurf der Blasphemie äußernde 'Mißverständnis' der Juden (31ff.) beruht natürlich nicht darauf, daß sie Jesu bloße 'Handlungseinheit' mit dem Vater mit einer 'Wesenseinheit' verwechseln[47] – eine m.E. absolut anachronistische Fragestellung –, sondern wie sonst im Evangelium darauf, daß sie ihn für einen bloßen Menschen (ἄνθρωπος ὤν V. 33) halten, für einen, der 'sich selbst zu Gott machen will', was er doch schon von Ewigkeit her ist. Bei Johannes ist Jesu Menschwerdung das Prädikat seiner Gottheit, und nicht umgekehrt: 'Nur als Gottessohn, aber eben als solcher, existiert Jesus Christus auch menschlich'.[48]

Darum darf das folgende Psalmzitat (Ps 82:6) auch nicht so verstanden werden, als verteidige Jesus hier seinen doch vergleichsweise bescheidenen eigenen Anspruch, der '*Sohn* Gottes' zu sein, damit, daß schließlich die Schrift, die doch wohl keiner seiner Zuhörer außer Kraft setzen wolle, Israels Richter sogar '*Götter*' genannt habe, und das doch gewiß nicht wegen deren 'Wesenseinheit' mit Gott, sondern allein aufgrund ihres richterlichen *Amtes* vor Gottes heiligem Gesetz.[49] Ehe man zu solcher vorgeblich rabbinischen Exegese von Psalm 82 seine Zuflucht nimmt, sollte genauer geprüft werden, was Johannes sagt. Da *werden* nicht 'Israels Richter', sondern da *wurden* diejenigen, πρὸς οὓς ὁ λόγος τοῦ θεοῦ ἐγένετο (10:35), 'Götter' genannt. Innerhalb der Textwelt des Johannesevangeliums ist man geneigt, das als Schluß 'vom Leichteren aufs Schwere' so zu verstehen: Wenn schon die, an die der Logos Gottes einst erging, im übertragenen Sinne – duldet das 'Höre Israel' doch keine Einschränkung! – 'Götter' genannt wurden, um wieviel mehr muß dann der in Wahrheit 'Sohn Gottes' sein, in dem dieser Logos endlich in Zeit und Geschichte erschienen ist! Mit der Differenz zwischen 'Gott' und 'Sohn Gottes' sollte man übrigens nicht spielen, denn der Psalm sagt im Parallelismus membrorum: ἐγὼ εἶπα Θεοί ἐστε / καὶ υἱοὶ ὑψίστου πάντες. Er fährt dann aber fort, indem er dieser 'göttlichen Vergangenheit' eine ganz und gar 'menschliche' Gegenwart und Zukunft gegenüberstellt: ὑμεῖς δὲ ὡς ἄνθρωποι ἀποθνῄσκετε / καὶ ὡς εἷς τῶν ἀρχόντων πίπτετε (Ps 82:6f.). Dies Todesgeschick, das über die einst 'Götter' Geheißenen gekommen ist, hat offenbar mit ihrem Verhalten dem Logos gegenüber zu tun, der an sie erging, damit, daß sie ihn nicht aufnahmen, als er in sein Eigentum kam (1:11), so daß sie nun 'in ihren Sünden sterben müssen' (8:21). Doch: die ihn aufnahmen, denen gab er die Vollmacht, Gottes Kinder zu werden, denen, die seine Stimme hören, gibt der gute Hirte das 'ewige Leben'.[50]

NOTES

1 Open questions on John 10

1 R. Schnackenburg, *Das Johannesevangelium* IV. 4, HThK IV. 4 (Freiburg, 1984), 131–43, discusses the most recent literature on John 10. Therefore it does not need to be mentioned here. Like E. Haenchen, *Das Johannes-evangelium. Ein Kommentar*, ed. U. Busse (Tübingen, 1980), 393, he also emphasises the numerous difficulties in interpreting the text properly.

2 The questions of predestination and also that of the 'Jews' are too extensive to be dealt with here. This is no attempt, however, to push them aside.

3 Thus J. Becker, *Das Evangelium des Johannes* 1, ÖTK 4/1 (Gütersloh/ Würzburg, 1979), 311; A. Becker, 'Über die Komposition des JE', *ThStKr*, 62 (1889), 117–40, 139; R. Bultmann, *Das Evangelium des Johannes*, KEK 2, 20th edn (Göttingen, 1941), 236; W. Langbrandtner, *Weltferner Gott oder Gott der Liebe* (Frankfurt, 1977), 46; F. Spitta, 'Die Hirtengleichnisse des vierten Evangeliums untersucht mit besonderer Berücksichtigung der neuesten Kritik', *ZNW*, 10 (1909), 59–80, 103–27, 63; idem, *Das Johannes-Evangelium als Quelle der Geschichte Jesu* (Göttingen, 1910), 209f.; H. Windisch, *Johannes und die Synoptiker*, UNT 12 (Leipzig, 1926), 65; idem, 'Der johanneische Erzählungsstil', *Eucharisterion, FS H. Gunkel*, ed. H. Schmidt; FRLANT n.s. 19 (Göttingen, 1923), II, 196; J. Schneider, *Das Evangelium nach Johannes*, 2nd edn (Berlin, 1978), 196; J. Wellhausen, *Das Evangelium Johannis* (Berlin, 1908), p. 47; J. H. Bernard, *A Critical and Exegetical Commentary on the Gospel According to St. John*, 2 vols., ed. A. H. McNeile (New York, 1929), I, xxiv f.; B. Bauer, *Kritik der evangelischen Geschichte des Johannes* (Bremen, 1840), 367; J. M. Thompson, 'Accidental Disarrangement in the Fourth Gospel', *Exp.*, 8 (1919), 47–54, 52; J. Jeremias, 'Johanneische Literarkritik', *ThBl*, 20 (1941), 33–46, 42; B. W. Bacon, *Jesus and Paul* (London: 1921), 226, note 2; idem, *The Gospel of the Hellenists*, ed. C. H. Kraeling (New York, 1933), 271–3; E. Schweizer, *Ego Eimi. Die religionsgeschichtliche Herkunft und theologische Bedeutung der johanneischen Bildreden*, FRLANT n.s. 38, 2nd edn (Göttingen, 1965), 141, 143; R. Bultmann, 'Hirsch's Auslegung des Johannes-Evangeliums', *EvTh*, 4, (1937), 115–42, 126; W. Soltau, *Das vierte Evangelium in seiner Entstehungsge-schichte dargelegt*, SHAW.PH 6. Abh. (Heidelberg, 1916), 10; M. Dibelius, 'Johannesevangelium', *RGG²* III (Tübingen, 1929), 349–63, 356; and others.

4 Cf. those mentioned in note 3 and also R. T. Fortna, 'Theological Use of Locale in the Fourth Gospel', *Gospel Studies in Honour of S. E. Johnson*,

AThR Suppl. Ser. 3; ed. M. H. Shepherd and E. C. Hobbs (Evanston: 1974), 58–95, 64; C. R. Bowen, 'The Fourth Gospel as Dramatic Material', *JBL*, 49 (1930), 292–305, 295; F. Hahn, 'Die Hirtenrede in Joh 10', *Theologia Crucis – Signum Crucis, FS E. Dinkler*, ed. C. Andresen and G. Klein (Tübingen, 1979), 185–200, 186.

5 Cf. Thompson, 'Disarrangement', 52; W. F. Howard/A. J. Gossip, *The Gospel According to St. John*, IntB VIII (New York/Nashville, 1952), 620f.; Bernard, *John*, xxivf.; and Jeremias, 'Literarkritik', 42; E. Schweizer, *Ego Eimi*, 141–51. F. R. Hoare, *The Original Order and Chapters of St. John's Gospel* (London, 1944), 129–31, 136, and Bultmann, *Evangelium*, 272ff. make far-reaching rearrangements; also Hoare on arithmetical grounds (exchange of sheets) and Bultmann, for the sake of harmonising his Johannine theology in terms of theological content.

6 Cf. A. Schweizer, *Das Evangelium Johannes nach seinem innern Werthe und seiner Bedeutung für das Leben Jesu kritisch untersucht* (Leipzig, 1841) and C. H. Weiße, *Die evangelische Geschichte kritisch und philosophisch bearbeitet*, 2 vols. (Leipzig, 1838), Book I, 103ff. and Book VI, 138–304.

7 See H. H. Wendt, *Die Lehre Jesu*, 2nd edn (Göttingen, 1901), 273f., 285; idem, *Das Johannesevangelium. Eine Untersuchung seiner Entstehung und seines geschichtlichen Wertes* (Göttingen, 1900), 138ff.; and idem, *Die Schichten im vierten Evangelium* (Göttingen, 1911), 43–9, 70f., 132–6.

8 Becker, *Johannes*, 311, and Langbrandtner, *Gott*, 46.

9 Cf. G. Richter, *Studien zum Johannesevangelium*, BU 13, ed. J. Hainz (Regensburg, 1977), 385; W. Heitmüller, *Das Evangelium des Johannes*, SNT vol. 2 (Göttingen, 1908), 799 and D. Völter, 'Grundlage und Überarbeitung im Evangelium des Johannes', *TThT*, 8 (1910), 447–93, 461.

10 Thus J. D. Schulze, *Der schriftstellerische Character und Werth des Johannes, zum Behuf der Specialhermeneutik seiner Schriften untersucht und bestimmt*, 2nd edn (Weißenfels and Leipzig, 1811), 78, 80; T. A. Seyfarth, *Ein Beitrag zur Special-Characteristik der Johanneischen Schriften besonders des Johanneischen Evangeliums* (Leipzig, 1823), 189; C. Weizsäcker, *Untersuchung über die evangelische Geschichte, ihre Quellen und den Gang ihrer Entwicklung*, 2nd edn, ed. A. Bilfinger (Tübingen, 1901), 163; M. de Jonge, 'Jesus as Prophet and King in the Fourth Gospel', *EThL*, 49 (1973), 160–77, 165; J. P. Martin, 'John 10, 1–10', *Interp*. 32 (1978), 171–5, 171; Windisch, 'Erzählungsstil', 196; Fischer, 'Über den Ausdruck Ἰουδαῖοι im Evangelium Johannis. Ein Beitrag zur Charakteristik desselben', *TZTh*, 11 (1840), 96–133, 100; B. Bauer, *Kritik*, 384; A. D. Loman, 'De bouw van het vierde evangelie', *ThT*, 11 (1877), 371–437, 417; A. Wild, 'Disposition und Zusammenhang des Logos-Evangeliums nach Johannes', *Jahrbuch der historischen Gesellschaft Züricher Theologen*, ed. G. Volkmar, vol. I (1877), 17–92, 66; G. Delling, *Der Kreuzestod Jesu in der urchristlichen Verkündigung* (Göttingen, Zürich, 1972), 98; A. Hilgenfeld, 'Das neueste Forscher-Paar über das Johannes-Evangelium', *ZWTh*, 28 (1885), 393–425, 402; Anonym (J. R. Tobler), *Die Evangelienfrage im Allgemeinen und die Johannisfrage insbesondere* (Zürich, 1858), 59; C. Weizsäcker, 'Beiträge zur Charakteristik des johanneischen Evangeliums', *JDTh*, 4 (1859), 685–767, 701; E. Schweizer, 'Jesus der Zeuge Gottes. Zum Problem des Doketismus im Johannesevangelium', *Studies in John. FS J. N. Sevenster*

(Leiden, 1970), 161–8, 163 (here Schweizer takes a different view from his earlier book *Ego Eimi*).

11 Division: 6: 52; 7: 43f.; 9: 16; 11: 54f.; intention to kill: 5: 18; 7: 20; intention to arrest: 7: 3, 32; 8: 20; 10: 39; intention to stone: 8: 59; 10: 31–3; 11: 8; charge of being possessed: 7: 20; 8: 48, 52.

12 F. C. Baur, *Kritische Untersuchungen über die kanonischen Evangelien, ihr Verhältnis zu einander, ihren Charakter und Ursprung* (Tübingen, 1847), 180; = idem, 'Über die Composition und den Charakter des johanneischen Evangeliums', *ThJb (T)*, 3 (1844), 1–191, 397–475, 615–700, 122f.; likewise K. R. Köstlin, 'Die pseudonyme Litteratur der ältesten Kirche', *ThJb (T)*, 10 (1851), 189; H. J. Holtzmann, 'Über die Disposition des vierten Evangeliums', *ZWTh*, 24 (1881), 257–90, 283; Tobler, *Evangelienfrage*, 59.

13 Even Spitta, *Johannesevangelium*, 213, who makes this observation, does not pay enough attention to it; cf. B. F. Westcott, *The Gospel According to St. John: The Authorised Version with Introduction and Notes* (London, 1920), 152, who speaks of the 'idea of separation' which he thinks is part of the parable's meaning.

14 In chapters 9–11 the 'Pharisees' constantly alternate with the 'Jews'.

15 Cf. the Johannine presentation of the 'Pharisees' as leaders: 1: 19; 3: 1; 7: 32, 45, 47f.; 9: 13; 11: 46f., 57; 12: 19, 42; 18: 3.

16 Read: C. T. Bretschneider, *Probabilia de Evangelii et Epistolarum Joannis Apostoli, indole et origine eruditorum judiciis modeste subjecit* (Leipzig, 1820), 20, 'Allegoria autem pastoris et ovium in V. et NT tam usitata est, ut nunquam necesse sit illam certae occasioni tribuere.' Already F. C. Bauer, *Untersuchungen*, 181, pointed to the proximity of the shepherd's motif; for the picture of the shepherd in the OT see the recent article: S. Mittmann, 'Aufbau und Einheit des Danklieds Psalm 23', *ZThK*, 77 (1980), 20f. and note 55, as well as B. Willmes, *Die sogenannte Hirtenallegorie Ez 34: Studien zum Bild des Hirten im AT*, BBET 19 (Frankfurt, 1984). The image of the shepherd is also found in hellenistic ideologies concerning the King: cf. only Dio Chry. I, 13–19. 28.

17 Thus H. Strathmann, *Das Evangelium nach Johannes*, NTD 4; 11th edn (Göttingen, 1968), 149, and W. Bousset, 'Johannesevangelium', *RGG¹ III* (Tübingen, 1912), 608–36, 619.

18 Cf. Strathmann, *Evangelium*, 149; E. Hoskyns, *The Fourth Gospel*, 2nd edn, ed. F. N. Davey (London, 1947), 366; Hahn, 'Hirtenrede', 195; A. H. Franke, 'Die Anlage des Johannes-Evangeliums', *ThStKr*, 57 (1884), 80–154, 119; B. Lindars, 'The Passion in the Fourth Gospel', *God's Christ and his People, FS N. A. Dahl*, ed. J. Jervell and W. A. Meeks (Oslo, 1977), 71–86, 80; H. Grotius, *Annotationes in Evangelium* κατα Ιωαννην (Amsterdam, 1679; reprint Stuttgart, 1972), II, 526; F. A. Lampe, *Commentarius Analytico-Exegeticus tam literalis quam realis Evangelii secundum Joannem*, vols. I–III (Basel, 1725–7), II, 609; F. Lücke, *Commentar über das Evangelium des Johannes*, 2nd edn (Bern, 1833–4), 342; O. Holtzmann, *Das Johannesevangelium untersucht und erklärt* (Darmstadt, 1887), 246.

19 Thus Hahn, 'Hirtenrede', 195 note 34; idem, 'Der Prozeß Jesu nach dem Johannesevangelium', *EKK. V*, 2 (1970), 23–96, 63; Schulze, *Charakter und Werth*, 233; A. Jülicher, *Einleitung in das Neue Testament*, 6th edn (Tübingen, 1906), 349; E. W. Hengstenberg, *Das Evangelium des heiligen*

Johannes erläutert, 3 vols (Berlin, 1867, 1869, 1870), vol. II, 156; Franke, 'Anlage', 119; Martin, 'Joh 10, 1–10', 171; C. T. Kuinoel, *Commentarius in libros Novi Testamenti historicos*, 4 vols., 3rd edn (Leipzig, 1823, 1818, 1824, 1825), vol. III, 487.

20 De Jonge, 'Prophet and King', 165; Windisch, *Johannes und die Synoptiker*, 60; G. Volkmar, 'Ein neu entdecktes Zeugnis für das Johannes-Evangelium', *ThJb (T)*, 13 (1854), 446–62, 452; Holtzmann, 'Disposition', 280; W. Hönig, 'Die Construction des vierten Evangeliums', *ZWTh*, 14 (1871), 535–66, 555f.; Loman, 'Bouw', 377; Wild, 'Disposition', 66; J. H. Neyrey, 'John III – A Debate over Johannine Epistemology and Christology, *NT*, 23 (1981), 115–27, 118; Baur, 'Composition', 123; C. E. Luthardt, *Die vier Evangelien verdeutscht und gemeinverständlich ausgelegt*, 4 vols., part IV: Das Evangelium des Johannes (Leipzig, 1899), 131; Heitmüller, *Evangelium*, 798; C. H. Dodd, *The Interpretation of the Fourth Gospel* (Cambridge, 1954), 358 ff.; Hahn, 'Prozeß', 28, 80.; O. Pfleiderer, *Das Urchristentum, seine Schriften und Lehren, in geschichtlichem Zusammenhang* (Berlin, 1887), II, 396; Lindars, 'Passion', 72; B. Jacobi, 'Über die Data zur Chronologie des Lebens Jesu in dem Evangelium des Johannes', *ThStKr*, 11 (1838), 845–916, 869; Weizsäcker, *Untersuchungen*, 166; Hilgenfeld, 'Forscher-Paar', 402; idem, 'Die neueste Evangelienforschung. I. Willibald Beyschlag und das Johannesevangelium', *ZWTh*, 20 (1877), 1–33, 29; H. J. Holtzmann, 'Unordnungen und Umordnungen im vierten Evangelium', *ZNW*, 3 (1902), 50–60, 54; B. Lindars, 'The Son of Man in the Johannine Christology', *Christ and Spirit in the New Testament*. FS C. F. D. Moule, ed. B. Lindars and S. S. Smalley (Cambridge, 1973), 43–60, 55; C. K. Barrett, *The Gospel According to St. John*, 2nd edn (London, 1978), 367; R. Kysar, *John's Story of Jesus* (Philadelphia, 1984), 51; R. H. Lightfoot, *St. John's Gospel. A Commentary*, ed. C. F. Evans (Oxford/London, 1956), 205; L. T. Brodie, 'Creative Rewriting: Key to a New Methodology', SBL.SP (1978), vol. II, 261–7, 264; W. A. Meeks, 'The Divine Agent and his Counterfeit in Philo and the Fourth Gospel', *Aspects of Religious Propaganda in Judaism and Early Christianity*, ed. E. Schüssler-Fiorenza (Notre Dame and London, 1976), 43–67, 55.

21 D. F. Strauß, *Das Leben Jesu, kritisch bearbeitet* (Tübingen, 1835), II, 376; H. J. Holtzmann, 'Disposition', 283; Windisch, *Johannes und die Synoptiker*, 82.

22 Cf. Martin, 'John 10, 1–10', 171; Weizsäcker, *Untersuchungen*, 160; H. J. Holtzmann, 'Die Gnosis und das johanneische Evangelium', *Die Anfänge des Christentums*, 7 (Berlin, 1877), 112–34, 120; Windisch, *Johannes und die Synoptiker*, 60, 82; Hahn, 'Prozeß', 62, 64, 68, 80, 84; W. Reiser, 'The Case of the Tidy Tomb: The Place of the Napkins of John 11, 44 and 20, 7', *HeyJ*, 14 (1973), 47–57, 53f.; G. W. Broomefield, 'John and Luke', *John, Peter and the Fourth Gospel* (London, 1934), 108–45, 125; Delling, *Kreuzestod*, 98; Windisch, 'Erzählungsstil', 201; R. Fuller, 'The "Jews" in the Fourth Gospel', *Dialog*, 16 (1977), 31–7, 34.

23 Lindars, 'Passion', 72; Hahn, 'Prozeß', 64f.; Meeks, 'Agent', 56; H. J. Holtzmann, 'Unordnungen und Umordnungen', 54; Windisch, 'Erzählungsstil', 201.

24 Vgl. P. W. Schmiedel, 'John, Son of Zebedee', *Encyclopaedia Biblica*, vol. II (London, 1891), 2502–62, 2530; Lindars, 'Passion', 80f.; Bousset, 'Johannesevangelium', 633; Hahn, 'Prozeß', 47; H. J. Holtzmann, 'Gnosis', 120.

25 Cf. Wendt, *Lehre Jesu*, 274; Bultmann, 'Hirsch's Auslegung', 125; Dibelius, 'Johannesevangelium', 352.

26 Haenchen, *Johannesevangelium*, 57; the following are against rearrangements: H. J. Holtzmann, 'Unordnungen und Umordnungen', 55, 59; Jülicher, *Einleitung*, 313; Hahn, 'Prozeß', 68; D. J. Hawkin, 'Orthodoxy and Heresy in John 10, 1–10 and 15, 1–17', *EvQ*, 47 (1975), 208–13, 209; Schmiedel, 'John', 2529; Lindars, 'Son of Man', 56 note 30.

27 Bultmann, *Evangelium*.

28 Thus B. M. Metzger, *A Textual Commentary on the Greek New Testament* (London/New York, 1971), 229; R. Schnackenburg, *Das Johannesevangelium* II, HThK 4.2 (Freiburg, 1971), 363f.; Barrett, *Gospel*, 370; W. Bauer, *Das Johannesevangelium*, HNT 6 (Tübingen, 1933), 139; R. E. Brown, *The Gospel According to John*, 2 vols (Garden City, 1966, 1970), I, 386; Hoskyns, *Gospel*, 373.

29 Thus Schnackenburg, *Johannesevangelium*, vol. II, 363; Heitmüller, *Evangelium*, 798–800; H. J. Holtzmann, *Evangelium, Briefe und Offenbarung des Johannes*, HC 4, 2nd edn (Freiburg/Leipzig, 1893), 146; O. Holtzmann, *Johannesevangelium*, 246f.; Lightfoot, *Gospel*, 210; J. F. O'Grady, 'Individualism and Johannine Ecclesiology', *BThB*, 5 (1975), 227–61, 241; H. J. Holtzmann, 'Disposition', 283; Langbrandtner/Becker see note 3.

30 B. Bauer, *Kritik*, 375, 377, 382; cf. also N. Walter, 'Die Auslegung überlieferter Wundererzählungen im Johannes-Evangelium', *Theologische Versuche*, II (Berlin, 1970), 93–107, 104 note 17; W. Soltau, 'Die Reden des vierten Evangeliums', *ZNW*, 17 (1916), 49–60, 53, 56; W. Bauer, *Johannesevangelium*, 139; B. Weiß, 'Rez.: W. Bäumlein, 'Kommentar über das Evangelium des Johannes' (Stuttgart, 1863), *ThStKr*, 38 (1865), 201–12, 208; W. A. Meeks, 'The Man from Heaven in Johannine Sectarianism', *JBL*, 91 (1972), 44–72, 65; Weiße, *Geschichte*, vol. VI, 254f.; K. L. Schmidt, 'Der johanneische Charackter der Erzählung vom Hochzeitswunder in Kana', *Beiträge zur Kirchengeschichte, Harnack-Ehrung* (Leipzig, 1921), 32–43, 41 note 1.

31 The following assume a copying mistake from an Aramaic Vorlage: C. C. Torrey, *The Four Gospels* (London, 1933), 108, 111–13; E. C. Broome, 'The Source of the Fourth Gospel', *JBL*, 63 (1944), 107–121, 116; and M. Black, *An Aramaic Approach to the Gospels and Acts* (Oxford, 1946), 193 note 1. In favour of viewing it as a stylistic device: E. Stange, *Die Eigenart der johanneischen Produktion* (Dresden, 1915), 16; J. Muilenburg, 'Literary Form in the Fourth Gospel', *JBL*, 51 (1932), 40–53, 45 note 24; Hoskyns, *Gospel*, 373.

32 Schnackenburg, *Johannesevangelium*, vol. II, 363.

33 Cf. 1 Clem 48, 4; Hermas, Sim. IX, 2, 12; X, 7, 9; Ign. Philad. 9, 1.2; Origenes, Philosophumena V, c. 16; Euseb. H. E. II. 23; pseudo-clem. Hom. III, 52; Tertullian, Adv. Marcionem III, 24; cf. J. Hellwag, 'Die Vorstellung von der Präexistenz Christi in der ältesten Kirche', *ThJb (T)*,

7 (1848), 144–61, 227–63, 257 note 1; Weiße, *Geschichte*, vol. VI, 255; and H. J. Holtzmann, 'Hermas und Johannes', *ZWTh*, 18 (1875), 47, writes: 'But precisely the concept of Christ as a door became in time a fixed element in Christian symbolism.'

34 Thus also Wellhausen, *Evangelium*, 48f.; E. Schwartz, 'Aporien im vierten Evangelium', NGWG.PH (1908), III, 149–88, 163f.; E. Schweizer, *Ego Eimi*, 142f.; Haenchen, *Johannesevangelium*, 388.

35 Thus also: Lindars, 'Son of Man', 55; idem, 'Passion', 80; H. J. Holtzmann, 'Unordnungen und Umordnungen', 55; P. S. Minear, 'The Audience of the Fourth Gospel', *Interp.*, 31 (1977), 339–54, 348; A. Schweizer, *Evangelium*, 30; Pfleiderer, *Urchristentum*, 368f.; W. Soltau, 'Reden', 57; idem, 'Das Problem des Johannesevangeliums und der Weg zu seiner Lösung', *ZNW*, 16 (1915), 24–53, 37; B. W. Bacon, 'The Johannine Problem', *HibJ*, 3 (1905), 353–75, 362; E. Reuss, 'Ideen zur Einleitung in das Evangelium Johannis', *Denkschrift der Theologischen Gesellschaft zu Strassburg*, 1 (1828–39), (Strassburg 1840), 7–60, 53; Strauß, *Leben Jesu*, I 653f.; Westcott, *Gospel*, 151.

36 Cf. Weiße, *Geschichte*, vol. VI, 254; Wild, 'Disposition', 66; E. Luthardt, ' Ἔργον τοῦ θεοῦ und πίστις in ihrem gegenseitigen Verhältnis nach der Darstellung des johanneischen Evangeliums', *ThStKr*, 25 (1852), 333–74, 346; Köstlin, 'Pseudonyme Literatur', 198; A. Schlatter, 'Der Bruch mit der Judenschaft (Joh 6 und 5), *Aus Schrift und Geschichte, FS Conrad von Orelli* (Basel, 1898), 1–23, 8; D. Schenkel, *Das Christusbild der Apostel und der nachapostolischen Zeit aus den Quellen dargestellt* (Leipzig, 1879), 183; B. Bauer, *Kritik*, 370.

37 Soltau, 'Entstehungsgeschichte', 10; J. F. O'Grady, 'Johannine Ecclesiology: A Critical Evaluation', *BThB* 7 (1977), 36–44, 40; Bousset, 'Johannesevangelium', 625.

38 Baur, 'Composition', 122.

39 A. Thoma, 'Das Alte Testament im Johannes-Evangelium', *ZWTh*, 22 (1879), 18–66, 171–223, 273–312, 202; Weizsäcker, *Untersuchungen*, 160; idem, 'Charakteristik', 757; M. Eberhardt, *Ev. Joh cap. 21 – Ein exegetischer Versuch als Beitrag zur johanneischen Frage* (Leipzig, 1897), 53; A. Hausrath, *Neutestamentliche Zeitgeschichte* (Heidelberg, 1877), vol. IV, 428; S. Sandmel, *Anti-Semitism in the NT?* (Philadelphia, 1978), 101–19, 110; J. Kreyenbühl, 'Kritische Randglossen zu Wellhausen's "Evangelium Johannis" ', *SThZ*, 30 (1913), 203; B. Bauer, *Kritik*, 370, 384; Luthardt, *Die vier Evangelien*, 127, 131; E. Schweizer, *Ego Eimi*, 146; Heitmüller, *Evangelium*, 798.

40 Strauß, *Leben Jesu*, I, 653; cf. Weizsäcker, *Untersuchungen*, 160; Weiße, *Geschichte*, vol. VI, 254.

41 B. Bauer, *Kritik*, 370.

42 K. Berger, *Formgeschichte des Neuen Testaments* (Heidelberg, 1984), 39.

43 Thus already K. L. Schmidt, 'Charakter', 41.

44 H. J. Holtzmann, 'Unordnungen und Umordnungen', 55; similarly: Hilgenfeld, 'Forscher-Paar', 399; W. Wrede, *Charakter und Tendenz des Johannesevangeliums* (Tübingen/Leipzig, 1903), 193; Reuss, *Ideen zur Einleitung*, 53; Schmiedel, 'John', 2529; Weizsäcker, *Untersuchungen*, 163; Franke,

'Anlage', 119; A. Loisy, *Evangelium und Kirche* (Munich, 1904), 23; E. Haupt, 'Wendts Stellung zur johanneischen Frage', *ThStKr*, 66 (1893), 217–50, 233; Strauß, *Leben Jesu*, I, 654 note 12; B. Bauer, *Kritik*, 392; Lindars, 'Son of Man', 56 note 30.

45 Weizsäcker, 'Charakteristik', 701.

46 So: Bousset, 'Johannesevangelium', 619; Hahn, 'Prozeß', 80, 92 and note 43.

47 There is almost unanimous agreement as to the present eschatology of this text: de Jonge, 'Prophet and King', 107f.; R. Kysar, 'The Eschatology of the Fourth Gospel – A Correction of Bultmann's Redactional Hypothesis', *Perspective*, 13 (1972), 23–33, 24f.; W. Hönig, 'Beiträge zur Aufklärung über das vierte Evangelium', *ZWTh*, 27 (1883), 83–125, 98; C. W. F. Smith, 'Fishers of Men – Footnotes on a Gospel Figure', *HThR*, 52 (1959), 187–203, 198; Meeks, 'Sectarianism', 61; Pfleiderer, *Urchristentum*, 386; C. H. Dodd, 'The Portrait of Jesus in John and in the Synoptics', *Christian History and Interpretation, FS John Knox*, ed. W. R. Farmer, C. F. D. Moule, R. R. Niebuhr (Cambridge, 1967), 183–98, 187; A. E. Garvie, 'The Evangelist's Experimental Reflexions in the Fourth Gospel', *Exp. 8. ser.* 10 (1915), 255–64, 260; Schenkel, 'Christusbild', 388; Bultmann, 'Hirsch's Auslegung', 130; Hahn, 'Hirtenrede', 195; W. R. Inge, 'The Theology of the Fourth Gospel', *Essays on Some Biblical Questions of the Day*, ed. H. B. Swete (London, 1909), 251–88, 282; Richter, *Studien*, 368, 223 note 163; R. T. Fortna, 'From Christology to Soteriology. A Redaction-Critical Study of Salvation in the Fourth Gospel', *Interp.* 27 (1973), 31–47, 44.

48 Cf. H. Windisch, 'Die Verstockungsidee in Mc 4,12 und das kausale ἵνα der späteren Koine', *ZNW*, 26 (1927), 203–9, 209.

49 Thus W. M. L. de Wette, 'Bemerkungen zu Stellen des Evangeliums Johannis', *ThStKr*, 7 (1834), 924–44, 929–31; cf. J. Blank, *Krisis. Untersuchungen zur johanneischen Christologie und Eschatologie* (Freiburg, 1964), 262f.

50 Cf. Dibelius, 'Johannesevangelium', 360; M. Dibelius, 'Die Isisweihe bei Apuleius und verwandte Initiations-Riten', *Botschaft und Geschichte. Gesammelte Aufsätze*, II, ed. H. Kraft/G. Bornkamm (Tübingen, 1956), 78; H. Windisch, 'Die Absolutheit des Johannesevangeliums', *ZSTh*, 5 (1928), 3–54, 9; B. Bauer, *Kritik*, 380.

51 Scholarship offers two options:
    a. Pharisees and chief priests and all teachers after the time of the prophets; Moses, Abraham and the prophets are excluded: Schenkel, 'Christusbild', 377f.; E. Abbot, *A Translation of the Gospels* (ed. C. E. Norton and E. Abbot (Boston, 1856), 1803f.; R. Schnackenburg, 'Das vierte Evangelium und die Johannesjünger', *HJ*, 77 (1958), 21–38, 37; J. B. Lightfoot, 'Internal Evidence for the Authenticity and Genuineness of St. John's Gospel III', *Biblical Essays* (London, 1904), 125–98, 146; B. Jacobi, 'Über die Erhöhung des Menschensohnes Joh 3,14.15', *ThStKr*, 8 (1835), 7–70, 38; Lücke, *Commentar*, 349;
    b. All bearers of revelation in the OT: Windisch, *Johannes und die Synoptiker*, 150; A. Hilgenfeld, 'Das Johannes-Evangelium und die neuesten Schriften von Hofstede de Groot, Keim und Scholten', *ZWTh*, 11 (1868), 213–31, 226; C. Weizsäcker, *Das apostolische Zeitalter der christlichen Kirche*, 3rd edn (Tübingen/Leipzig, 1902),

522; idem, 'Die johanneische Logoslehre', *JDTh*, 7 (1862), 619–708, 677;

c. Pseudo-messiahs and zealots: Grotius, *Annotationes*, and Well-hausen, *Evangelium*.

52 The following rightly agree: J. Wichelhaus, *Akademische Vorlesungen über das Neue Testament. III. Bd.: Das Evangelium des Johannes* ed. A. Zahn (Halle, 1884), 188; Schweizer, *Ego Eimi*, 148; B. Bauer, *Kritik*, 380; J. C. K. von Hofmann, *Die heilige Schrift neuen Testaments zusammenhängend untersucht*, revised by W. Wolck (Nördlingen, 1881), 361; Jülicher, *Einleitung*, 359.

53 In favour of the idea of an atonement offering: B. Bauer, *Kritik*, 385; J. H. Roberts, 'The Lamb of God', *Neotestamentica*, 2 (1968), 41–56, 48. Allusions of this sort are assumed by: M. Dibelius, 'Joh 15, 13. Eine Studie zum Traditionsproblem des Johannes-Evangeliums', *FS A. Deissmann* (Tübingen, 1927), 168–86, 182 note 2; Delling, *Kreuzestod*, 105; U. B. Müller, 'Die Bedeutung des Kreuzestodes im Johannesevangelium', *KuD*, 21 (1975), 49–71, 63. Since the soteriological dimension of Jesus' death could only be perceived in this light by the early generations, owing to their strong cultural roots in the religious world-view, this view is widely held. It is explicitly rejected by H. Thyen, ' "Niemand hat größere Liebe als die, daß er sein Leben für seine Freunde hingibt" (Joh 15, 13). Das johanneische Verständnis des Kreuzestodes Jesu', *Theologia Crucis – Signum Crucis, FS E. Dinkler*, ed. C. Andresen and G. Klein (Tübingen, 1979), 467–81, 476; P. Winter, 'Zum Verständnis des Johannesevangeliums', *VoxTh*, 25 (1955), 149–59, 157; Hahn, 'Prozeß', 26 note 14; C. H. Dodd, 'The First Epistle of John and the Fourth Gospel', *BJRL*, 21 (1937), 129–56, 145; H. H. Cludius, *Uransichten des Christenthums nebst Untersuchungen über einige Bücher des neuen Testaments* (Altona, 1808), 54f.; Schenkel, 'Christusbild', 386.

54 B. de Pinto, 'Word and Wisdom in St. John', *Scrip.*, 19 (1967), 107–22, 117; B. Weiß, *Das Johannesevangelium als einheitliches Werk geschichtlich erklärt* (Berlin, 1912), 196; N. A. Dahl, 'The Johannine Church and History', *Current Issues in New Testament Interpretation: Essays in Honor of O. A. Piper*, ed. W. Klassen (New York, 1962), 124–42, 126.

55 Cf. Bultmann, *Evangelium*, 523.

56 H. J. Holtzmann, 'Das Problem des ersten johanneischen Briefes in seinem Verhältnis zum Evangelium', *JPTh*, 8 (1882), 128–52, 146.

57 So Schenkel, 'Christusbild', 391; W. Baldensperger, *Der Prolog des vierten Evangeliums. Sein polemisch-apologetischer Zweck* (Freiburg/Leipzig/Tübingen, 1898), 168f.; E. Käsemann, *Jesu letzter Wille nach Johannes 17*, 4th edn (Tübingen, 1980), *passim*; Heitmüller, *Evangelium*, 800; M. D. Smith, 'The Presentation of Jesus in the Fourth Gospel', *Interp.*, 31 (1977), 367–78, 370; Müller, 'Bedeutung', 63. It is rejected by Thyen, 'Kreuzestod', 467 and Haenchen, *Johannesevangelium*, 561f.

58 Cf. A. Meyer, *Die Auferstehung Christi* (Tübingen, 1905) 52 and Minear, 'Audience', 348; the latter writes: 'The "other sheep" are the disciples at second hand, whose place in a united flock is here assured to be the will and work of this selfsacrificing shepherd.'

59 Already Bretschneider, *Probabilia*, 20, wrote: 'Quae c. x, 22 seqq. leguntur nil nisi repetitio sunt antea jam dictorum, haud paulo post in templo praesentibus pharisaeis facta.'

60 F. C. Baur, *Vorlesungen über neutestamentliche Theologie*, Bibliothek Theologischer Klassiker 45, 46; ed. F. F. Baur (Gotha, 1892), II, 169; Heitmüller, *Evangelium*, 801; Pfleiderer, *Urchristentum*, 475; Schmiedel, 'John', 2533; Schenkel, 'Christusbild', 378; B. Bauer, *Kritik*, 392; A. Hilgenfeld, 'Das Johannes-Evangelium und seine gegenwärtigen Auffassungen', *ZWTh*, 2 (1859), 281–348, 296, 346.

61 H. J. Holtzmann, 'Der Logos und der eingeborene Gottessohn im vierten Evangelium', *ZWTh*, 36 (1893), 385–407, 402; A. von Harnack, 'Über das Verhältnis des Prologs des vierten Evangeliums zum ganzen Werk', *ZThK*, 2 (1892), 189–231, 196f.; T. Zahn, *Das Evangelium des Johannes*, KNTIV, 6th edn (Leipzig, 1921), 467; B. Weiß, *Johannesevangelium*, 202; Hellwag, 'Vorstellungen', 262f.; F. Gumlich, 'Die Räthsel der Erweckung Lazari', *ThStKr*, 35 (1862), 65–110, 248–336, 320; Schulze, *Charakter und Werth*, 74; J. C. R. Eckermann, 'Wollte Jesus Wunder und Zeichen als Beweise seiner göttlichen Sendung betrachtet wissen?', *Theologische Beyträge, 5. Bd. 2. Stück* (Altona, 1796), 5–105, 78; Cludius, *Uransichten*, 68, 77; in this century the following declare for unity: R. Schnackenburg: 'Die Messiasfrage im Johannesevangelium', *Neutestamentliche Aufsätze*, FS J. Schmid, ed. J. Blinzler, O. Kuss, F. Mussner (Regensburg, 1963), 240–64, 255; Richter, *Studien*, 41; P. Riga, 'Signs of Glory. The Use of "Semeion" in St. John's Gospel', *Interp.*, 17 (1963), 402–24, 419; those against are: Lindars, 'Passion', 80; A. C. Sundberg, 'Christology in the Fourth Gospel', *BR*, 21 (1976), 29–37, 30; O. Michel, 'Das Gebet des scheidenden Erlösers', *ZSTh*, 18 (1941), 521–34, 531; T. Onuki, 'Die johanneischen Abschiedsreden und die synoptische Tradition', *AJBI*, 3 (1977), 157–268, 228; Walter, 'Auslegung', 99; O'Grady, 'Individualism', 233; Strathmann, *Evangelium*, 149; Lindars, 'Son of Man', 55; Meeks, 'Agent', 55.

62 Cludius, *Uransichten*, 77.

63 Cf. Schlatter, 'Bruch Jesu', 8.

64 Cf. D. B. Woll, *Johannine Christianity in Conflict*, SBL.DS 60 (Chico, 1981), 44; Hilgenfeld, 'Auffassungen', 296; R. Schnackenburg, 'Logos-Hymnus und johanneischer Prolog', *BZ*, 1 (1957), 69–109, 76; H. Spaeth, 'Nathanael: Ein Beitrag zum Verständnis der Composition des Logos-Evangeliums', *ZWTh*, 11 (1868), 168–213, 309–43, 319 with B. Weiß, *Johannesevangelium*, 201f.

65 Bultmann, *Evangelium*, 64 note 3, rightly argues thus.

66 C. Weizsäcker, 'Das Selbstzeugnis des johanneischen Christus. Ein Beitrag zur Christologie', *JDTh* 2 (1857), 154–208, 198.

67 A one-sided ecclesiological explanation of the chapter should with Richter, *Studien* 386, be regarded as *ad acta*. It is only of interest if one holds the 'ecclesiastical redactor' to be a valid possibility.

68 Wrede, *Charakter*, 212.

69 Haenchen, *Johannesevangelium*, 388.

2 Der alttestmentlich-jüdische Hintergrund der Hirtenrede in Joh 10

1 'Die Hirtenrede in Joh 10' in R. Schnackenburg, *Das Johannesevangelium IV*, HThK IV/4 (Freiburg–Basel–Wien, 1984), 131–43.
2 Vgl. die Kommentare von Hoskyns-Davey, Strathmann, R. E. Brown u.a.
3 Vgl. die Kommentare von Bauer, Bultmann und Schulz.
4 Vgl. etwa die Einleitung von J. M. Robinson zu E. Haenchen, *Das Johannesevangelium*, hrsg. v. U. Busse (Tübingen, 1980). Er spricht hier vom 'gnostischen Endpunkt der johanneischen Entwicklungslinie' (vi).
5 Vor einem Nebeneinander verschiedener 'Hintergründe', etwa des jüdischen und des gnostischen, warnt J. M. Robinson in: H. Koester – J. M. Robinson, *Entwicklungslinien durch die Welt des frühen Christentums* (Tübingen, 1971), 8–19.
6 Zum Aufkommen dieses Begriffes vgl. die Anm. 4 erwähnte Einleitung von J. M. Robinson zu Haenchens Johanneskommentar sowie die in Anm. 5 genannte Arbeit.
7 Vgl. zuletzt Schnackenburg, *Johannesevangelium IV* (Anm. 1), 133–4.
8 Schnackenburg, *Johannesevangelium IV* (Anm. 1), 135–40.
9 Vgl. zuletzt F. Hahn, 'Die Hirtenrede in Joh 10', *Theologia crucis – signum crucis. Festschrift für E. Dinkler zum 70. Geburtstag*, hrsg. v. C. Andresen u. G. Klein (Tübingen, 1979), 185–200; E. Haenchen, *Johannesevangelium* (Anm. 4) und J. Becker, *Das Johannesevangelium I*, ÖTK 4/1 (Gütersloh–Würzburg, 1979), z. St.
10 Vgl. Anm. 7. R. Schnackenburg weist hier vor allem auf die neueren angelsächsischen Kommentare hin.
11 Dies wird mit Ausnahme von J. H. Bernard, *The Gospel of St. John*, ICC (Edinburgh, 1928), der gleichfalls Umstellungen vornimmt, durchweg in den angelsächsischen Kommentaren gesehen. Vgl. besonders C. H. Dodd, *The Interpretation of the Fourth Gospel* (Cambridge, 1953), 354–62, der den Abschnitt 9: 1 – 10: 21 zu einer Einheit 'Judgment by the Light' zusammenfaßt. Zur Überleitungsfunktion von 9: 39–41 ebd., 358.
12 Vgl. zu dieser Einteilung etwa H. van den Bussche, *Jean. Commentaire de l'évangile spirituel* (Brügge, 1967). Er überschreibt den Abschnitt Joh 5–12: 'Le livre des oeuvres'.
13 Vgl. zuletzt E. Haenchen, *Johannesevangelium* (Anm. 4), z. St.
14 P. Weigandt, 'Zum Text von Joh 10,7. Ein Beitrag zum Problem der koptischen Bibelübersetzung', *NT*, 9 (1967), 43–51.
15 Weigandt, 'Text Joh 10,7' (Anm. 14), 49–50.
16 E. Fascher, 'Ich bin die Tür! Eine Studie zu Joh 10: 1–8', *DTh*, 9 (1942), 33–57, 118–33.
17 Vgl. J. Schneider, 'Zur Komposition von Joh 10', *CNT*, 11 (1947), 220–5; O. Kiefer, *Die Hirtenrede*, SBS 23 (Stuttgart, 1967); A. J. Simonis, *Die Hirtenrede im Johannes-Evangelium. Versuch einer Analyse von Joh 10, 1–18 nach Entstehung, Hintergrund und Inhalt*, AnBib 29 (Rom, 1967), der freilich ein kompliziertes Strukturmodell vorlegt.
18 Das 'vor mir' unterliegt textkritischen Bedenken und ist für den Sinn nicht erforderlich, da es hier um ein qualifiziertes 'Kommen' im Sinne des Kommens Jesu geht.

19 Becker, *Johannesevangelium I* (Anm. 9) schreibt den Vers einer sekundären Bearbeitung der johanneischen Redaktion zu (332–3), Hahn 'Hirtenrede' (Anm. 9), 198 and Haenchen, *Johannesevangelium* (Anm. 4), 394 sehen in ihm einen Zusatz der kirchlichen bzw. deuterojohanneischen Redaktion zum Evangelisten.

20 Er führt schon bei J. H. Bernard, *John* (Anm. 11) zur Umstellung von V. 19–29 vor 10: 1–18, seitdem mehrfach nachgeahmt.

21 P.-R. Tragan, 'La parabole du "pasteur" et ses explications Jean 10,1–18. La genèse, les milieux littéraires' (Diss. Strasbourg 1976; Lille 1977 (Rom, 1980)), 131–5.

22 Wir lesen dabei in V. 22 den von Nestle-Aland[26] bevorzugten Text, trotz des neuerlichen Gegenvorschlags von J. A. Whittaker, 'A Hellenistic Context for Joh 10,29', *VigChr*, 24 (1970), 241–60.

23 Vgl. Anm. 21. Bezüglich der bei ihm in V. 7 vorausgesetzten Lesart 'Ich bin der Hirt der Schafe' vgl. das oben, 1.2, Gesagte.

24 Eine breiter als bei Bultmann anzusetzende nachjohanneische Redaktion wird u.a. angenommen in den Kommentaren von Becker, *Johannesevangelium I* (Anm. 9), Haenchen, *Johannesevangelium* (Anm. 4) und neuerdings auch bei Schnackenburg, *Johannesevangelium IV* (Anm. 1), 185–234, auch die Nachträge zu Band I–III, 1965–1975. Ferner H. Thyen, 'Johannes 13 und die "Kirchliche Redaktion" des vierten Evangeliums', *Tradition und Glaube. Das frühe Christentum in seiner Umwelt. Festschrift K. G. Kuhn*, hrsg. v. J. Jeremias u.a. (Göttingen, 1971), 343–56; ders., 'Aus der Literatur zum Johannesevangelium', *ThR*, 39 (1974), 1–69, 222–52, 289–330; 42 (1977), 211–70; G. Richter, *Studien zum Johannesevangelium*, BU 13, hrsg. v. J. Hainz (Regensburg, 1977), passim.

25 Zum frühjüdischen und rabbinischen Verständnis von Ps 82: 6 an dieser Stelle vgl. E. A. Emerton, *JTS*, 11 (1966), 329–32; 17 (1966), 399–401; A. Hanson, *NTS*, 11 (1964–5), 158–62; 13 (1967), 363–7; J. S. Ackerman, *HThR*, 59 (1966), 186–91.

26 So vermutet – im Anschluß an R. Bultmann, *Das Evangelium nach Johannes*, KEK 2 (Göttingen, 1957), 296–7 – etwas unschlüssig Becker, *Johannesevangelium I* (Anm. 9), 339.

27 Zu beiden Gründen vgl. J. Jeremias, 'ποιμήν κτλ.', *ThWNT*, 6 (1959), 484–501, hier 487–8. – Der Versuch von J. D. M. Derrett, Joh 10: 1–18 aus jüdischer Halakhah abzuleiten (J. D. M. Derrett, 'The Good Shepherd: St. John's Use of Jewish Halakah and Haggadah', *StTh*, 27 (1973), 25–50) bleibt problematisch.

28 Vgl. J. Jeremias, 'ποιμήν' (Anm. 27), 488–9.

29 Es sind dies: θύρα, αὐλή, κλέπτης, λῃστής, πρόβατον, θυρωρός, παροιμία, ἀπόλλυμι, καλός, ψυχὴν τιθέναι, ἁρπάζω, σκορπίχω, μέλει (περί). Vgl. die Konkordanzen.

30 Dies spricht gegen eine zu enge Zuordnung der Hirtenrede zu 'pastoralen' Abschnitten des NT, wie sie Tragan, *Parabole* (Anm. 21), vorsieht.

31 E. D. Freed, *Old Testament Quotations in the Gospel of John*, NT.S 11 (Leiden, 1965).

32 G. Reim, *Studien zum alttestamentlichen Hintergrund des Johannesevangeliums*, SNTSMS 22 (Cambridge, 1974), vgl. etwa 188.

33 Tragan, *Parabole* (Anm. 21), 242–3.

34 Jeremias, 'ποιμήν' (Anm. 27), 486–7.
35 A. Weiser, *Der Prophet Jeremia. Kap. 1–25, 13*, ATD 20 (Göttingen, 1952), 206, datiert es auf die Spätzeit des Jeremia; W. Thiel, *Die deuteronomische Redaktion von Jeremia 1–25*, WMANT 41 (Neukirchen, 1973), 246–7, schreibt es der deuteronomischen Redaktion des Jeremiabuches zu.
36 Den neuesten Stand vermittelt B. Willmes, *Die sogenannte Hirtenallegorie Ez 34*, BBET 19 (Frankfurt a.M. – Bern – New York – Nancy, 1984). Er unterscheidet in Ez 34 zwei Grundberichte und mehrere Überarbeitungen. Von einem Grundwort und dessen sukzessiver Erweiterung geht aus F. L. Hossfeld, *Untersuchungen zu Komposition und Theologie des Ezechielbuches*, FzB 20 (Stuttgart–Würzburg, 1976).
37 Willmes, *Hirtenallegorie* (Anm. 36), 419ff.
38 Willmes, *Hirtenallegorie* (Anm. 36), 335–9.
39 Übersetzung und Abgrenzung nach M. Black, *The Book of Enoch or I Enoch*, SVTP 1 (Leiden, 1985).
40 Black, *Enoch* (Anm. 39), 19–20.
41 A.-M. Denis, *Introduction aux pseudépigraphes grecs d'Ancien Testament*, SVTP 7 (Leiden, 1970), 190.
42 A.-M. Denis, *Fragmenta pseudepigraphorum quae supersunt graeca* (zusammen mit M. Black, *Apocalypsis Henochi graece*), PVTG 3 (Leiden, 1970), 125ff. (= Papyrus Chester Beatty 185). Der Text ist noch nicht berücksichtigt in: K. G. Eckart, *Das Apokryphon Ezechiel*, JSHRZ V/1 (Gütersloh, 1974), 45–55.
43 Vgl. Denis, *Introduction* (Anm. 41), 200.
44 Text nach M. De Jonge, *The Testaments of the Twelve Patriarchs*, PVTG I/2 (Leiden, 1978).
45 Willmes, *Hirtenallegorie* (Anm. 36), 279–311.
46 Willmes, *Hirtenallegorie* (Anm. 36), 342–7.
47 Willmes, *Hirtenallegorie* (Anm. 36), 208–12.
48 Zu politischen Führern der Vergangenheit als Hirten vgl. noch Jes 63:11 (Mose), Ps 78:70, 72 (David), vorausschauend Jes 44:28 (Kyrus).
49 Vgl. dazu ausführlicher W. Jost, ΠΟΙΜΗΝ. *Das Bild vom Hirten in der biblischen Überlieferung und seine christologische Bedeutung* (Gießen, 1939), 37–41.
50 Abweichend vom TM oder über ihn hinaus hat die LXX das Verb ποιμαίνειν noch in Ex 2:16; Spr 9:12; 22:11; Jer 6:18.
51 Vgl. Anm. 42.
52 Vgl. J. F. Priest, 'Mebaqqer, Paqid, and the Messiah', *JBL*, 81 (1962), 55–61, hier 60.
53 Ch. Rabin, *The Zadokite Documents*, I–II (Oxford, 1958), zitiert bei C. Dupont-Sommer, *Die essenischen Schriften vom Toten Meer* (Tübingen, 1960), 173. Vgl. E. Cothenet, 'Le document de Damas', *Les textes de Qumran, traduits et annotés*, II, ed. J. Carmignac, E. Cothenet, H. Lignée (Paris, 1963), 129–204, hier 201 (n. 16).
54 Im Sinne einer Untersuchung oder Unterscheidung steht es Lev 13:63; 27:33; im Sinne des Überlegens 2 Kön 16:5; Spr 20:25; Ps 27:4.
55 Übersetzung und Datierung nach A. F. J. Klijn, *Die syrische Baruch-Apokalypse*, JSHRZ 5/2 (Gütersloh, 1976), 103–91.
56 So J. Jeremias, 'ποιμήν' (Anm. 27), 487.

57 Vgl. Cothenet, 'Damas' (Anm. 53), z. St.
58 Zum nachjohanneischen Charakter der Abschiedsrede Jesu in Joh 15–17 vgl. zuletzt J. Beutler, *Habt keine Angst. Die erste johanneische Abschiedsrede (Joh 14)*, SBS 116 (Stuttgart, 1984), 9–10.
59 Zur Schwierigkeit, hier die genaue alttestamentliche Textvorlage zu ermitteln, vgl. Freed, *Quotations* (Anm. 31), 114ff. Nach Reim, *Hintergrund* (Anm. 32), 54ff. hat der Evangelist aus christlicher Tradition geschöpft (vgl. Offb 1:7).
60 Vgl. zuletzt die Einheitsübersetzung der Heiligen Schrift und die ausführliche Diskussion bei R. Schnackenburg, *Das Johannesevangelium II*, HThK IV/2 (Freiburg–Basel–Wien, 1971), z. St.
61 J. Jeremias, 'θύρα', *ThWNT*, 3 (1938), 173–80, hier 178–80.
62 Jeremias, 'θύρα' (Anm. 61), 179–80.
63 Brieflicher Hinweis von P. Stuhlmacher vom 7.3.1986, für den ich P. S. danke. Auf die Offenheit der Gemeinde für Außenstehende deutet das Türmotiv J. P. Martin, 'John 10:1–10', *Interpr.*, 32 (1978), 171–5.

3 The history of religions background of John 10

1 Liddell–Scott–Jones, *Greek–English Lexicon*, 1471a.
2 *Statesman*, 271–6; cf. *Republic*, 343, 345, 359, 370, 440; *Critias*, 109; *Theaetetus*, 174; *Laws*, 677, 713, 735, for similar metaphors of the ruled and the ruler.
3 Cf. H. Preisker and S. Schulz, 'πρόβατον', *TDNT*, 6 (1968), 689, citing Epictetus, *Dissertationes* I. 23.7–7; 28.15 and III.22.35.
4 Vol. I, Handbuch der Altertumswissenschaft V, 2; 2nd edn (Munich, 1955).
5 Vols. 4 and 5 (Oxford, 1909).
6 See M. Fränkel, *Die Inschriften von Pergamon*, Altertümer von Pergamon VIII (Berlin, 1890–5), 329; cf. Suidas: Στροφαῖον' ἐπωνυμία εστὶν Ἑρμοῦ παρά τὸ ταῖς θύραις ἱδρῦσθαι ἐπὶ φυλακῇ τῶν ἄλλων κλεπτῶν ('Standing-at-the-door [hinges]' is an epithet of Hermes seated by the doors for the purpose of protection from other thieves, a play on the 'twisty' character and thievery of Hermes).
7 *Praetera aedes ut ovium pastoris sunt apud Camirenses* ἐπιμηλίου, *apud Naxios* ποιμνίου, *itemque deus* ἀρνοκόμης *colitur ... quapropter universi pecoris antistes et vere pastor agnoscitur* ('Moreover, there are temples [to Apollo] as Feeder of Sheep, at Camirus with the title Guardian of Flocks, and at Naxos with the title Patron of Shepherds; and he is worshipped also as the God with the Lamb's Fleece ... so that he is recognised to be the overseer of all flocks and herds and in very truth to feed them').
8 H. Kees *apud* J. Jeremias, 'ποιμήν', *TDNT*, 6 (1968), 486–7, citing K. Sethe, *Die altaegyptischen Pyramidentexte*, I, 771b; II, 1533b; A. Bertholet, ed., *Aegyptisches Religionsgeschichtliches Lesebuch*, X, 44.
9 S. N. Kramer, *The Sumerians: Their History, Culture and Character* (Chicago, 1963), 116; 328–9; Pritchard, *ANET*, 574, 590.
10 E.g. Psalms 23:1–4; 74:1; 77:20–1; 78:52; 79:13; 80:1; 95:7; 100:3; 121:4; Gen. 49:24; Is. 40:10–11; 49:9; Jer. 23:3; Ezek. 34 (*passim*); Zech. 11: 4–17; Mic. 2:12.

11 1 Kings 14:8; 18:21; 2 Kings 23:3 = 2 Chron. 31:34; Deut. 31:1—4; Psalm
    68:7; Jer. 2:2—8; 3:15; 10:21; 22:22; 25:34—6; 50:6.
12 J. Jeremias, 'ποιμήν', *TDNT*, 6 (1968), 487—8.
13 Ibid., 488—9.
14 Ibid., 491—4.
15 Ibid., 494.
16 D. Halperin, *Before Pastoral: Theocritus and the Ancient Origin of Bucolic
    Poetry* (New Haven, 1983), 85—117, to whom I am indebted for the following
    observation on the liminal position of the shepherd.
17 O. Betz, 'φωνή', *TDNT*, 9 (1973), 280—4.
18 'I am a Voice (ⲀⲢⲞⲞⲨ = ἦχος, φθόγγος, φωνή) [speaking softly]. I exist
    [from the first. I dwell] within the Silence [that envelops each] of them. And
    [it is] the hidden Voice that [indwells] me, [within the] incomprehensible,
    immeasurable [Thought], within the immeasurable Silence. It is I who am
    laden with the Voice; it is through me that Gnosis proceeds. [I] dwell among
    the ineffable and unknowable. I am perception and Gnosis, uttering Voice
    by virtue of Thought. [I] am the true Voice; I cry out in everyone and they
    recognise [me] since a seed indwells [them]. I am the Thought of the Father
    and through me proceeded the Voice, that is, the knowledge of the ever-
    lasting things. I exist as Thought for the [All], joined with the unknowable
    and incomprehensible Thought. I revealed myself, even I, among all those
    who recognised me, for it is I who am joined with everyone by virtue of the
    hidden Thought and exalted ‹Voice› , even a Voice from the hidden Thought
    (35:32—36:27)... Now the Voice that originated through my Thought subsists
    as three abiding entities: the Father, the Mother, the Son. Existing perceptibly
    as Speech (ⲤⲘⲎ = φωνή) it has within it a Logos (37,20—4) ... I am the
    Voice that appeared through my Thought, for I am the male consort insofar
    as I am called the "the Thought of the Invisible One"; insofar as I am called
    "the unchanging Speech", I am called the female consort (44,29—31) ...
    I am the Mother of the Voice, speaking in many ways, completing the All.
    It is in me that knowledge inheres, the knowledge of things everlasting.
    [It is] I [who] speak in every creature, and I was known by the All. It is I
    who lift up the Speech of the Voice to the ears of those who have known
    me, that is the Sons of the Light. Now I have come the second time in the
    likeness of a female and have spoken with them (45,25—30) ... So now, O
    Sons of the Thought, listen to me, the Speech of your merciful Mother ...
    It is through me that the Voice originated and it is I who put the breath within
    my own. And I cast upon them the eternally holy Spirit and I ascended and
    I entered my Light ... (At first) I taught [them the mysteries] through the
    [Voice that indwells] a perfect Intellect [and I] became a foundation for the
    All, and [I empowered] them. The second time I came in the [Speech] of
    my Voice and I gave shape to those who [took] shape until their consum-
    mation. The third time I revealed myself to them [in their tents] as the Logos
    and I revealed myself in the likeness of their shape (47,7—16).'
19 This can be seen by the following chain of metaphors (NHC XIII,1:
    46,11—32): 'But there is a Light [that] dwells hidden in Silence, and it was
    first to [come] forth. Whereas she (the Mother) alone exists as Silence, I
    alone am the Word, ineffable, incorruptible, immeasurable, inconceivable.
    It (the Word) is a hidden Light, bearing living fruit, pouring forth living

water from the invisible, unpolluted, immeasurable Spring, that is the unreproducible Voice of the glory of the Mother, the glorious offspring of God, a male Virgin by virtue of hidden Intellect, that is the Silence hidden from the All, being an unreproducible, immeasurable Light, the source of the All, the root of the entire Aeon. It is the foundation that supports every movement of the Aeons that belong to the mighty Glory; it is the foundation of every foundation; it is the breath of the powers; it is the eye of the three abiding entities which exist as Voice by virtue of Thought and is Logos by virtue of Speech; it was sent to illumine those who dwell in the [darkness].'

20 C. K. Barrett, 'The Old Testament in the Fourth Gospel', *JTS*, 48 (1947), 163–4; J. Jeremias, 'ποιμήν', *TDNT*, 6 (1968), 494–7; R. E. Brown, *The Gospel According to John (xiii–xxi)*, Anchor Bible 29 (Garden City, NY, 1966), 390–400.

21 Ibid., 90–1.

22 Bultmann, *The Gospel of John: A Commentary* (Oxford, 1971), 364–70.

23 *In Parables: The Challenge of the Historical Jesus* (New York, 1963).

24 *The Gospel of John*, 367.

25 Ibid., 367–70.

26 'Everything indicates that the image of the shepherd is an integral part of early Mandaean figurative language. Here we discover again traits which are important for the Johannine discourse on the Good Shepherd, not only in the shepherd's care for pasture and water, the fold, the protection from the wolf and thief, but notably the most important, namely that the shepherd is not a regal figure, but the Redeemer sent from the heavenly world. It is not a people that he gathers together, but his own, who are lost and in danger in the world. He "loves" the sheep and carries them "on his shoulders" (Joh B. 44:27f.), he calls them (48:2ff.), and they are rescued when they hear his voice (48:11f.) ... The only element which does not occur in the Mandaean shepherd-texts is the contrasted picture of the hireling [10:12–13], and consequently the fact that the shepherd risks his life for the sheep ... It is surely not without significance that in Hermetic Gnosticism the god to whom the role of the Revealer was specifically attributed was the god who, from of old, had been cast in the role of the shepherd, namely Hermes ... he was also the messenger of the gods and the guide of souls. The fact that nevertheless the figure of the shepherd and the Revealer are closely related is shown by the name Ποιμάνδρης, which is given to the Revealer in C. Herm. 1, and also by the shepherd's costume of the revealing angel, Herm. Vis. 5 [Reitzenstein *Poimandres* 1904, 11f., 32f.].'

27 'Der johanneische Christus und der gnostische Erlöser: Überlegungen auf Grund von Joh 10', *Gnosis und Neues Testament: Studien aus Religions-wissenschaft und Theologie*, ed. K. W. Tröger (Berlin, 1973), 245–66.

28 Fischer refers to *Auth. Teach* NHC VI, *3*: 32, 10 as an instance of the gnostic use of this term, but here it actually refers to the light-world, not this world; cf. Mandaean Joh B., Lidzbarski 45.

29 Fischer cites in addition to the Mandaean passages on the shepherd: *Auth. Teach.* NHC VI, *3*: 32, 9–11; 33, 1–3; *Gos. Tr.* NHC I, *3*: 31, 35 – 32, 30; *Gos. Thom.* 107, NHC II, *2*: 50, 22–7).

30 *Exc. Theod.* 42, 1–3; *Od. Sol.* 22, 1–2; *1 Apoc. Jas.* NHC V, *3 passim.*

31 Citing *Exeg. Soul*, NHC II, 6: 127, 26–32; *Gos. Thom.* 21, NHC II, 2: 37, 6–16; *Gos. Phil.* NHC II, 3: 52, 13–54, 19 (note here also the motif of the saviour's laying down his life).

32 *The Gospel of John*, 376. One also notes that Bodmer papyrus p⁷⁵ and the Sahidic Coptic read ὁ ποιμήν for ἡ θύρα; in the course of transmission, the former could have been substituted for the latter on similar grounds to those Bultmann expresses, yet one might also argue that the latter was substituted for the former by a later redactor or scribe who wished to apply the door symbolism to Christ as the only legitimate way or means to salvation (cf. Ignatius, *Phil* 9, 1; 1 Clement 48, 4; Hermas, *Sim.* 9, 2 and 10, 7 etc.).

33 'But the soul ... learns about her light, as she goes about stripping off this world, while her true garment clothes her within, [and] her bridal clothing is placed upon her in the beauty of mind, not in pride of flesh. And she learns about her depth and runs into her *fold*, while her *shepherd* stands at the *door*. In return for the shame and scorn, then, that she received in this world, she receives ten thousand times the grace and glory. She gave the body to those who had given it to her ... They did not realise that she has an invisible spiritual body, thinking, "We are her *shepherd* who feeds her." But they did not realise that she knows another *way* [Copt. 2IH for Gk. ὁδός, cf. John 14. 6 and this discourse's use of θύρα], which is hidden from them. This her *true shepherd* taught her in knowledge.'

34 Bultmann, *The Gospel of John*, 383–4, attributes this verse to the later ecclesiastical redaction of the gospel.

35 C. H. Dodd, *The Bible and the Greeks* (London, 1954); *The Interpretation of the Fourth Gospel* (Cambridge, 1953).

4 Tradition, history and interpretation in John 10

1 In both chapters 5 and 10 Jesus speaks of the Father/Son relation in the third person as well as the first; 'my father (5: 17; 10: 25, 29); the Father's love for the Son (5: 20; 10: 17); and of his own works (ἔργα) as the works of God (5: 17, 19–21, 30, 36; 10: 32–3, 37–8, and see 7: 21–4). The works demonstrate that he has been sent by the Father (5: 23–4, 36–8; 10: 36; and see 7: 16, 18, 28, 33; 8: 16, 26, 29).

2 In 10: 33, the evangelist may well have introduced a tradition from the passion story, compare 19: 7.

3 'Works' (ἔργα) is a key term in the gospel. It is, to some extent, the equivalent of 'signs' (σημεῖα). In 6: 30 the crowd asked Jesus, 'What sign (σημεῖον) do you do ... what do you work (ἐργάζῃ)?' But the term sign is not specifically Johannine, being used thirteen times in Matt. compared with seventeen times in John. In the Synoptics the term 'sign' is frequently used in the demand for a sign, as it is in John 6: 30. In John Jesus characteristically describes his miracles as his 'works'. The noun ἔργον and the verb ἐργάζεσθαι are used thirty-four times compared with a total use of sixteen times in the Synoptics. In John the works are part of the manifold witness to Jesus, 5: 36; 10: 25. See my *John: Witness and Theologian* (London, 1975), 10–11, 23, 52–3, 72, 73, 75; and 'Text and Context in John 5', *ABR*, 35 (Oct. 1987), 28–34. John 5 provides the first extended treatment of 'works', and the term is given its peculiar Johannine resonance in the context of the charge that Jesus worked on the Sabbath thus breaking the fourth commandment.

4 See the emphasis on making the man whole (ὑγιής) in 5:6, 9, 11, 14, 15; 7:23 and the reference to *'good* works' in 10:32.

5 This form, found in chapters 5, 6, and 9, around which the discourses of chapters 7, 8, and 10 are arranged, signals conflict material, as do the 'Pronouncement Stories' of Mark. John 11:1–12, 36 also include conflict material, but the summary of 10:40–2 was probably the original transition to the Passion account.

6 Conflict is expressed in the murmuring (γογγυσμός) of the crowd (6:41–43, 61; 7:12–13); division (σχίσμα) caused by Jesus' word (7:43; 9:16; 10:19), the charge of demon possession brought against Jesus (7:20; 8:48–52; 10:20–1), and fear of the Jews (7:13; 9:22), which inhibited open confession of faith. In spite of this, many believed (6:14–15; 7:31; 8:30; 10:42, and see 2:23; 11:45, 47–8; 12:42).

7 In this regard John follows the general order of Mark: Prologue and call of the disciples (Mark 1:1–20; John 1:1–51); the revelation of Jesus through word and action (Mark 1:21–45; John 2:1–4:54); conflict stories and disputations (Mark 2:1–3:30; John 5:1–10:39). In both Mark 3 and John 10 Jesus is accused of demon possession.

8 The ἀμήν-sayings in John, of which there are twenty-five, always double, are to be found in 1:51; 3:3, 5, 11; 5:19, 24, 25; 6:26, 32, 47, 53; 8:34, 51, 58; 10:1, 7; 12:24; 13:16, 20, 21, 38; 14:12; 16:20, 23; 21:28. They are always placed on the lips of Jesus.

9 Reference to a σχίσμα also occurs in 9:16. There it is the Pharisees who are divided whereas, in 10:19–21 it is the Jews. In 9:40 reference is again made to the Pharisees so that it can be asked if the group in 9:16 and 9:40 is the same and whether reference to 'the Jews' (in 10:19–21) is simply a variation without distinction. But there is no σχίσμα amongst the Pharisees of 9:40. The dialogue of 9:39–41 indicates that this group contains only those who have rejected Jesus.

10 Jesus answered the Jews, 'You are not able to believe because you are not my sheep.' J. Jeremias, *TDNT*, 6 (1968), 494–5, rightly concludes that the rearrangement is unconvincing.

11 For examples of studies based on this approach see my articles on the 'Prologue', *NTS*, 30 (1984), 460–74; the 'Farewell Discourses', *NTS*, 27 (1981), 525–43; 'John 9 and the Interpretation of the Fourth Gospel' in *JSNT*, 28 (1986), 31–61; 'Text and Context in John 5', and 'Tradition and Interpretation in John 6', *NTS*, 35 (1989), 421–50.

12 Naturally parable and allegory are not alien categories, so there could be 'mixed forms'. In John 10 the παροιμία is separated from the allegorical interpretation by an editorial note (10:6), as is the parable of 'the soils' (Mark 4:11–12). Since I prepared this paper for *SNTS* Atlanta (1986), Richard Bauckham's 'Rediscovering a Lost Parable of Jesus' has appeared, *NTS*, 33 (1987), 84–101. There Bauckham compares John 10 and 15, noting similarities and the implied parable of 15:1–11.

13 See Matt. 5:18. In Luke ἀμήν is sometimes translated as ἀληθῶς, Luke 9:27; Mark 9:1.

14 *The Gospel of John* (London, 1972), 355. Lindars has made use of the work of Klaus Berger on the ἀμήν-sayings of Jesus.

15 C. H. Dodd, *Interpretation of the Fourth Gospel* (Cambridge, 1953), 358–9, rightly stresses the importance of Ezek. 34. See also C. K. Barrett, *The Gospel according to St. John* (London, 1978), 373–5; and the articles in this volume by Beutler and Turner.

16 Especially in Pss. 23:1; 80:2 and implied in 74:1, 79:13; 95:7; 100:3. See also Isaiah 40:11; Jer. 31:9.

17 Ps. 78:70–2; Jer. 2:8; 10:20; 12:10; Ezek. 34; 37:24; Micah 5:3; Pss. of Solomon 17:45. See also Num. 27:17.

18 This is true of J. A. T. Robinson, C. H. Dodd, and B. Lindars. Even if it could be shown that the παροιμία was traditional, it need not follow that it goes back to Jesus.

19 In classical historiography a degree of freedom was often taken in placing speeches on the lips of the actors.

20 'The Parable of the Shepherd', *ZNW*, 46 (1955), 233–40. Both Dodd and Lindars accepted Robinson's argument about the merging of two parables. More recently Robert Kysar, *John* (Minneapolis, 1986), 159 has argued that the evangelist wove together as many as four distinct allegories in John 10:1–16.

21 By the addition of πρὸ ἐμοῦ (verse 8) and by the addition of ἐγὼ ἦλθον ἵνα ζωὴν ἔχωσιν καὶ περισσὸν ἔχωσιν (verse 10b). Hence the πρὸ ἐμοῦ (verse 8) is original, though omitted by some subsequent editors because it does not fit the affirmation identifying Jesus with the door. The implications of πρὸ ἐμοῦ are taken up again and more fully in verse 10b. These additions were made by the evangelist to prepare the way for the second interpretation and are part of the original version of the completed gospel.

22 The saying in 10:7–10 is dependent on the παροιμία for the use of θύρα as a symbol. If Jesus came to be identified with the θυρωρὸς this might have determined the evangelist's choice of θύρα rather than πύλη. The two words are used as alternatives in the Q tradition (Luke 13:24 = Matt. 7:13–14).

23 Reference to thieves and robbers might have arisen from the use of Jer. 7:11 in the gospel tradition of the cleansing of the Temple (Mark 11:17 and parallels). John does not refer to this tradition in his account though οἶκον ἐμπορίου (2:16) might be a Johannine interpretation, assuming the identification of the Jewish leaders with the robbers.

24 'John 9'.

25 There are good reasons for thinking that the evangelist became dissatisfied with this approach and its christology. It would probably be right to say that it did not go far enough for him rather than that he rejected it. See section 5 below.

26 The note indicates that 'This παροιμία Jesus spoke to them (αὐτοῖς) but they did not know what it was he spoke to them (αὐτοῖς).' Presumably 'them' refers to the unbelieving group of Pharisees to whom 9:39, 41 were addressed.

27 R. Brown, *The Gospel According to John* (Garden City, NY, 1966), I, 386, notes that 'The manuscript tradition on the inclusion, omission, and order of these words [to them again] is very confused.' The words are part of the quotation formula of 10:7. They are probably original since it is easier to explain their omission than their addition. The πάλιν may have been omitted by an overly literalistic scribe who noted that this was in fact the first time Jesus had solemnly affirmed 'I am the door'. The αὐτοῖς may have been

omitted because it obviously referred to the unbelieving Pharisees, to whom the αὐτοῖς of 10:6 also refers, while the scribe thought that the words of Jesus in 10:7–18 were more appropriately addressed to believers. The original order of the words is more problematical.

28 *The Gospel According to St John,* II (New York, 1980), 288.

29 On the formal parallel between the first two and second two sayings see ibid, 289–90, 294–5; also Beutler, in this volume.

30 The double ἀμήν of 10:7 is followed by ὅτι and an ἐγώ εἰμι saying. The ὅτι clause following the double ἀμήν is unusual in John and is sometimes taken to indicate that the saying, as it stands, is not the work of the evangelist. This argument is often combined with the view that the door symbol is not original but has displaced the shepherd motif. But a ὅτι clause does follow the double ἀμήν in 8:34 and 13:21. These peculiarities are not sufficient ground for questioning the authority of the reading, especially as the door motif is reintroduced in 10:9, where it is characteristic of a number of symbolic 'I am' sayings, especially 'I am the way ...', 14:6. On the relation to 14:6 see J. Jeremias, *TDNT,* 3 (1965), 179–80. It could be that 14:6 influenced the evangelist in his choice of the symbol of the door. More of a problem is the change of use from 10:7 to 10:9. In the former it is 'the door of the sheep', which is consistent with the meaning in the παροιμία if the 'of' is taken to mean 'to the sheep'. But in the latter it is the door to life or salvation which the sheep enter, a meaning which can also be conveyed by the first statement of the theme in 10:7.

31 That the Matthean form has influenced John is perhaps indicated by the association of false prophets with 'ravening wolves' in 7:15. But Matthew uses πύλη rather than θύρα (which is used also by Luke). Consequently we can assume only a general influence of the gospel tradition on John at this point.

32 The precise meaning of καλός in this phrase is debated. In John the term is used also of the 'good wine', 2:10; and Jesus' 'good work(s)', 10:32, 33. Matthew's use of 'good tree' using both καλός and ἀγαθός (Matt. 7:17–18) suggests that 'good' is the correct rendering, but there are arguments for relating the term to John's use of ἀληθῶς, ἀληθινός, which would bring the saying into line with John 15:1 ('I am the true vine ...'), etc.

33 This emphasis has already been foreshadowed by 10:3b–4a in the παροιμία.

34 The figures of the hireling and the wolf are not necessary for the evangelist to develop the role of the good shepherd in giving his life for his sheep. This was already possible in relation to the thieves and robbers who have no other purpose than κλέψῃ καὶ θύσῃ καὶ ἀπολέσῃ. Indeed, as John attributes the responsibility for Jesus' death to the Jewish authorities, it would have been appropriate for the thieves and robbers to be responsible for the death of the good shepherd. Thus, the introduction of the hireling and the wolf requires explanation.

35 While the term μισθωτός refers to a hired worker (compare Mark 1:20 with John 10:12–13), it is not the emphasis on payment that is in view in John 10. Those who are paid are not those to whom the sheep belong. Hence it is unlikely that the figure of the hireling signals a conflict between Christian

leaders who were paid and the unpaid leaders of the Johannine community. The word has no different meaning than μίσθιος, which is used only in Luke 15:17, 19, 21. More interesting is the fact that the μισθωτὸς is contrasted with the θεῖος ἡγεμών in Plut., Mor., 37E. In the standard literature there is a lack of attention to the question why the evangelist has introduced the figures of the μισθωτὸς and the λύκος into his interpretation of the παροιμία. These figures, not mentioned in the παροιμία, signal the influence of the history of the Johannine Christians on the interpretation.

36 Here again we find evidence that the evangelist saw Jesus' saving work as involving his death for 'his own'. See also 1:29, 36. Hence it is not correct to say that John portrays Jesus simply as the revealer, even if it is not clear how the death of Jesus is thought to be a saving act.

37 It might be objected that, in the dialogue of John 21:15–17, Peter is instructed not only to feed (βόσκε, 21:15, 17), but also to shepherd the sheep (ποίμαινε, 21:16), implying that he is portrayed as a shepherd. But those who are hired to look after the sheep also shepherd them. Further, in each of the three instances it is emphasised in the words of Jesus, 'Feed (or shepherd) *my* sheep'. Since it is emphasised that the sheep belong to Jesus, Peter is a hireling (see 10:12).

38 See John 10:16, in which the work of the good shepherd leads to the creation of one flock (μία ποίμνη).

39 The question now to be answered is, where and how is the voice of the good shepherd to be heard?

40 *The Gospel of John* (Oxford, 1971), 380–1.

41 By this I mean the consciousness of those who have been rejected by, and have rejected the world and who think of themselves and the world in terms that justify this separation.

42 On this see my *John: Witness and Theologian*, 98–100. It should be noted that the mutuality formula is also expressed in terms of love, the love of the Father for the Son and the Son for the Father; and the love of the Son for his own and his own for him and for one another. Both sides of the relation are not, however, expressed in the same text. The emphasis is on a descending order of love, of the Father for the Son, of the Son for his own, and of the disciples for each other.

43 By definition 'the sheep' are his sheep. The sheep belong to the shepherd. But saying that the good shepherd gives his life for *the* sheep has a less exclusive ring about it than saying that he gives his life for *his* sheep. That this impression is intended is borne out by 10:16. There are other sheep which must be brought into the one fold.

44 On this see my 'The Opponents in 1 John', *NTS*, 32 (1986), 48–71.

45 The hope of regathering the scattered might indicate that this discourse is earlier than 1 John where the scattering appears to have hardened into a schism with no hope of a reconstituted unity (1 John 2:19).

46 Interestingly it is διὰ τοὺς λογοὺς τούτους that the schism occurred (10:19), while those who reject the view that Jesus was demon-possessed asserted ταῦτα τὰ ῥήματα οὐκ ἔστιν δαιμονιζομένου (10:21). Consequently it seems unlikely that the evangelist distinguished between λόγος and ῥῆμα.

47 Reference to the σχίσμα occurs in 9:16 and 7:43. In 9:16 the σχίσμα is in response to the word of the healed Man. He represents the Johannine

Christians who have been ejected from the synagogue because of their witness to Jesus. The focus in 10:19 and 7:43 is on the σχίσμα resulting from Jesus' words.

48 John 10:18 is the equivalent of Mark 8:31, etc. See also John 6:51–9.

49 It seems that 'demon possession' was a theological diagnosis and madness a popular diagnosis; see also 7:20; 8:48–53 and Mark 3:22–30. It is possible that the charge of demon possession is intended to recall the context in which it was first made in 7:20. There it was a consequence of Jesus' asking why 'the Jews' sought to kill him. Though they deny the charge, it is accepted as true in 7:25; see also 5:18.

50 The reference is a generalisation, using the plural τυφλῶν, hence making the case in chapter 9 typical. As such the response seems to be a reflection of the early Christian preaching rather than a response to the event narrated in chapter 9. Interestingly, in the schism of chapter 9, those who defended Jesus did so by an appeal to his signs (σημεῖα, 9:16). Again it is a generalisation, not referring specifically to the healing of the man in question.

51 See now my 'Tradition and Interpretation in John 6'.

52 The decision to cast out of the synagogue anyone who confessed Christ (= 'Jesus is the Christ', 9:22) is strange because no one in the story of John 9 has suggested this. It represents the confession of faith of Jewish Christians not the evangelist. See my article on 'John 9'.

53 John 10:31, 33 and for a previous attempt to stone Jesus see 8:59. Attempts to arrest or kill Jesus occur frequently in chapters 5–11 (5:16, 18; 7:19, 20, 25, 30, 32, 44; 8:20; 10:39; 11:57).

54 As in the designation 'good shepherd', the evangelist uses the adjective καλός (here the neuter plural καλά), rather than ἀγαθός.

55 In 10:25 Jesus refers to 'the works I do in the name of my Father', and in 10:35 he answers, 'Many good works I showed you from (ἐκ) the [or my] Father.' In the former we have the language of agency, depicting Jesus as the emissary of the Father, while, in the latter, language of ontological unity, asserting that the works done by Jesus originate in the Father.

56 See Phil. 2:6 and my 'Text and Context in John 5' for a more extensive treatment of John 5:17.

57 'Is it not written in *your* Law (ἐν τῷ νόμῳ ὑμῶν)', and what follows is an appeal to Ps. 82:6. On the significance of this see the articles by Anthony Hanson, 'John's Citation of Psalm 82', *NTS*, 11 (1964–65), 158–62 and 'John's Citation of Psalm 82 Reconsidered', *NTS*, 13 (1966–67), 363–7. It is rightly noticed that, in these words, Jesus has distanced himself from the Jews by disavowing that it is also his Law.

58 This form of argument may be dependent on tradition. It is similar to Mark 12:35–7 in the way it uses a scriptural precedent as justification.

59 The choice of one or other of these verbs in John appears to be based on preference for grammatical forms. Πέμπω supplies the present and future indicative active, and the aorist active participle, while ἀλοστέλλω supplies the aorist and perfect indicative active and the passive participle. On the language of 'agency' and precedent for it in Jewish sources see Peder Borgen, *Logos Was the True Light* (Trondheim, 1983), especially 121–32.

60 A collection of signs might have originated in a Palestinian mission to Baptist loyalists, though the evangelist would have used it in the dialogues and disputes with the synagogue.

61 Although this is a significant word for the evangelist it is unlikely that any overtone is intended here. Perhaps it was already to be found in the tradition used by the evangelist.

62 On the use of this phrase see, 2:23; 7:31; 8:30; 11:45, 47–8; 12:42. Another use of πολλοὶ in the gospel (10:20) indicates that 'many' reject Jesus. The evangelist's own perspective involves reserve about the mass response of belief in his signs and it is for this reason that the faith of the many is called into question.

63 On a possible relation of this stratum of the gospel to the opponents in 1 John see my article '1 John'.

5 John 10 and its relation to the Synoptic Gospels

1 See M. Sabbe, 'The Arrest of Jesus in Jn 18, 1–11 and Its Relation to the Synoptic Gospels. A Critical Evaluation of A. Dauer's Hypothesis', *L'évangile de Jean*, ed. M. de Jonge, BETL 44 (Leuven, 1977), 203–34; M. Sabbe, 'The Footwashing in Jn 13 and Its Relation to the Synoptic Gospels', *EThL*, 58 (1982), 279–308.

2 Boismard suggests a possible allusion to Ps. 22:17 (ἐκύκλωσάν με κύνες πολλοί, συναγωγὴ πονηρομένων περιέσχον με), a Psalm which offers more links with the Passion Narrative (John 19:24). Cf. M.-E. Boismard and A. Lamouille, *L'évangile de Jean. Commentaire*, Synopse des quatre évangiles en français 3 (Paris, 1977), 274.

3 Cf. also Acts 7:58–60, the stoning of Stephen within the framework of a Passion Narrative, likewise dependent upon the Passion Narrative of Jesus. Cf. M. Sabbe, 'The Son of Man Saying in Acts 7, 56', *Les Actes des Apôtres. Traditions, rédaction, théologie*, ed. J. Kremer, BETL 48 (Leuven, 1979), 241–79, esp. 251.

4 See A. Dauer, *Die Passionsgeschichte im Johannesevangelium. Eine traditionsgeschichtliche und theologische Untersuchung zu Joh 18,1–19,30*, SANT 30 (Munich, 1972), 83, 87.

5 Ibid., esp. 88. In note 164 he also refers to his own Excursus 'Spuren des Kaiphasverhörs im 4. Evangelium' of his dissertation (Würzburg, 1969), 117–131. See also *Passionsgeschichte* 87: 'Ja, 10, 22–38 ist geradezu die joh Vorwegnahme des synoptischen Synedriumsverhörs' and again note 159 'Wir können hier auf diesen Abschnitt und besonders auch auf die wichtigen Parallelen zu den synoptischen Berichten der Synedriumsverhandlung nicht eingehen. Doch vgl. die maschinengeschriebene Dissertation des Verfassers S. 119–131.'

6 Cf. Mark 14:61 (ὁ ἀρχιερεὺς ἐπηρώτα αὐτὸν) with John 18:19 (ὁ οὖν ἀρχιερεὺς ἠρώτησεν τὸν Ἰησοῦν).

7 Even the reference to 'the temple where all the Jews come together' (18:20) reminds us of John 10:23–24a.

8 The question of the Pharisees in John 8:25 (σὺ τίς εἶ;) shows some similarity with the query regarding Jesus' proclamation of Messiahship (cf. 7:40–1 and 7:26 – using the χριστός title as well as the word παρρησία) as in 10:24, all the more since some similar background of a trial scene before the Jews is equally discernible in chapter 8. In 7:51 the perspective of an official interrogation of Jesus is opened, and the whole section ends with an attempt at stoning Jesus (verse 59).

9 See S. Temple, *The Core of the Fourth Gospel* (London, 1975), esp. 180. Boismard and Lamouille (*Jean*, 272–3), on the contrary, think that John (John II–B *in casu*) was here mostly inspired by the narrative of Luke (and did not depend upon a proto-Luke).

10 Stylistic characteristic no. 53, used forty-five times in John, as in 10:32, 33, 34. The stylistic characteristics are referred to with the numbers given by Neirynck (to the most extensive list of Boismard and Lamouille, *Jean*) and published in the alphabetic order of the Greek words in F. Neirynck et al., *Jean et les Synoptiques. Examen critique de l'exégèse de M.-É. Boismard*, BETL 49 (Leuven, 1979), 45–66. See also G. Van Belle, *Les parenthèses dans l'évangile de Jean. Aperçu historique et classification. Texte grec de Jean*, SNTA 11 (Leuven, 1985), 124–155 where the list of stylistic characteristics, present in the parenthetical texts, is given with all the references to the gospel of John for each of them.

11 Compare with the way Boismard and Lamouille (*Jean*, 274) express this idea: 'ou peut-être pense-t-il (the evangelist) aux Juifs de son temps qui n'ont pas voulu croire à la déclaration faite par Jésus devant le Sanhédrin, lors de son procès raconté dans les Synoptiques.'

12 Although the saying concerning Jesus' speaking and the unbelief on the part of the Jews has an immediate parallel to the text of Luke, there are other parallels in the gospel of John itself: 3:12 (εἰ τὰ ἐπίγεια εἶπον ὑμῖν καὶ οὐ πιστεύετε, πῶς ἐὰν εἴπω ὑμῖν τὰ ἐπουράνια πιστεύσετε;) 6:36 (ἀλλ᾿ εἶπον ὑμῖν ὅτι καὶ ἑωράκατέ με καὶ οὐ πιστεύετε).

13 Mark 14:55, 56–7, 59, 60, 63; Matt. 26:59, 62, 65; Luke 22:71.

14 Just as he who is of God can hear the words of God (8:47), or he who is of the truth can hear my voice (18:37). For τῆς φωνῆς αὐτοῦ (μου) ἀκούω, cf. Exod. 3:18; 4:1, 8, 9; 5:2; 15:26; 19:5; 23:22, meaning obey or believe.

15 Cf. John 18:8–9 and 3:16–17; 6:39; 17:12. This protection given by Jesus to his disciples, to his sheep who follow him, is in harmony with 18:8–9 where in the scene of the arrest, Jesus in fact intervenes in their favour.

16 Cf. verse 28 (καὶ οὐχ ἁρπάσει τις αὐτὰ ἐκ τῆς χειρός μου) and verse 29 (καὶ οὐδεὶς δύναται ἁρπάζειν ἐκ τῆς χειρὸς τοῦ πατρός). Cf. also 'I give them eternal life' (verse 28) and 'My Father who has given them to me' (verse 29).

17 Cf. Acts 7:55 (᾿Ιησοῦν ἑστῶτα ἐκ δεξιῶν τοῦ θεοῦ) and 7:56 (καὶ τὸν υἱὸν τοῦ ἀνθρώπου ἐκ δεξιῶν ἑστῶτα τοῦ θεοῦ). Cf. Sabbe, 'Son of Man', 260–3. One could object that my linking of verse 30 with Luke 24:69 is an easy affirmation and that it does not fully explain the absence of the Son of Man title in the Johannine pericope under consideration, and that it overlooks the significance of the Son of Man title used elsewhere in the Johannine gospel. In my opinion, John 10:30 is rather a clear example of Johannine interpretation of a text of Luke and of its use of the Son of Man title. It conforms to the general Johannine use of the Son of Man title, which no longer has specific eschatological meaning but which is now heightened as an equivalent of the Son of God title in its full significance. The oneness of Jesus and the Father is a Johannine interpretation of the Son of Man at the right hand of the power of God.

18 *Rückverweisung* of previous words or facts of Jesus as in 4:46 (cf. 2:1–11); 18:9 (cf. 6:39; 17:12); 19:39 (cf. 3:2).

19 The confession of Nathaneal in John 1:49 is, of course, interesting (σὺ εἶ ὁ υἱὸς τοῦ θεοῦ). Such an early confession on the lips of Jesus' disciples is surely surprising, but again can we not see in it, taken together with the other half of the saying (σὺ βασιλεὺς εἶ τοῦ Ἰσραήλ) an elaboration inspired by the self-proclamations of Jesus in the Synoptic trial narrative before the Jews and before Pilate? See also John 1:34; 5:18.

20 The reason Luke dropped both the accusation of blasphemy and the condemnation to death – thus having no formal conclusion to the session before the Sanhedrin – is not clear. Perhaps he was in a hurry to come to the trial before Pilate. In the latter Luke has an introduction of his own (Luke 23:2), in which he explicitly formulates the accusations of the whole company of the Sanhedrin, which in fact can be considered as the conclusion of the preceding trial before 'the Jews' which is now redacted in view of the Romans. (It is as if we hear an echo of Luke 23:2 [ἤρξαντο δὲ κατηγορεῖν] in John 18:29 [τίνα κατηγορίαν φέρετε κατὰ τοῦ ἀνθρώπου τούτου] – see ἄνθρωπος in Luke 23:4, 6, 14 [bis].) With his own redaction of 10:33–6, John puts the motif of accusation of blasphemy back in its normal place. The other motif, the condemnation to death, implied in the attempt to stone Jesus (verses 31–3), will further be formally expressed in John 11:47–53 (cf. Mark 15:1; Matt. 26:3–4; 27:1–2; Luke 22:66).

21 It is interesting to observe with Dauer ('Spuren des Kaiphasverhörs', 118) that in the Johannine narrative of the trial before Pilate it is possible to discover various elements which seem to originate in or to be inspired by the Synoptic narrative of the trial before Caiaphas in the pre-Johannine source. He mentions John 18:31, 33 and 19:7 as presupposing respectively a condemnation to death, an accusation of admitted Messiahship and a law against blasphemy.

22 Cf. also John 8:53 (τίνα σεαυτὸν ποιεῖς;) 'Who do you claim to be? Are you greater than our father Abraham, who died?'

23 For the Johannine stylistic characteristics of the pericope see the list already referred to in note 10. Equally, the structure of the pericope has some typically Johannine features: themes developed at length, a consistency of its own, a complexity of a spiral (or sometimes more chiastic) evolution of ideas and a number of parenthetical elements amplifying and reflecting on previous literary data.

24 Dauer accepts for the source of John 10:22–8 the existence of a narrative of the trial before Caiaphas which should not differ greatly from that of the Synoptics. Nevertheless, because of what he considers to be the partially uncertain Lukan character of the trial narrative (redactional or traditional) on the one hand, and the complex character of the Johannine elaboration on the other hand, he accepts an intermediate, probably written, Johannine source which explains both the similarities with the Synoptists and the complexity of the gospel of John. According to Dauer, the possibility of a direct dependence of John upon the Synoptic Gospels cannot be excluded in principle; however, perhaps in view of his general theory, he prefers to see in the whole of a pre-Johannine Passion Narrative a slowly evolving process of the oral tradition which ends in a probably written separate trial narrative. Cf. A. Dauer, 'Spuren des Kaiphasverhörs', 119: 'Eine verblüffende Ähnlichkeit zu den syn Versionen vom Synedriumsverhör'; p. 120:

'Als Grundbestand des von Johannes stark überarbeiteten Abschnittes 10, 22–38 schält sich eine Verhörszene heraus, deren Ähnlichkeit mit dem syn Synedriumsverhör beachtlich ist'; p. 130: 'der Grundbestand der Szene ... setzt die uns bekannten Syn voraus'.

25 See Sabbe, 'Footwashing', 289.

26 The discourse of Jesus (10: 1–17) makes no formal mention of the addressees. They could be the Jews of 9: 18–34; 10: 19 or the Pharisees of 9: 13–17, 40, but the disciples of Jesus cannot be excluded. The introductory discourse of the parable terminates with a vague suggestion as to the identity of the public which surely must include them. See John 10: 6 (ταύτην τὴν παροιμίαν εἶπεν αὐτοῖς), comparable to John 16: 25, 29.

27 See also Zech. 9: 9 in John 12: 15 and Zech. 11: 12–13 in Matt. 27: 9–10; 26: 15.

28 The verb σκορπίζω is used only twice in John (10: 12 and the already-mentioned 16: 32) and echoes well the text of the Beelzebul controversy: ὁ μὴ συνάγων μετ' ἐμοῦ σκορπίζει (Matt. 12: 30; Luke 11: 23). Also ἁρπάζω occurs there in Matt. 12: 29 and διαρπάζω in Mark 3: 27 = Matt. 12: 29. For the wolf, cf. also Matt. 7: 15 and Matt. 10: 16; Luke 10: 3.

29 Rather than a tradition bringing the citation closer to the Hebrew or to one of the Septuagintal texts, we are dealing with a Matthean redactional adaptation in line with his perspective of the relation of Jesus to his disciples – see for instance 26: 31 – and also with Matt. 9: 36 (cf. Mark 6: 34): the sheep without shepherd, and Matt. 25: 32: the shepherd who separates the sheep from the goats. See D. P. Senior, *The Passion Narrative According to Matthew. A Redactional Study*, BETL 39 (Leuven, 1975), esp. 91–4.

30 The saying using the verb διεσκορπισμένα echoes the Zechariah text (διασκορπισθήσονται) and receives a Johannine flavour with an emphasis on the more abstract ἕν, as highlighted in the union of Jesus with his Father and thus with the faithful of John 17: 21–3. One is also tempted to compare it with προάξω ὑμᾶς εἰς τὴν Γαλιλαίαν.

31 In this case with the accent on the flock and on Caiaphas – see Matt. 26: 3, 57 – again closer to the Matthean redaction. Compare also John 11: 53 (ἐβουλεύσαντο ἵνα ἀποκτείνωσιν αὐτόν) with Matt. 26: 4 (συνεβουλεύσαντο ἵνα τὸν Ἰησοῦν ... ἀποκτείνωσιν).

32 Luke has a certain preference for ἀπόλλυμι, sometimes in opposition to his other favoured verb σώζω, as in Luke 6: 9; 9: 24 and above all in 19: 10 (ἦλθεν γὰρ ὁ υἱὸς τοῦ ἀνθρώπου ... σῶσαι τὸ ἀπολωλός).

33 The other reading (τοῦ πατρός μου – cf. Matt. 18: 10, 35) is also well attested. Matthew has nineteen instances of 'my Father' and eighteen of 'your Father'. See B. M. Metzger, *A Textual Commentary on the Greek New Testament* (London, 1975), 45.

34 R. Schnackenburg, on the contrary, sees therein a difficulty in accepting any direct influence of the parable: *Das Johannesevangelium*, HThK 4 (Freiburg, 1971), 2, 359–60.

35 See J. Dupont, 'Les implications christologiques de la parabole de la brebis perdue,' in J. Dupont, ed., *Jésus aux origines de la Christologie*, BETL 40 (Leuven, 1975), 331–50 and esp. 347–9.

36 See R. Brown, *The Gospel According to John* (Garden City, NY, 1971), I, 398. He nevertheless also refers to 1 Sam. 17: 34–5 where David, risking

his life for the sheep, kills the attacking bear. The other image of Jesus as 'the lamb ... being their shepherd – τὸ ἀρνίον ... ποιμανεῖ αὐτούς – and who will guide them to the springs of the water of life' (Rev. 7:17; cf. Rev. 22:1), has a lot in common (it has even been slain in Rev. 5:6 and its blood is mentioned in Rev. 7:14; see also John 1:29) but is secondary.

37 Jesus has power (ἐξουσίαν ἔχω) over his life – not as Pilate thinks he has over him (John 19:10–11) – which results from a commandment he has received from his Father. Compare with Mark 2:10 and 3:15, the power Jesus has to forgive sins or to cast out demons, and with Mark 1:27, his teaching as one who has authority and with Mark 11:28–33, the discussion on his authority.

38 The alternative reading for verse 11 (δίδωσιν) and verse 15 (δίδωμι – pap. 45, D, al) is a good exegesis of the text.

39 See Sabbe, 'Footwashing', 295–6.

40 Ibid., 290. The way Peter is described in the dialogue of John 21:15–22, as tending the sheep of Jesus and following him into death, may be seen in the same perspective.

41 Compare, with Ch. Maurer, 'τίθημι', in G. Kittel – G. Friedrich, *ThWNT*, 8 (1966), 152–8, esp. 155–6. According to Maurer the peculiar formula of John has Greek–Hellenistic parallels meaning 'risking his own life' (παρατίθημι τὴν ψυχήν) as in the OT τίθεναι τὴν ψυχὴν ἐν χειρὶ αὐτοῦ (Judg. 12:3; 1 Sam. 19:5; 28:21). 'To lay down his life' (including the actual death), however, is found in terms such as ἀφίημι, προβάλλω, et al., and also δίδωμι τὴν ψυχήν (Eur. Phoen. 998; Jos. Bell. 2, 201). John probably also has the first meaning in mind ('um mindestens den Sinn *sein Leben aufs Spiel setzen* anklingen zu lassen') although his main intention will have been the real laying down, the offering of his life, thus paraphrasing the Synoptic formula of Mark 10:45 ('um damit auf seine Weise das synoptische ... zu umschreiben lassen'), while the Greek vocabulary τίθημι ... ὑπέρ is a perfect rendering of the Hebrew of Isa. 53:10.

42 Cf. Sabbe, 'Footwashing', 295–6. See no. 134 (ἐντολή of Christ); no. 135 (δίδωμι ἐντολήν); no. 136 (λαμβάνω ἐντολήν) and no. 313 (παρά [τοῦ] πατρός). See also the ὑπόδειγμα of Jesus in 13:15.

43 See K. M. Fischer, 'Der johanneische Christus und der gnostische Erlöser. Überlegungen auf Grund von Joh 10', *Gnosis und Neues Testament. Studien aus Religionswissenschaft und Theologie*, ed. K. W. Troeger (Gütersloh, 1973), 245–66, esp. 260 and 264–5.

44 Similar to passages such as John 10:27, 38; 17:2–3, 6–8, 21, 25–6 and 3:35; 5:20; 13:3.

45 See M. Sabbe, 'Can Mt 11, 25–27 and Lk 10, 22 Be Called a Johannine Logion?', *Logia. Les Paroles de Jésus – The Sayings of Jesus*, ed. J. Delobel, BETL 59 (Leuven, 1982), 363–71.

46 See Fischer, 'Der johanneische Christus', 259. For instance: 'The soul learns about her light ... and runs into her fold, while her shepherd stands at the door ... she receives ten thousand times the grace and glory' (NHC VI, 32 *Authoritative Teaching*).

47 For the similarity between John 10:9 and 14:6, see Boismard Lamouille, *Commentaire*, 265, 269.

48 See L. Cerfaux, 'Le thème littéraire parabolique dans l'évangile de saint Jean', *Con Neotest* 11 (FS A. Fridrichsen, 1947), 15–25 also in *Recueil L. Cerfaux*, BETL 7 (Leuven, 1954), 2, 17–26.

49 Cf. σχίσμα ἐν (no. 370) of John 7:43; 9:16.

50 The expression is also found in Matt. 11:18 = Luke 7:33; Luke 8:27 (cf. Luke 4:33).

51 Mark 3:23a explains how Jesus speaks in parables about division. For a survey of the history of the exegesis of John 10:1–18, which notes that authors often repeat one another in methods and results, see P.-R. Tragan, *La parabole du 'pasteur' et ses explications: Jean 10, 1–18. La genèse, les milieux littéraires* (Diss. Strasbourg, 1976; Studia Anselmiana 67; Rome, 1980), esp. 55–175. As a result of a text and literary-critical analysis, the author proposes a genesis of the pericope on different levels of the Johannine tradition with a final expression of it in the gospel itself. He simply lists the Synoptic analogies on pp. 239–42, studies in particular the pastoral and antiheretical paraenesis of the Apostolic churches and the Johannine communities, and gives a synopsis of the principal themes and of the main vocabulary on pp. 441–5.

6 A syntactical and narratological reading of John 10 in coherence with chapter 9

1 See R. E. Brown, *The Gospel According to John* (Garden City, NY, 1966), I, 414, who suggests that 10:40–2 could be the original conclusion to the Johannine sketch of the public ministry of Jesus. Cf. in general R. T. Fortna, *The Gospel of Signs: A reconstruction of the narrative source underlying the Fourth Gospel* (Cambridge, 1970; SNTSMS 11).

2 Cf. Brown, *John*, I, 389. He places chapter 9 and 10:1–21 in the general co-text of Tabernacles but says that these chapters are not so tightly tied to the feast as are chapters 7–8.

3 See J. L. Martyn, 'Glimpses into the History of the Johannine Community', *L'Evangile de Jean: Sources, rédaction, théologie*, ed. M. de Jonge (Gembloux, 1977), 149–75; R. E. Brown, *The Community of the Beloved Disciple* (New York, 1979), 62.

4 Guilding, quoted by Brown, *John*, I, 389, has interestingly shown that all the regular readings on the Sabbath nearest Dedication were concerned with the imagery of the sheep and shepherd.

5 Cf. 5:17, 18, 19–23, 30, 36; 7:16, 18, 28, 33; 8:16, 26, 29.

6 So Dodd, Feuillet, Schneider (quoted by Brown, *John*, I, 390), in spite of Bernard's proposed order (9; 10:19–29, 1–18, 30–9) and Bultmann's (9:39–41; added material from chapters 8 and 12; 10:19–21, 22–6, 11–13, 1–10, 14–18, 27–30, 31–9). F. Hahn, 'Die Hirtenrede in Joh. 10', *Theologia crusis – signum crusis* (Tübingen, 1979), 186, comes to the conclusion: 'Der Aufbau von 9, 1–10, 39 ist wohlüberlegt und bis zu einem gewissen Grade durchaus sinnvoll.' Cf. J. Becker, *Das Evangelium des Johannes, Kap. 1–10* (Gütersloh, 1979), 311.

7 See among others the reviews by B. Olsson, 'A Decade of Text-linguistic Analyses of Biblical Texts at Uppsala', *Studia Theologica*, 39 (1985), 107–26; L. Hartman, 'New Testament Exegesis', *Uppsala University 500 years*, vol. 1,

Faculty of Theology (Uppsala, 1976), 51−65; J. A. Du Rand, 'Plot and Point of View in the Gospel of John', *A South African Perspective on the New Testament*, ed. J. H. Petzer (Grand Rapids, 1986), 149−69; R. A. Culpepper, *Anatomy of the Fourth Gospel. A study in literary design* (Philadelphia, 1983).

8 See Olsson, 'A decade', 114−15.
9 Cf. S. J. Greimas, *Sémantique structural* (Paris: Larousse, 1966); idem, 'Narrative Grammar: Units and levels', *Modern Language Notes*, 86 (1971), 793−806; C. Bremond, 'De logika van de narrative mogelijkheden', *Teksboek algemene literatuurwetenschap*, ed. W. J. M. Bronzwaer, D. W. Fokkema, E. Ibish (Baarn, 1977), 183−207; G. Genette, *Narrative Discourse* (Oxford, 1980); S. Rimmon-Kenan, *Narrative Fiction: Contemporary Poetics* (London, 1983). The basic aspects of a narrative literary text are *histoire, récit* and *narration* (Genette), or story, text and narration (Rimmon-Kenan).
10 See Rimmon-Kenan, *Narrative Fiction*, 20−2.
11 For a discussion of these three levels, cf. W. S. Vorster, 'De Structuuranalyse', *Inleiding tot de studie van het Nieuwe Testament*, ed. A. F. J. Klijn (Kampen, 1982), 127−52, esp. 139−50. J. P. Louw, 'A Semiotic Approach to Discourse Analysis with Reference to Translation Theory', *The Bible Translator*, 36 (1985), 101−7, distinguishes among: the syntactical declarative level, which lays out the bare facts; the structural level, which involves the compositional interrelationships in order to signify the focus of the written text; and the intentional level, which conveys the message as purpose of the discourse.
12 Cf. J. A. Du Rand, 'Die Evangelie van Johannes as getuigende vertelling', *NGTT*, 24 (1983), 383−97; idem, 'Die leser in die Evangelie volgens Johannes', *Fax Theologica*, 4 (1984), 45−63; S. S. Lanser, *The Narrative Act: Point of view in prose fiction* (Princeton, 1981); S. Chatman, *Story and Discourse: Narrative structure in fiction and film* (Ithaca, 1978); Culpepper, *Anatomy*; W. S. Vorster, 'The Reader in the Text: Reflections on the interpretation of the New Testament' (paper read at SNTS Seminar on The Role of the Reader, Atlanta, 1986); Ina Gräbe, 'Narratologiese ondersoek en eksegese van die boodskap van die evangelies', *HTS*, 42 (1986), 151−68.
13 The narratological model of B. Uspensky favours this perspective. Cf. his *A Poetics of Composition. The structure of the artistic text and typology of a compositional form* (Berkeley, 1973). Cf. further N. R. Petersen, *Literary Criticism for New Testament Critics* (Philadelphia, 1978), and Culpepper, *Anatomy*, 13−50.
14 Cf. J. L. Martyn, 'Glimpses', 149−75; J. Painter, 'The farewell discourses and the history of Johannine Christianity', *NTS*, 27 (1981), 525−43; A. G. van Aarde, 'Die outeurskapvraagstuk van die Johannesevangelie met die oog op interpretasie of resepsie', *Skrif en Kerk*, 6 (1985), 45−62; Du Rand, 'Plot'.
15 The surface-level syntactic structures reflect the underlying semantic structures as well as the possible meaningful relations among the various structures. Cf. further E. A. Nida, J. P. Louw, et al., *Style and Discourse* (Cape Town, 1983), 99−109.
16 For a theoretical discussion of speech act theory, cf. J. L. Austin, *How to Do Things with Words* (Oxford, 1962); M. Stubbs, *Discourse Analysis: the sociolinguistic analysis of natural language* (London, 1983).

17 *Narrative Fiction*, 46–7. She defines an *analepsis* as 'a narration of a story-event at a point in the text after later events have been told. The narration returns, as it were, to a past point in the story.' On the other hand a *prolepsis* is 'a narration of a story-event at a point before earlier events have been mentioned. The narration, as it were, takes an excursion into the future of the story.' An example of an analepsis can be found in John 9:2: 'Who sinned, this man or his parents?' And a prolepsis in 9:3: 'that the works of God might be made manifest in him'.
18 Cf. Culpepper, *Anatomy*, 70–3, and Genette, *Narrative Discourse*, 87–8.
19 See 9:16, 18. Culpepper, *Anatomy*, also sees the escalation of unbelief especially from chapters 5–10 (91–4), and R. Kysar, *Augsburg Commentary on the NT: John* (Minneapolis, 1986), 114–71, discusses chapters 7–10 as a unit. Cf. Kysar's *John's Story of Jesus* (Philadelphia, 1984), 39–54.

7 Johannes 10 im Kontext des vierten Evangeliums

1 Nicht nur die Existenz von Bultmanns 'Offenbarungsreden-Quelle', sondern auch seine breit rezipierte und bis in die Kommentare hinein fast als 'Tatsache' gewertete Hypothese einer *'Semeia*-Quelle' ist mir höchst unwahrscheinlich. Was den destruktiven Part seiner Untersuchung angeht, stimme ich da voll H.-P. Heekerens, *Die Zeichen-Quelle der johanneischen Redaktion*, SBS 113 (Stuttgart, 1984) zu: Die Existenz *einer* Quelle, der *alle* joh. Wunder-erzählungen entstammen, läßt sich nicht wahrscheinlich machen, geschweige denn erweisen. Das meiste stammt wohl aus den Synoptikern. Ist es aber schon historisch zumindest abenteuerlich, auf derart schwankendem Boden die Intentionen eines vergangenen Autors aus den vermeintlichen Korrekturen seiner mutmaßlichen Quellen erschließen zu wollen, so ist jedes derartige Verfahren textlinguistisch *unmöglich*. Denn Texte sind einzig aus ihrer syntaktischen, semantischen und pragmatischen Struktur, niemals jedoch aus ihrer Genese zu entschlüsseln. Mag z.B. Joh 1.1–18 ein wie immer geartetes Quellenstück zugrundeliegen – wiewohl mir das immer unwahr-scheinlicher wird –, so will der Text jetzt jedoch als die über alles weitere entscheidende Leseanweisung und als der 'Prolog' des Evangeliums beim Wort genommen werden. Mit den vermeintlichen 'Quellen' steht dann natürlich auch die Basis für die Konstruktion einer 'johanneischen Entwicklungslinie' auf dem Spiel!
2 Außer E. Betti, *Teoria generale della interpretazione*, 2 Bde. (Mailand, 1955); ders., *Die Hermeneutik als allgemeine Methode der Geisteswissenschaften* (Tübingen, 1972) jagt diesem Phantom zumal E. D. Hirsch, *Validity in Inter-pretation* (Yale University Press, 1967) nach. Als ob es sich bei ihm nicht seinerseits um ein veränderliches *Produkt* handelte, muß bei Hirsch das 'Genre' dafür herhalten, den 'objektiven Sinn' des Textes sicherzustellen. Vgl. zur Kritik vor allem M. Frank, *Das individuelle Allgemeine* (Frankfurt, 1977), 250ff.
3 U. Eco, *Nachschrift zum 'Namen der Rose'* (München und Wien, 1984), 9–10, 13–14.
4 R. M. Frye, 'A Literary Perspective for the Criticism of the Gospels', *Jesus and Man's Hope*, II, ed. D. B. Miller (Pittsburgh, 1971), 193–221; vgl. ebd. 201ff.

5 Vgl. dazu z.B. W. Schmithals, *Einleitung in die drei ersten Evangelien* (Berlin, 1985).

6 E. C. Hoskyns, *The Fourth Gospel*, ed. F. N. Davey (London, 1947), 82.

7 F. Neirynck, 'John and the Synoptics', *L'Evangile de Jean. Sources, rédaction, théologie*, ed. M. de Jonge, BETL 44 (Gembloux–Leuven, 1977), 73–106: ders., 'John and the Synoptics: The Empty Tomb Stories', *NTS*, 30 (1984), 161–87; ders., 'Les Femmes au Tombeau: Etude de la rédaction Matthéenne (Matt. XXVIII.1–10)', *NTS*, 15 (1968–9), 168–90. M. Sabbe, 'The Arrest of Jesus in Jn 18.1–11 and its Relation to the Synoptic Gospels. A Critical Examination of A. Dauer's Hypothesis', BETL 44 (Gembloux–Leuven, 1977), 203–34; ders., 'John 10 and its Relation to the Synoptic Gospels', *in diesem Bande*.

8 A. Dauer, *Die Passionsgeschichte im Johannesevangelium*, SANT 30 (München, 1972).

9 F. Neirynck u.a., 'L'évangile de Jean. Examen critique du commentaire de M.-E. Boismard et A. Lamouille', *EThL*, 53 (1977), 363–478; ders. u.a., *Jean et les synoptiques. Examen critique de l'exégèse de M.-E. Boismard*, BETL 49 (Leuven, 1979).

10 Vgl. Hoskyns, *Fourth Gospel*, 67ff. Erst daß das Johannesevangelium als literarischer zugleich ein *kanonischer* Text ist, macht den theologischen Rang seiner Lektüre aus. Vor allen möglichen 'religionsgeschichtlichen Analogien' ist deshalb die Kontextualität der gesamten Bibel sein primärer 'Sitz im Leben'. Daß erst das restriktive Vorgehen Marcions den Anstoß zur Kanonbildung gegeben haben soll (so z.B. H. von Campenhausen, *Die Entstehung der christlichen Bibel*, BHTh 39 (Tübingen, 1968), 173ff.; und H. Köster, *Einführung in das Neue Testament* (Berlin, 1980), 436), ist mir wenig wahrscheinlich. Denn schon die Sammlung der Paulusbriefe und die Schriftlichkeit und Struktur der Evangelien sind erkennbare Stadien im Prozeß der Kanonbildung, den Justin deutlich reflektiert. – Keinesfalls zustimmen kann ich den Sätzen: 'Die Unterscheidungen zwischen kanonischer und nichtkanonischer, rechtgläubiger und häretischer Literatur sind überholt. Die klassische "Einleitung in das Neue Testament" hat ihre wissenschaftliche Berechtigung verloren' (H. Köster in: ders. und J. M. Robinson, *Entwicklungslinien durch die Welt des frühen Christentums* (Tübingen, 1971), 252). Denn der geistliche Grundkonsensus der Kirche über die Kanonizität der Bibel ist durch keine sachgemäß-theologische Wissenschaft je überholbar. Die historische Kritik am Kanon ist nichts anderes als die neuzeitliche Gestalt des alten Widerspruchs gegen das 'Ärgernis des Kreuzes', wiederholt sich doch am ausgegrenzten und singulären Bibelkanon als dem mittelbaren Zeugnis dieses Skandalons nur der Einspruch der Vernunft gegen das Partikulare, Zufällige und Negative der Wahrheit Gottes, die jenseits der Relativität solcher Vermittlungen zur nominalistischen Ideologie wird. Zudem ist der Kanon ja nicht nur Dekret der Kirche und damit der Triumph der Sieger, sondern längst zuvor als die Stimme der Märtyrer schon der Grund der Kirche, deren geistliche Erfahrung mit seinen Schriften um nichts weniger historisches Geschehen ist als der förmliche Kanonisierungsprozeß, in den sie mündete, auch wenn diese Erfahrung aufgrund der Prinzipien historischer Kritik den Maschen von deren Netz entgleiten muß. Vgl. im übrigen zur Sache jetzt B. S. Childs, *The New Testament as Canon* (London, 1984).

11 Auf den Spuren des völlig zu Unrecht weithin vergessenen A. Wurm, *Die Irrlehrer im ersten Johannesbrief*, BSt 8,1 (Freiburg, 1903) hat E. Stegemann in seiner Heidelberger Habilitationsvorlesung, 'Christusbekenntnis und Bruderliebe', die Johannesbriefe einleuchtend aus der gleichen Situation wie das Evangelium begriffen, nämlich aus dem Streit mit der Synagoge um das messianische Bekenntnis. In den vermeintlich doketistischen 'Irrlehrern' sieht er mit guten Gründen Apostaten von dem lebensgefährlich gewordenen Christusbekenntnis. Vgl. H. Thyen, 'Johannesbriefe', *TRE* 17 (1990), 186–200 und siehe auch: E. Stegemann, ' "Kindlein, hütet euch vor den Götterbildern!" ', *ThZ*, 41 (1985), 284–94.

12 Vgl. G. R. O'Day, *Revelation in the Fourth Gospel. Narrative Mode and Theological Claim* (Philadelphia, 1986).

13 U. Eco, *Semiotik und Philosophie der Sprache* (München, 1985), 222. Eco fährt ebd. fort: 'Die einzig mögliche Antwort auf diese Frage war praktischer Natur: die Regeln für gute Interpretationen wurden von den Türhütern der Orthodoxie geliefert, und die Türhüter der Orthodoxie waren die Sieger (politisch und kulturell gesehen) im Kampf um die Durchsetzung ihrer eigenen Interpretation ...'.

14 Vgl. J. L. Martyn, *History and Theologie in the Fourth Gospel* (Nashville, [2]1979). – F. Vouga, *Le cadre historique et l'intention théologique de Jean* (Paris, 1977). – K. Wengst, *Bedrängte Gemeinde und verherrlichter Christus* (Neukirchen, [2]1983).

15 Vgl. Stegemann, ' 'Kindlein, hütet euch vor den Götterbildern!'' '.

16 Vgl. H. Timm, *Geist der Liebe* (Gütersloh, 1978), 88ff.; H. Thyen, ' "... denn wir lieben die Brüder" (1 Joh 3:14)', hg. J. Friedrich u.a., *Rechtfertigung. FS-E. Käsemann* (Tübingen und Göttingen, 1976), 527–42. Die namentlich von E. Haenchen, *Der Vater, der mich gesandt hat: Gott und Mensch. Gesammelte Aufsätze* (Tübingen, 1965), 68–77; ders., *Johannesevangelium. Ein Kommentar*, hg. U. Busse (Tübingen, 1980) pass. dem Evangelium unterstellte subordinatianische Christologie ist samt dem ihr zugehörigen nominalistischen Gottesbegriff der typische Fall einer *unmöglichen* Johanneslektüre. Das gilt auch U. Busses Versuch gegenüber, die göttliche Wesenseinheit des Vaters und des Sohnes gegen deren angeblich bloße 'Funktionseinheit' auszuspielen (siehe *in diesem Bande* 15–16). Nirgends ist bei Johannes 'etwa von einem μαρτυρεῖν oder einer μαρτυρία Jesu περὶ πατρός die Rede'. Vielmehr ist stets der bekannte Vater Zeuge seines unbekannten Sohnes, der nicht etwa zur Heimkehr zum Schöpfer ruft, sondern 'exklusiv und definitiv zu *sich*'. 'Man findet im Sohn den Vater wieder, sofern man eben im Sohn durch den Vater gesucht und gefunden wird' (K. Barth, *Johannesevangelium*, Gesamtausgabe II/9 (Zürich, 1976), 364f. Vgl. M. L. Appold, *The Oneness Motif in the Fourth Gospel*, WUNT 2/1 (Tübingen, 1976), pass.

17 W. A. Meeks, 'The Man from Heaven in Johannine Sectarianism', *JBL*, 91 (1972), 44–72. Deutsch: 'Die Funktion des vom Himmel herabgestiegenen Offenbarers für das Selbstverständnis der johanneischen Gemeinde', *Zur Soziologie des Urchristentums*, hrsg. v. W. A. Meeks (München, 1979), 245–83.

18 So behauptet Meeks etwa: 'Bloßer Glaube ohne den Anschluß and die johanneische Gemeinschaft, ohne den entscheidenden Bruch mit "der Welt",

speziell der Welt des Judentums, ist eine teuflische Lüge'; Meeks, 'Funktion' (Anm. 17), 279. Damit verkennt er aber die forensische Rolle des Bekenntnisses bei Johannes und verwechselt Ursache und Wirkung. Denn nirgends fordert Johannes den Bruch mit der 'jüdischen Frömmigkeit'. Er rät vielmehr zu ihrer rechten Wahrnehmung im messianischen Bekenntnis, selbst wenn das den schmerzlichen Ausschluß aus der Synagoge und das Martyrium zur Folge haben sollte.

19 Obgleich bei Johannes nirgends expliziert, treten bei Meeks ekklosiologische Themen unangemessen in den Vordergrund. Er begrift das Evangelium weithin nach Analogie der 'Sammelliteratur von Sekten' und redet von dem Evangelisten 'vorgegebenen' untereinander widerspruchsvollen 'didaktischen Einheiten', die auf 'von der Gemeinschaft hervorgebrachten Formulierungen' (!) beruhen sollen; Meeks, 'Funktion' (Anm. 17), 260. Meeks belastet seine fruchtbare Fragestellung unnötig mit dem fragwürdigen Konstrukt einer 'johanneischen Entwicklungslinie'.

20 Vgl. R. Bultmann z.St. und siehe H. Thyen, 'ΒΑΠΤΙΣΜΑ ΜΕΤΑΝΟΙΑΣ ΕΙΣΑΦΕΣΙΝ ΑΜΑΡΤΙΩΝ', *Zeit und Geschichte. FS-R. Bultmann*, hrsg. v. E. Dinkler (Tübingen, 1964), 97–125.

21 W. Wrede, *Charakter und Tendenz des Johannesevangeliums* (Tübingen, 1903), 64–5.

22 M. Rissi, 'Der Aufbau des vierten Evangeliums', *NTS*, 29 (1983), 48–54; vgl. dazu jedoch J. Staley, 'The Structure of John's Prologue: Its Implications for the Gospel's Narrative Structure', *CBQ*, 48 (1986), 241–64.

23 Vgl. dazu Staley, 'Structure', 249ff.

24 Nach 6.1 begibt sich Jesus – offenbar vom tiberianischen Ufer aus – ja erst auf die andere Seite des Sees. R. Kieffer, 'Rum och tid i johannesevangeliets teologiska struktur', *SEÅ*, 49 (1984), 109–25, gliedert aufgrund des Gebrauchs von πέραν in diese vier Teile: 1.19 – 3.21 (I), 3.22 – 5.47 (II), 6.1 – 10.39 (III) und 10.40 – 21.23 (IV).

25 Vgl. Staley, 'Structure', 258ff.

26 M. Sabbe,

27 Vgl. W. Wilkens, *Die Entstehungsgeschichte des vierten Evangeliums* (Zollikon, 1958), 123ff.; und siehe dazu H. Thyen, 'Aus der Literatur zum Johannesevangelium', *ThR*, 39 (1974), 308ff.

28 'Alle Texte, die eine symbolische Lektüre verlangen, sind nicht dekodierbar, sondern appellieren an die Freiheit ... des Lesers' (M. Frank, *Das individuelle Allgemeine* (Frankfurt, 1977), 353). Das gilt im übrigen auch und gerade für die Hirtenrede.

29 W. Schenk, *Evangelium – Evangelien – Evangeliologie*, TEH 216 (München, 1983), 73.

30 Vgl. die Kommentare von C. K. Barrett und R. E. Brown z.St. und siehe B. Olsson, *Structure and Meaning in the Fourth Gospel*, CB. NT 6 (Lund, 1974), 21ff.

31 O. Kiefer, *Die Hirtenrede*, SBS 23 (Stuttgart, 1967).

32 U. Busse, 'Open questions on John 10', *in diesem Bande* 7–8.

33 B. M. Metzger, *A Textual Commentary on the Greek New Testament* (London–New York, corrected edition, 1975), 229.

34 Vgl. O. Kiefer, *Hirtenrede*, 16.

35 Zur Differenz zwischen allegorischem und symbolischem Modus der Rede vgl. U. Eco, *Semiotik und Philosophie der Sprache* (München, 1985), 212ff.

36 Vgl. nur die phantastische Rekonstruktion der Hirtenrede als eines Echos Jesu auf einen Zelotenaufstand während eines Laubhüttenfestes in Jerusalem durch A. J. Simonis, *Die Hirtenrede im Johannes-Evangelium*, AnBib 29 (Rom, 1967).

37 H. Odeberg, *The Fourth Gospel interpreted in its relation to contemporaneous religious currents in Palestine and the hellenistic-oriental world* (Unchanged reprint of the edition Uppsala, 1929; Amsterdam, 1974), 313.

38 K. Bornhäuser, *Das Johannesevangelium eine Missionsschrift für Israel*, BFChTh.M 15 (Gütersloh, 1928), 58–9. Vgl. P. Fiebig, 'Die Mekhilta und das Johannesevangelium', *Angelos*, 1 (1925), 57–9.

39 S. Anm. 38 und vgl. Odeberg, *Fourth Gospel*, 314.

40 Ebd.

41 Vgl. das Material bei Odeberg, *Fourth Gospel*, 313ff.

42 Vgl. W. A. Meeks, *The Prophet-King. Moses Traditions and the Johannine Christology*, NT.S 14 (Leiden, 1967).

43 *In diesem Bande*, 83–5.

44 Daß nur Lukas (3.2 und Apg 4.6) neben dem auch Mt 26.3, 57 genannten 'Kaiphas' als Hoherpriester 'Hannas' nennt, gehört zu den oft beobachteten besonderen Affinitäten zwischen drittem und viertem Evangelium.

45 S.o. S. 124.

46 Vgl. Bultmann and Barrett z.St. u. siehe J. Whittaker, 'A Hellenistic Context for John 10,29', *VigChr*, 24 (1970), 241–60.

47 So u.a. Haenchen, *Johannesevangelium*, 392; Busse, 'Open questions', 16.

48 K. Barth, *KD* IV/2, 100. Der Kenosisgedanke, daß der Logos sein präexistentes 'Sein bei seiner Inkarnation...abgelegt' habe, Busse, 'Open questions', 16, darf keinesfalls an das Johannesevangelium herangetragen werden.

49 Daß Jesus die Psalmstelle als 'in eurem Gesetz geschrieben' bezeichnet, indiziert zweierlei: *Einmal*, sofern er sagt 'euer *Gesetz*', daß Johannes, wie lange vor ihm schon Paulus, als γραφή einen (jüdischen) Kanon voraussetzt, der den Psalter einschließt und umgangssprachlich Tora (νόμος) heißt. Und, sofern es heißt '*euer* Gesetz', *zum andern*, daß Jesus hier aus der hoheitlichen Distanz Gottes über Israels Tora spricht, wie Odeberg, *Fourth Gospel*, 292, aus rabbinischen Texten belegt hat. 'Euer Gesetz' zumal es ja nicht auf aufgelöst werden kann (V. 35!), darf also nicht als Makel und aus der Position eines 'gesetzesfreien Heidenchristentums' interpretiert werden.

Im übrigen hat J. S. Ackerman, 'The Rabbinic Interpretation of Psalm 82 and the Gospel of John', *HThR*, 59 (1966), 186–91, zu Recht darauf aufmerksam gemacht, daß die Rabbinen wohl die Verse 1–4 von Psalm 82 auf Israels Richter bezogen haben, niemals jedoch die Verse 6–7. Für diese vermag er dagegen eine sehr breite rabbinische Tradition nachzuweisen, wonach Israel die ihm mit der ursprünglichen Tora vom Sinai verliehene Unsterblichkeit durch die Anbetung des Stierbildes verwirkt hat. 'Götter' heißen sie also im Unterschied zu allen Völkern, sofern der an sie ergangene Logos ihnen Unsterblichkeit verlieh.

Nicht der ursprüngliche Sinaibund von Ex 19f., sondern der erneuerte mit seinem nach und wegen der Sünde Israels erneut gegebenen Gesetz von

Ex 33f. ist auch die Folie von Joh 1: 14–18; vgl. W. J. Dumbrell, 'Law and Grace: The Nature of the Contrast in John 1: 17', *EvQ*, 58 (1986), 25–37).

50 Gerade die kühne und fast absurde Durchbrechung der Metapher, wonach Jesus als der gute Hirte seinen Schafen nicht nur Weide, sondern das 'ewige Leben' gibt und sich dafür verbürgt, daß sie *in Ewigkeit* nicht verloren gehen, noch seiner schützenden Hand entrissen werden können (10: 28), bestätigt den von Ackerman, 'Interpretation', aufgewiesenen Zusammenhang als den aktuellen Hintergrund der Auseinandersetzung.

INDEX OF MODERN AUTHORS

Made in the USA
Las Vegas, NV
03 March 2022

44906528R00111